Estimating and Costing for the Metal Manufacturing Industries

COST ENGINEERING

A Series of Reference Books and Textbooks

Editor

KENNETH K. HUMPHREYS
American Association of Cost Engineers
Morgantown, West Virginia

1. Applied Cost Engineering, *Forrest D. Clark and A. B. Lorenzoni*
2. Basic Cost Engineering, *Kenneth K. Humphreys and Sidney Katell*
3. Applied Cost and Schedule Control, *James A. Bent*
4. Cost Engineering Management Techniques, *James H. Black*
5. Manufacturing Cost Engineering Handbook, *edited by Eric M. Malstrom*
6. Project and Cost Engineers' Handbook: Second Edition, Revised and Expanded, *edited by Kenneth K. Humphreys*
7. How to Keep Product Costs in Line, *Nathan Gutman*
8. Applied Cost Engineering: Second Edition, Revised and Expanded, *Forrest D. Clark and A. B. Lorenzoni*
9. Managing the Engineering and Construction of Small Projects: Practical Techniques for Planning, Estimating, Project Control, and Computer Applications, *Richard E. Westney*
10. Basic Cost Engineering: Second Edition, Revised and Expanded, *Kenneth K. Humphreys and Paul Wellman*
11. Cost Engineering in Printed Circuit Board Manufacturing, *Robert P. Hedden*
12. Construction Cost Engineering Handbook, *Anghel Patrascu*
13. Computerized Project Control, *Fulvio Drigani*
14. Cost Analysis for Capital Investment Decisions, *Hans J. Lang*
15. Computer-Organized Cost Engineering, *Gideon Samid*
16. Engineering Project Management, *Frederick L. Blanchard*
17. Computerized Management of Multiple Small Projects: Planning, Task and Resource Scheduling, Estimating, Design Optimization, and Project Control, *Richard E. Westney*
18. Estimating and Costing for the Metal Manufacturing Industries, *Robert C. Creese, M. Adithan, and B. S. Pabla*

Additional Volumes in Preparation

Project and Cost Engineers' Handbook, Third Edition, Revised and Expanded, *Kenneth K. Humphreys and Lloyd M. English*

Estimating and Costing for the Metal Manufacturing Industries

Robert C. Creese
Department of Industrial Engineering
College of Engineering
West Virginia University
Morgantown, West Virginia

M. Adithan
B.S. Pabla
Department of Mechanical Engineering
Technical Teachers Training Institute
Chandigarh, India

MARCEL DEKKER, INC.   NEW YORK · BASEL

Library of Congress Cataloging-in-Publication Data

Creese, Robert C.
    Estimating and costing for the metal manufacturing industries /
Robert C. Creese, M. Adithan, and B.S. Pabla.
        p.   cm. -- (Cost engineering ; 18)
    Includes bibliographical references and index.
    ISBN 0-8247-8712-9
    1. Metal-work--Estimates.   I. Adithan, M.   II. Pabla, B. S.
III. Title.   IV. Series: Cost engineering (Marcel Dekker, Inc.) ; 18.
TS213.C74   1992
671'.0681--dc20   92-20774
                                                                      CIP

This book is printed on acid-free paper.

MARCEL DEKKER, INC.
270 Madison Avenue, New York, New York 10016

Current printing (last digit):
10 9 8 7 6

PRINTED IN THE UNITED STATES OF AMERICA

Preface

Most engineers and managers have not had a course on cost estimating and costing, although they may have studied engineering economy or cost accounting. There are few textbooks on these topics, and one purpose of this book is to provide a basic introduction. The book is intentionally brief so the reader can start applying the principles quickly. It is essential that engineers and managers develop their own systems to meet their particular needs, and we believe enough information is presented here to enable them to better estimate and analyze their costs.

The second purpose of this book is to serve as a supplementary textbook in engineering economics courses, production management courses, and senior project courses in which economic evaluations are required. The example problems and study problems are presented to illustrate potential applications and to present the methodology involved in estimating costs. This book can be used as a textbook for a separate course on cost estimating techniques or the analysis of overhead. The goal has been to keep the book compact so it will be used, as thick textbooks discourage students and people in industry from reading them. The authors, particularly Robert Creese, would like to receive comments, corrections, and illustrative examples and applications by the readers from industry or academia for consideration in future editions.

The problems used in the book are for illustrative purposes only. The values in the tables and figures are typical values and do not represent those of any particular shop or foundry; however the problems should illustrate the type of information necessary for cost estimating purposes. We recommend that readers gather the information required for their own tasks from their own facility.

iii

The primary author, Robert Creese, would like to thank his wife, Natalie, for her patience during the writing of this book. He will get to those various household tasks he put off because of the book. He also expresses thanks for the moral support of Kenneth Humphreys and comments by Ted Moore. Several graduate students were helpful in the production of the figures, in particular B. P. Madhu Sudhan and Sarmad Vali. John Mansuy, also a graduate student, has developed a solutions manual (available to teachers from the publisher) for most of the evaluative questions at the end of each chapter.

Robert C. Creese
M. Adithan
B. S. Pabla

Contents

1
Introduction

IMPORTANCE OF COST ESTIMATION AND COSTING

Cost estimation and costing are two of the most critical factors for the continued success of a manufacturing enterprise. The world is an international marketplace. For a company to be competitive in the international marketplace, its costs must be accurately estimated, in order to secure business; its costing must also be accurate, to correctly determine the profitability of the various products produced.

The economic strength of a nation has been related to the gross national product (GNP) on a per capita basis. It has been noted (1) that as the percentage contribution of manufacturing to the GNP increases, the GNP per capita increases. Thus most countries are trying to increase their manufacturing capabilities to improve their GNP and economic base.

In order to have a strong economic base, several economic conditions and factors are necessary. Two of the important factors are good cost estimating and costing systems, and these two factors are the emphasis of this book. For example, in *Concurrent Engineering* the key objectives stated are reduced time to production, improved quality, and reduced cost (2). In order to determine the cost reductions obtained by concurrent engineering, cost databases, cost estimating relationships, and costing systems will be required. This book provides an introduction to the costing systems and basic cost estimating relationships for manufacturing. Figure 1-1 shows the information presented in this book and the relationships between the various items. This book indicates the types of basic relationships used for costing and cost estimating and illustrates how they can be used.

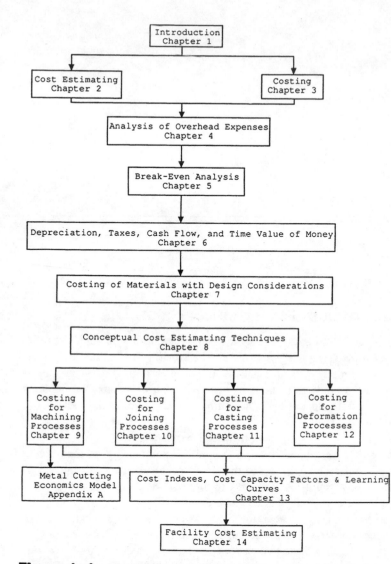

Figure 1–1   Hierarchical organization of the contents of "estimating and costing for engineers and managers in the metal manufacturing industries."

CONCURRENT ENGINEERING AND COST ESTIMATION

Concurrent engineering is one of the new concepts being applied to improve the competitiveness of the U.S. manufacturing sector. It is a management and engineering philosophy used to improve product quality, decrease costs, and reduce the lead time to develop new products (3). The philosophy is not new, but it was lost as companies became larger and communications between marketing, sales, design, production, and assembly broke down. Departments became concerned with their specific task and were not concerned with the overall product. Higher scrap rates, higher costs, longer schedules, and poorer product quality was the result. A major goal of concurrent engineering is to shift the focus to overall product optimization rather than the optimization of individual department performance. Overall product optimization is an integrated optimization of design, materials, processing, assembly, marketing, sales, and servicing.

Smaller companies tend to practice concurrent engineering as a natural mode of communication, as departments are physically closer together. In addition, one person may perform several functions in the small company and thus product optimization is more focused and accomplished more easily.

There are many other terms which imply one or more aspects of concurrent engineering: systems engineering, design for manufacturing, flexible manufacturing, simultaneous engineering, rapid prototyping, computer integrated manufacturing, horizontally integrated manufacturing, integrated cross-functional engineering, art-to-part, and productibility engineering. The definition of concurrent engineering given by the Institute of Defense Analysis (2) in 1988 was:

"Concurrent engineering is a systematic approach to the integrated, concurrent design of products and their related processes, including manufacturing and support. This approach is intended to cause the developers, from the outset, to consider all elements of the product life cycle, including quality, cost, schedule, and user requirements."

One of the key items in the understanding of concurrent engineering is to realize that it is a philosophy, and it is difficult to formulate a specific, detailed definition. Concurrent engineering *is not* a specific tool, architecture, technique, system, or process. A major difficulty in the implementation of concurrent engineering is the failure of management to recognize that it is a management and engineering philosophy which must be implemented at the top levels first. Concurrent engineering must be implemented through leadership rather than dictates, and the main cause of failure of concurrent engineering programs is the failure of management to provide appropriate leadership.

COST TERMINOLOGY

There are different interpretations of some terms in costing, so the following definitions are presented for a common understanding. Most of these definitions were developed by the American Association of Cost Engineers recently appeared in *Cost Engineering* (4), and are reprinted with the permission of AACE.

Cost Engineering—The area of engineering practice where engineering judgment and experience are utilized in the application of scientific principles and techniques to problems of cost estimation, cost control, business planning and management, profitability analysis, and project management, planning and scheduling (4).

Cost Estimation—The determination of quantity and the predicting or forecasting, within a defined scope, of the costs required to construct and equip a facility, to manufacture goods, or to furnish a service. Costs are determined utilizing past experience and calculating and forecasting the future cost of resources, methods, and management within a scheduled time frame. Included in these costs are assessments and evaluation of risks and uncertainties. Cost estimation provides the basis for project management, business planning, budget preparation, and cost and schedule control (4).

Cost Control—Procedures to monitor expenditures and performance against progress of projects and manufacturing operations with projected completion to measure variances from authorized budgets and allow effective action to be taken to achieve minimum cost (4).

Business Planning—The determination of financial, production and sales goals of a business organization; and the identification of resources, methods, and procedures required to achieve the established objectives within specified budgets and timetables (4).

Management Science—The application of methods and procedures including sophisticated mathematical techniques to facilitate decision-making in the handling, direction, and control of projects and manufacturing operations (4).

Profitability Analysis—The evaluation of the economics of a project, manufactured product or service within a specific time frame (4).

Project Management—The utilization of skills and knowledge in coordinating the organizing, planning, scheduling, directing, controlling, monitoring and evaluating of prescribed activities to ensure that the stated objectives of a project, manufactured product, or service, are achieved (4).

Planning—The determination of a project's objectives with identification of the activities to be performed, methods and resources to be used for accomplishing the tasks, assignment of responsibility and accountability, and establishment of an integrated plan to achieve completion as required (4).

Scheduling—The assignment of desired start and finish times to each activity in the project within the overall time cycle required for completion according to plan (4).

Costing—Costing, also called cost accounting, is the methodology for classifying, recording, and allocating the appropriate expenditure incurred for the determination of the cost of construction, production, or service performed. Costing is achieved by keeping a continuous record of all the costs involved in the facility constructed, goods manufactured, or service provided. It is the historical reporting of disbursements, costs, or expenditures for a project, product, or service.

Value Engineering—Value engineering is an organized effort analyzing the functions of equipment, facilities, and procedures for the purpose of achieving the required functions at the lowest total cost, consistent with the requirements for performance, reliability, quality, maintainability, and safety.

PUBLICATIONS AND SOCIETIES FOR COST ESTIMATING AND COSTING

There are several professional societies and publications which emphasize costing and cost estimating. Some of the more notable organizations with publications in English are: American Association of Cost Engineers (AACE)—AACE is an international nonprofit organization founded in 1956 to advance the science and art of cost engineering. It represents cost engineers, cost estimators, project managers, planners and schedulers, and other professionals engaged in work related to business costs and profitability. AACE has certification programs for Certified Cost Engineers and Certified Cost Consultants. The address of AACE is:

AACE
P.O. Box 1557
Morgantown, WV 26507–1557
USA

American Association of Professional Estimators (APE)—This organization is located near Washington, D.C. and has emphasized estimating for government and military projects. This organization also has a certification program for professional estimators. The address of APE is:

American Association of Professional Estimators
11141 Georgia Ave., Suite 412
Wheaton, MD 20902
USA

Institute of Industrial Engineers (IIE)—This organization was founded in 1948 as the professional society for the field of industrial engineering. Two of the areas of industrial engineering closely related to costing are engineering economy and management. The address of IIE is:

Institute of Industrial Engineers
25 Technology Park/Atlanta
Norcross, GA 30092
USA

The Association of Cost Engineers (ACE)—This is the primary organization
for cost engineering in the United Kingdom. Their address is:

Association of Cost Engineers
Lea House, 5 Middlewich Road
Sandbach, Cheshire CW11 9XL
United Kingdom

The Society of American Value Engineers (SAVE)—This organization pro-
motes the use value engineering to reduce product costs. Their address is:

Society of American Value Engineers
60 Revere Drive, Suite 500
Northbrook, IL 60062
USA

The Society of Cost Estimating and Analysis—This is a new organization that
is the result of the merger of the National Estimating Society and the Institute
of Cost Analysis. The primary areas of concern are the military/defense and
aerospace industries. Their address is:

Society of Cost Estimating and Analysis
101 S. Whiting Street, Suite 313
Alexandria, VA 22304
USA

There are other cost estimating societies throughout the world, primarily in
most first world nations. For specific societies in other nations, one can contact
the International Cost Engineering Council. Their current address is:

International Cost Engineering Council
P.O. Box 1557
Morgantown, WV 26507-1557
USA

The International Society of Parametric Analysts—This society was formed in
the late 1970s. It emphasizes the use of parametric analysis for forecasting and

planning the outcome of new projects. The primary areas of concern have been military/defense, NASA projects, and the aerospace industries.

International Society of Parametric Analysts
P.O. Box 1056
Germantown, MD 20875–1056
USA

It is difficult to obtain publications on cost engineering and costing that are published on a regular basis. There are only a few journals or magazines that address cost engineering and costing problems on a regular basis and some of them are:
Cost Engineering—Published by the American Association of Cost Engineers.
The Cost Engineer—Published by the Association of Cost Engineers.
The Estimator—Published by the American Association of Professional Estimators.
Industrial Engineering—Published by the Institute of Industrial Engineers.
Journal of Parametrics—Published by the International Society of Parametric Analysts.
International Journal of Production Economics—Published by Elsevier Science Publishers. Their address is:

Elsevier Science Publishers
P.O. Box 1991
1000 BZ Amsterdam
The Netherlands

International Journal of Project Management—This journal is published by Butterworth-Heinenann and their address is:

Butterworth-Heinenann Limited
P.O. Box 63
Westbury House, Bury Street
Guildford, Surry GU2 5BH
United Kingdom

Engineering News-Record—This journal is published by McGraw-Hill and their address is:

McGraw-Hill Inc.
1221 Ave. of the Americas
New York, NY 10020
USA

Chemical Engineering—This is also published by McGraw-Hill Inc.

Three companies which publish a wide variety of cost estimating information and cost indices, primarily for the construction industry are:

R. S. Means Co.
100 Construction Plaza
Kingston, MA 02364

Richardson Engineering Services
1742 Fraser Drive
P.O. Box 9103
Mesa, AZ 85214–2062

Marshall & Swift
1200 Route 22
Bridgewater, NJ 08807

There are only some of the societies and publications which emphasize cost engineering and costing. There are also a number of accounting and management societies which deal with these topics, but they generally do not emphasize the cost engineering aspects.

TEXT OVERVIEW

The overview of the entire text is presented in Figure 1–1. The purpose of Chapter 1 is to indicate the overall importance of costing and cost estimating in the global sense and to emphasize that we are competing in an international market, not just a domestic market.

Chapter 2 presents a more detailed explanation of cost estimating and illustrates different types of cost estimates. Cost estimating, in the area of manufacturing, is the prediction of the expected cost of producing a product or manufacturing order before the actual production starts.

Chapter 3 presents the other major component, that is costing or cost accounting. Costing is a historical process in that is gives the expenses incurred after the item has been produced, whereas cost estimating is the prediction of the cost before it occurs.

One of the important aspects of costing is the determination of overhead expenses, and this is discussed in Chapter 4. In the early 1900s direct labor was the major cost item, whereas today, administrative, sales, research and development, legal expenses, and other items which cannot be directly associated with the specific product are greater than the direct labor costs.

Chapter 5 indicates how costs are divided into fixed and variable costs so a break-even analysis can be made.

The topics of depreciation, taxes, cash flow, and the time value of money are introduced in Chapter 6. These topics can have a large impact on economic evaluations.

Chapter 7 introduces methods for selecting and costing materials while simultaneously considering performance factors. The effects of scrap upon product cost are also presented.

Chapter 8 illustrates some estimating techniques that can be used when all the information about the product is not known, but a cost estimate is required. The techniques are frequently used in the conceptual design stage and are called conceptual cost estimating techniques.

Chapter 9, 10, 11, and 12 present basic costing methods for machining, joining, casting, and deformation processes. These methods indicate the cost driving elements for the selected processes. The methods are presented for only a few of the processes, but the approaches can be extended to other processes.

Chapter 13 addresses other costing issues such as cost indexes, cost capacity factors, and the effect of learning upon productivity.

Chapter 14 presents an approach to determine the cost of a manufacturing facility. This approach was designed for conducting technical and economic evaluations in the process (chemical) and utility industries, but it can also be used, with appropriate modification, for the manufacturing industries.

Appendix A is the machining economics optimization relationships developed for the metal cutting economics model.

UNITS

Although the United States officially uses the metric system, industry still utilizes the English system of pounds, inches, and etc. rather than kilograms, meters, and etc. Since this book will be primarily utilized in the United States, the system primarily used will be the English system, although some problems will be illustrated for the metric or ISO systems. Tables of data will be expressed in both systems and the figures will attempt to use both systems, with the English units on the bottom and left axes and the corresponding ISO units on the top and right axes.

SUMMARY

Cost engineering, cost estimation, and costing are emerging as integrated disciplines to control costs so companies can be competitive in national and international markets. The continued economic success of the free world depends upon more competitive manufacturing. Two critical tools for more competitive manufacturing are cost estimating and costing. The basic terms in cost estimating and costing have been presented as well as a list of publications and professional societies which emphasize cost estimating and costing.

EVALUATIVE QUESTIONS

1. What are the definitions for cost estimating and costing?
2. Find an article on cost estimating or costing in one of the references and write a summary of the article.
3. What are the process categories that are covered in detail on costing?

BIBLIOGRAPHY

1. Schey, John A., *Introduction to Manufacturing Processes*, McGraw-Hill, 1987, p. 6.
2. Winner, R. I., et al., *The Role of Concurrent Engineering in Weapons Systems Acquisition,* IDA Report R-338, December, 1988, Institute for Defense Analysis, Alexandria, VA.
3. Creese, R. C. and Moore, L. T., "Cost Modeling for Concurrent Engineering", *Cost Engineering*, June 1990, pp. 23–27.
4. "American Association of Cost Engineers — Constitution and By-Laws", *Cost Engineering*, September 1990, pp. D-xix to D-xxii.

2

Cost Estimation

INTRODUCTION

Cost estimating is the estimation of the cost likely to be incurred in producing a product before the actual production is started. It is a prediction of what products will cost and is one of the main inputs for economic evaluations (1,2,3).

Cost accounting or costing is different from cost estimating in that this is a determination of what the costs were to make a product. It occurs after the product has been made, whereas cost estimating is a prediction of what the costs will be before the product is made. The cost items may be the same items for a cost estimation and for a costing report, but the first is a prediction whereas the second is an accounting of what expenses actually were incurred.

Cost estimation of any product is a complex process and requires engineering skills, as the process involves understanding the following items:

1. The product design.
2. The suitability of alternative materials which will satisfy the functional requirements and the processing methods.
3. The alternative technologies available for processing the material of concern and the cost of each process.
4. The costs involved in ensuring the quality of the product in all stages of production.
5. The costs of servicing the product during its usage.
6. The implications and costs involved in product liability suits in case of the failure of the product.
7. The environmental effects and costs of product disposal at the end of the product life.

An understanding of these items requires a knowledge of the principles of engineering, materials, manufacturing processing, inspection methods, quality control, repair and servicing, product safety, and environmental safety as well as the principles of costing. It is essential that engineers have a leading role in the determination of cost estimates and that they work with professional cost accountants to obtain realistic cost estimates.

PROFIT IMPROVEMENT AND COST REDUCTION

A necessary objective for a commercial enterprise is to make a profit if that enterprise plans to remain in business. One of the uses of cost estimation is to plan and evaluate cost reductions. There are several methods used to improve profitability, and it is important to realize the impact of cost reduction upon profitability. The four methods commonly considered for profit improvement are:

1. Increased Prices
2. Increased Sales
3. Improved Product Mix
4. Reduced Costs

To illustrate the effect of the four methods, a problem is presented in Table 2-1 showing the effects of a 10 percent price increase, a 10 percent sales increase, a doubling of sales of the most profitable product with a corresponding decrease of sales of the other product, and a 10 percent cost reduction. Two products are considered, Product A which has a high sales volume with a small percentage profit and Product B, which has a low sales volume but a higher profit percentage.

The results indicate that the 10 percent price increase would give the largest increase (125 percent) in profits. However, it is extremely difficult to increase prices unless there is little competition. The next greatest increase in profits (115 percent) was obtained with the 10 percent decrease in costs. Cost reduction is something that the manufacturer can better control and, to be competitive in the international marketplace, continuous cost reduction is a way of life. The other two methods of profit improvement, a 10 percent sales increase and the improvement in product mix, gave considerably smaller increases in profitability.

These results indicate why cost reduction is so critical to the long-term survival of a company. Cost reductions frequently require the purchases of new equipment and the evaluation of savings with new methods and new processes. Cost estimating and costing are necessary tools for the evaluation of cost reductions.

Table 2–1 Gross Profit Improvement Analysis for a Two Product System

	Current Practice	10% Price Increase	10% Sales Increase	Double Sales of B & Decrease Sales of A by Equal Amt	10% Cost Reduction
Sales					
Product A	80	88	88	60	80
Product B	20	22	22	40	20
Costs					
Variable Cost					
Product A	57	57	62.7	42.75	51.3
Product B	12	12	13.2	24	10.8
Fixed Cost					
Product A	19	19	19	19	17.1
Product B	4	4	4	4	3.6
Total Cost					
Product A	76	76	81.7	61.75	68.4
Product B	16	16	17.2	28	14.4
Gross Profit					
Product A	4	12	6.3	(−1.75)	11.6
Product B	4	6	4.8	12.0	5.6
Total	8	18	11.1	10.25	17.2
Profit Increase					
Product A	Base	8	2.3	(−5.75)	7.6
Product B	Case	2	.8	8.0	1.6
Total		10	3.1	2.25	9.2
% Product A		200	57.5	(−143.75)	190
% Product B		50	20.	200	40
Total Percent		125	38.8	28.1	115

TYPES OF COST ESTIMATES

One classification system for cost estimates was presented by Wierda (4) and is based upon design level. The three levels of design considered were conceptual design, preliminary design, and detailed design.

The conceptual design stage is that stage at which the geometry and materials are unknown, except when they dictate essential product functions. Techniques such as feature-based design or solid modeling are used by the designer at this stage and an order of magnitude estimate can be obtained. The accuracy of such estimates are approximately minus 30 percent to plus 50 percent (5). The cost estimation methods used at this level are the factor method, the material cost method, and the function method(6). The factor method, as illustrated in its simplest form is

$$C = F \times AM \tag{2-1}$$

where

   C = Estimated Cost of item
   F = Factor for total cost estimate
AM = Amount of Major cost item

Some examples of the factor F would be:

- Cost per mile of highway
- Cost of fabricated component per pound of casting
- Cost of house construction per square foot of livable space

Example Problem 2-1

If a casting weighed 15 kilograms and the factor of the cost of casting per kilogram of casting is $ 1.50, what is the estimated cost of the casting? Solution:

$$C = \$ 1.50/\text{kg of casting} \times 15 \text{ kg casting}$$
$$= \$ 22.50 \text{ per casting}$$

The material cost method predicts the total cost of the product based upon the ratio of the material cost of the product to the material cost share of the total cost. This can be represented in equation form by:

$$C = MC/MCS \tag{2-2}$$

where

    C = Estimated Cost of item
  MC = Material Cost of item being estimated
MCS = Material Cost Share of item being estimated

The material cost share is used for complex assemblies and some examples of the material cost share for three items are:

ITEM	MATERIAL COST SHARE
Passenger Car	65%
Diesel Engine	50%
Glass Products	10%

Example Problem 2-2

If the material cost of an automobile was $ 2,500, what would be the total cost: Solution:

  C = $ 2,500 / 0.65

    = $ 3,850 (total cost of automobile)

The function method is similar to the factor method, but more variables are used. The function method uses a mathematical expression with constants and parameters derived for specific processes, such as machining or casting, or for specific classes of parts based upon size, alloy, weight or other cost parameters. Parametric cost estimating is generally considered to be a function method, but it tends to be more detailed and is used for design or detailed design. An example of the function method for a machining problem is:

$$C = G \times (a+b) + (R \times c) + (N \times d) \qquad (2\text{-}3)$$

where

  C = Estimated Cost of item
  G = Weight of item in pounds
  a = Material cost per pound
  b = Tolerance cost per pound
  R = Weight of material removed
  c = Cost per pound of material removed
  N = Number of dimensions for a product surface
  d = Cost per dimension

In the preliminary design stage all of the materials and dimensions of the product are known. The cost estimates in this stage are sufficiently accurate to determine project feasibility and are for budgetary estimates. The accuracy is in the minus 15 to plus 30 percent range. The methods frequently used for cost estimating in this stage are:

1. Product Comparison—the product is compared with classes of existing products and adjustments are made for the differences.
2. Database Calculations—the product cost estimate is determined from cost databases such as those developed by Ostwald (7), Boothroyd/ Dewhurst (8), or Ehrlenspiel (9).
3. Detailed Cost Functions and/or Parametric Cost Estimating—the product cost estimate is determined from detailed programs such as PRICE (10).

In the final detailed design stage, all of the information about the product and how it is to be manufactured must be known. This includes complete design details including dimensions, tolerances, and finishes; the product support requirements and even the product disposal requirements; production details, such as material and process standards, scheduling, lot sizes, process and product quality requirements, testing costs, overhead rates, etc. The detailed cost estimate should be within minus five to plus 15 percent accuracy.

The cost estimating methods used for the detailed design stage are either a detailed cost function method such as PRICE (10) or the traditional approach of estimating the costs of the materials and operations for each step and including loss and yield factors, testing, packaging, inspection, overheads, etc.

COSTS OF ESTIMATES

The more accurate the cost estimate, the higher the cost of the estimate. As the accuracy increases, the time required, the design data required, and the details required to prepare the estimate increase. The estimator's skill, estimator's time, data availability, and quality of data are critical factors in the cost and accuracy of an estimate.

An expression has been developed from the data of Park and Jackson (11) to estimate the cost of an estimate in terms of its accuracy for the total project cost. The expression presented is for a project with a value of one million dollars. The expression is:

$$CE = 700,000 \times A^{-1.7} \qquad (2\text{--}4)$$

where

    CE = Cost of the Estimate in dollars
    A = Accuracy of estimate (lower value)

Example Problem 2-3

If the accuracy level of the estimate is minus 5 to plus 10 percent, what would be the cost of the estimate for a $1,000,000 project?
Solution:

$$CE = 700,000 \times 5^{-1.7} = \$45,400$$

If an order of magnitude estimate is desired, that is a -30 to plus 50 percent, the cost of the estimate would be:

$$CE = 700,000 \times 30^{-1.7} = \$2,200$$

This means that cost of a detailed estimate on a $1,000,000 is 4.54 percent of the total cost or $45,400. For smaller projects, the percentage cost increases while the dollar value decreases. If the expression of Equation 2–4 is extended to give only a percentage cost for the estimate, the expression is:

$$CE(\%) = 70 \times A^{-1.7}$$

The cost of conceptual and budget estimates at Kodak were presented by Lukas (12). After three years of developing estimating aids, the cost of a conceptual estimate was approximately 0.005 percent of the project estimate and the cost of a preliminary design or budget estimate (minus 15 to plus 30 percent) was slightly over 0.4 percent of the project estimate. These costs were initially 0.08 and 0.8 percent of the project estimate, but dropped considerably after three years to the levels stated. In general, a detailed estimate costs 4–6 percent; a budget estimate from 0.5 to 1.5 percent; and a conceptual estimate from 0.005 to 0.20 percent.

PURPOSES OF ESTIMATING

There are numerous reasons for cost estimating. Some of the major purposes, according to Adithan and Pabla (13), are that it:

1. Indicates to the manufacturer whether the project under consideration is economical.
2. Enables a manufacturer to choose from various alternatives of production the one which is likely to be most economical.

3. Enables the manufacturer to fix a selling price in advance of actual production.
4. Enables manufacturer to decide whether to buy or to manufacture the product, and at what price to buy.
5. Enables management to plan for procurement of tools and raw materials.
6. Enables manufacturer to set standards for production to be achieved in actual practice.
7. Helps management plan what type of equipment is needed, what labor requirements are, and what the capital requirements are.

The value of an estimate lies in its accuracy, and carelessly prepared estimates can be extremely harmful to an organization. If the cost is overestimated, then the work can be lost to competitors. If the cost is underestimated, then the work will be done at a loss, and a company must make profits rather than losses.

COMPONENTS OF A COST ESTIMATE

There are numerous components for cost estimating and the ones presented are those that typically occur. There are others which are critical for special products and processes and they must be included in those special cases. The typical components of a cost estimate are (13):

1. Design Cost
2. Engineering/Drafting Cost
3. Research and Development Cost
4. Materials Cost
5. Labor Cost
6. Quality Cost
7. Tooling Cost
8. Overhead Cost

The design cost is estimated from the expected time for the design of that component. This may be done on the basis of similar jobs previously done, but for new or complicated jobs the estimator would need to consult with the designer. If the design is done by an outside contractor, the amount paid to that contractor would be the design cost.

The engineering/drafting cost includes the engineering time in simulations and modeling to validate the design and to prepare the engineering drawings needed for production. This would be primarily engineering man-hours and computer time costs.

The cost of research and development work can be theoretical, experimental, developmental, and/or prototype. These costs are difficult to estimate, especially for new products, and are often included in the overhead costs. The developmental and prototype costs can often be attributed to a particular product during its development, but it is difficult to estimate these costs prior to the start of development.

The cost of materials can be estimated from the design by determining the types, amounts, and shapes required in production. Allowances for wastage, spoilage, and scrap must also be included in the cost estimate.

The cost of labor includes the direct labor time and rate for the product. The determination of these values will require a thorough knowledge of the operations performed, sequence of operations, machines used, and tools used. Some of these costs will be included in the overhead costs, but the cost estimator must be certain that all costs are included.

The quality costs include the cost of inspection, the cost of the inspection equipment, the cost of maintaining process control charts, and costs associated with improving product quality.

The tooling cost includes the tool costs, the costs for fixtures, the cost of sharpening tools, tool storage costs, etc. Cutting fluid costs may be included in the material costs, tooling costs, or as part of overhead costs.

The overhead costs include all costs which cannot be charged to a specific product. These costs are often the largest cost component and more work needs to be done to assign costs to specific products rather than use general overhead rates.

ESTIMATING PROCEDURE

The estimating procedure can be illustrated by using a general estimating form and a discussion of the items on that form. The form is presented in Figure 2-1 and includes the estimating components in the previous section.

The major cost items in Figure 2-1 are the design costs, engineering/drafting costs, research and development costs, material costs, labor costs, other direct costs, and overhead costs. Prime cost is the sum of all the direct costs and would include the design, engineering/drafting, and research and development costs if these can be associated with the specific product; frequently these costs are included in the overhead rates.

EVALUATIVE QUESTIONS

1. What is the difference between cost estimating and cost accounting?
2. What are the three types of cost estimates and their levels of accuracy?

```
Product Description _____        Date        _____
Product Number _____            Customer #_____
Quality_____                           Customer Name_____
Estimator _____                 Customer Contact_____
                                          Customer Telephone_____


Item of Expenditure                       Item Cost    Total Cost

1) Design Costs
      Design Time (hr.) & Rate ($/hr.)    _____

      _____    _____
      Computer Time (hr.) & Rate ($/hr.)

      _____    _____
      Outside Costs ($) _____   _____
      Total Design Costs                  _____    _____

2) Engineering/Drafting Costs
      Engineering (hr.) & Rate ($/hr.)
      _____    _____               _____

      Engineering Computer
      (hr.)_____    Rate ($/hr.)____   _____
      Drafting Computer
      (hr.)_____    Rate($/hr.)____    _____
      Total Engineering Cost              _____    _____

3) Research & Development Costs
      Engineering (hr.) & Rate ($/hr.)
      _____    _____
      Technician (hr.) & Rate ($/hr.)     _____

      _____    _____
      Material Costs                      _____
          Amount (lb.)    _____        _____
          Cost ($/lb)     _____        _____
          Amount (lb)     _____        _____
          Costs ($/lb)    _____        _____

      Total R & D Cost                    _____    _____

4) Direct Material Costs
      Material   Amt. (lb.)     Costs ($/lb.)
      _____   _____       ____  _____
      _____   _____       ____  _____
      _____   _____       ____  _____
      Total Material Costs            _____    _____
```

Figure 2–1   Generalized cost estimating form (Adapted from Ref. 13).

3. If the factor for total cost estimating for complex castings is $ 2.50 per kilogram, what is the expected cost of a 7 kilogram casting?

4. If the material cost share for a television set is 20 percent and the total materials cost for the television set is $ 25.00, what is the expected cost of the television set?

```
5) Direct Labor Costs                    Item Cost    Total Cost
      Operations Time (hr.)    Rate($/hr.)
      _____  _____       _____      _____
      _____  _____       _____      _____
      _____  _____       _____      _____

      Total Labor Costs                    _____    _____

6) Other Direct Expenses
Machine Costs
      Operation        Time (hr.)    Rate($/hr)        .
      _____         _____      _____   _____
      _____         _____      _____   _____
      _____         _____      _____   _____

Tooling Costs (Jigs, Fixtures, Dies)
      Tool      Quality    Costs ($/unit)
      ___ __               _____      _____
      ___ __               _____      _____

Inspection Costs
      Operation        Frequency Costs ($/test)
      _____         _____         _____
      _____         _____         _____

      Inspector (hr.)       Rate ($/hr.)
      _____              _____

      Total Other Direct Costs          _____    _____

7) Overhead Costs
      Plant Overhead
      Hours      Rate ($/hr.)
      _____     _____                 _____
      or
      Rate (%)   Prime Cost ($)
      _____                            _____
      Office & Administrative Overhead
      Hours      Rate ($/hr.)
      _____     _____                 _____
      or
      Rate (%)   Factory Cost ($)
      _____                            _____
      Sales Expenses
      Rate (%)   Production Cost ($)
      _____                            _____

      Total Overhead Costs              _____    _____
8) Total Costs (Sum 1-7)                            _____
9) Profit
      Rate (%)   Total Costs ($)
      _____     _____                 _____

      Total Profit                      _____    _____
10) Total Selling price ($)                         _____
```

Figure 2–1 Continued.

5. What is the expected cost of an estimate for a $ 1,000,000 order if the accuracy is minus 10 to plus 15 percent?
6. Explain why engineers should play a leading role in determining the cost estimates.
7. What are the purposes of cost estimating?

8. What are the different components of a cost estimate?
9. Outline a procedure for estimating the cost of an industrial product.

BIBLIOGRAPHY

1. Humphreys, K. K. and Katell, S., *Basic Cost Engineering*, 1981, Dekker, New York p.218.
2. Ostwald, P. *Cost Estimating*, 2nd Edition, 1984, Prentice-Hall, Englewood Cliffs, New Jersey, pp. 41.
3. Park, W. R., and Jackson, D. E., *Cost Engineering Analysis*, 2nd Edition, 1984, John Wiley & Sons, New York, p. 335.
4. Wierda, L. F., 1988, "Detailed Cost Estimation Concept and Database Structure for DIDACOE", Report IM K177, Aug., Delft University of Technology, The Netherlands, p. 122.
5. Humphreys, K. K., and Katell, S., 1981, *Basic Cost Engineering*, Marcel Dekker, New York, p. 1.
6. Creese, R. C., and Moore, L. T., "Cost Modeling for Concurrent Engineering", *Cost Engineering*, June 1990, pp. 23–7.
7. Ostwald, P. F., *American Machinist Manufacturing Cost Estimation Guide*, 1983, McGraw-Hill Book Company, New York.
8. Boothroyd, J. "Estimate Costs at an Early Stage", *American Machinist*, Aug. 1988, pp. 54–57.
9. Ehrlenspiel, K. and Hillebrand, A., "Konstruieren und Kalkulieren am Bildschirm", *Systec'86 Proceedings*, München, VDI-Verlag, Düsseldorf, 1986, pp. 1–24.
10. RCA PRICE SYSTEMS, *An Executive Guide to PRICE*, 1987, Moorestown NJ, p. 76.
11. Park, W. R., and Jackson, D. E., *Cost Engineering Analysis*, 2nd Edition, 1984, John Wiley & Sons, New York, p. 128.
12. Lukas, J. A., "Conceptual Estimating: Productivity Improvements at Kodak", *1991 Transactions of AACE*, American Association of Cost Engineers, Morgantown, WV, pp. F.5.1–F.5.5.
13. Adithan, M. and Pabla, B. S., *Production Engineering, Estimating, and Costing*, Konark Publishers Pvt. Ltd., Delhi, India, pp. 98,99.

3
Costing

INTRODUCTION

Costing is similar to cost accounting in that it is a process of recording the expenses after they been incurred in producing the product. It is not identical to accounting in that it does not use the debit-credit transaction account analysis, but it does use the same type of cost information and uses this information for the same purposes of evaluating profitability. Similarly, costing can be used to evaluate the cost of a service by adding all the expenses incurred in providing the service. Although there are many purposes for costing, as indicated by Adithan and Pabla(1), some of the more important ones are:

1. To determine the actual cost of each component and the total cost of the final product.
2. To form a basis for fixing the selling price.
3. To determine the expenses incurred in production so the critical operations on a cost basis can be controlled.
4. To evaluate the accuracy of estimates.
5. To determine which products are profitable to manufacture.
6. To determine which components to manufacture and which ones to purchase from outside vendors.
7. To determine the purchase price limits for components.
8. To compare manufacturing products by different processes to determine most efficient and most economical process.

There are many other reasons for costing, but this list indicates that costing is an essential function for a company to be profitable.

CLASSIFICATION OF COSTS

Fixed and Variable Costs

Costs are generally classified as to whether or not they vary with the quantity being manufactured or level of production. A fixed cost is a cost that is unaffected by the level of production. Some examples of fixed costs are plant security, property taxes, insurance, and administrative salaries. A variable cost is one that varies with the level of production. Some examples of variable costs are direct material costs and direct labor costs.

In some cases, the costs partially fixed and partially variable and may be called semi-variable. The fuel needed may be used to heat the plant as well as for production and thus it could have a fixed component (heat the plant) as well as a variable component (heat a part for forming). Another example is maintenance, where a minimal staff is needed, but for high production levels more staff may be needed. For this type of situation, the cost may be divided into two components, a fixed portion and a variable portion.

Direct and Indirect Costs

Costs are also generally classified as to whether they are direct or indirect costs. Direct costs can be directly related to a specific product whereas indirect costs cannot be determined for specific products.

Direct costs are costs which directly contribute to the final product and can be directly allocated to the manufacture of a specific product. Direct costs include the cost of raw materials, labor processing the materials, cost of the equipment, special tooling, and engineering costs used in the manufacturing of the product.

Indirect costs are the costs which cannot be directly allocated to the manufacture of a particular product. These costs usually are combined together and allocated to a number of products manufactured in the plant in a specific time period, usually in the form of overhead charges. Indirect costs include the wages of supervisory and inspection staff, selling and distribution expenses, administrative expenses, basic research and development, and the costs of indirect materials like greases, lubricants, coolants, as well as repair and maintenance costs.

COST ELEMENTS

For the purpose of calculations, the total cost of the product is divided into the following elements: material cost, labor cost, engineering cost, burden (other expenses).

Material Cost

Material cost consists of the cost of materials which are used in the manufacture of the product. It is divided into the categories of direct and indirect material costs.

Direct Material Cost

Direct material costs are the costs of those materials which are directly used for the manufacture of the product and become part of the finished product. This expenditure can be directly allocated and charged to the manufacture of a specific product or job and includes the scrap and losses that occur in the process. One procedure for calculating the direct material cost is as follows:

1. From the engineering drawings, make a list of all the components required to make the final product.
2. Calculate the volume of each component from the drawing after adding allowances for the processes, such as machining, casting, forming, etc.
3. The weight of the component is the component volume times the material density.
4. Adjust the quantities for process yield, projected scrap rates, and other material losses such as melt loss, to obtain the gross weight of the component. Some items, such as the gates and risers/feeders of castings, are recirculated and are not losses.
5. Multiply the gross weight by the material cost per unit weight to obtain the cost of raw material per component.
6. The sum of the component raw material costs equals the total direct material cost per component.

Indirect Material Cost

In addition to direct materials, a number of other materials are necessary for the conversion of the direct materials into the final shape. Although these materials are consumed in the production process, they do not become part of the finished product, and their cost cannot be directly related to the manufacture of a specific product; therefore, these materials are called indirect materials. The indirect materials include oils and lubricants in machining or forming, sand in casting for molds and cores, etc.

In some cases direct materials like nails, screws, glue, etc., which are used in small quantities are charged as indirect materials because the additional recordkeeping is too expensive. Depending upon the product manufactured, the same items may be direct materials for one company and indirect for another.

Labor Costs

Direct Labor Cost

Direct labor consists of that labor performed on the product to convert it into its final shape. The direct labor cost for a task is the product of the direct labor time and the direct labor rate for that task. The total direct labor cost is the sum of the direct labor costs for the individual tasks to make the product. Examples of direct labor are machine operators, such as lathe operators, CNC machine operators, press operators, assemblers, etc. who are directly involved in the conversion from raw material to finished product. The direct labor costs include all costs, not just the wages but also the benefit costs such as vacation, FICA, retirement, etc.

Indirect Labor Costs

Indirect labor is that labor effort that is not directly tied to a specific product but whose labor is used indirectly in the manufacture of a product. The indirect labor cost is the product of the indirect labor hours and the indirect labor rate. Some examples of indirect labor are the janitorial staff who keep the workplace clean and the maintenance staff who repair the equipment when needed. The indirect labor hours generally cannot be identified with a specific product, but are charged to the total number of products produced and then allocated to specific products by some type of distribution factor.

Engineering Cost

Direct Engineering Costs

The engineering costs of high technology products are now a substantial portion of the total product costs and can no longer be included in the burden or overhead. Although all of the engineering costs cannot be identified with a particular item, many of them can be and they should be costed to that product. Costs such as design and drafting, tooling, prototype construction and testing, etc., can be identified with a particular product and should be identified with its cost. With small production runs, it is critical that the costs be identified with a specific product rather than lumped into a general overhead.

Indirect Engineering Costs

Indirect engineering costs includes computers and software packages that have been purchased to assist in the design of the part and control of a process. For example a finite element program may be used to perform stress analyses for various products, not just one. Expert system packages may be developed to improve the operation of the machines for a family of products, not just a single product. The cost of such packages and program development may be rather high and should be shared by the products that use these tools.

Burden (Other Expenses)

Direct Burden Expenses

Direct burden expenses include all expenditures, other than expenditures in the three previous categories, which can be directly allocated and charged to a particular job. The direct expenses include jigs and fixtures, patterns, etc., which have not been included as engineering expenses. Other items are marketing and sales expenses, advertising, and shipping expenses attributed to a particular product.

Indirect Burden Expenses

All expenses except direct expenses are classified as indirect expenses. These expenses are also called overhead expenses or on-cost. These expenses are usually further classified as factory expenses, selling and distribution expenses, and administrative expenses.

Factory expenses include the indirect material costs, indirect labor costs, indirect engineering costs, and all other expenses involved in the manufacture of the product at the factory, such as rent or depreciation of the factory building and equipment, utilities, insurance, and license fees. This also includes factory administrative expenses, such as supervisors, and foreman, as these are part of the indirect labor expenses.

Selling and distribution expenses include all expenses related to marketing, sales, and distribution of the product from the factory. This includes salaries, commissions, travel expenses, advertising, and delivery of the product to the customer. It includes marketing research to determine what products to produce for current and prospective customers.

Administrative expenses include those administrative costs that are not at the factory, but at the corporate level. This would include executive salaries, legal and accounting costs, corporate office and utility expenses, basic research and development expenses that are not product specific, and all expenses that are not factory or selling expenses.

MARKUP RATE (PROFIT)

The markup rate includes the profit and the taxes that must be paid when a profit is made. The AACE definitions for the different types of profit are (2):

Gross Profit—earnings from an ongoing business after direct costs of goods sold have been deducted from sales revenue for a given period.

Operating Profit—earnings or income after all expenses(selling, administrative, depreciation) have been deducted from the gross profit.

Net Profit—earnings or income after subtracting miscellaneous income and expenses(patent royalties, interest, capital gains) and federal income tax from operating profit.

It can be seen that the markup rate would be considerably higher than the net profit, as no consideration has been made for income tax as a cost item. The operating profit would be the closest value to the markup rate. Although the markup rate is not really a cost item, it is an item that appears in the cost relationships.

COST RELATIONSHIPS

The basic relationships between costs and expenses are presented in Figures 3-1 and 3-2. These figures illustrate how the terms are related and the use of

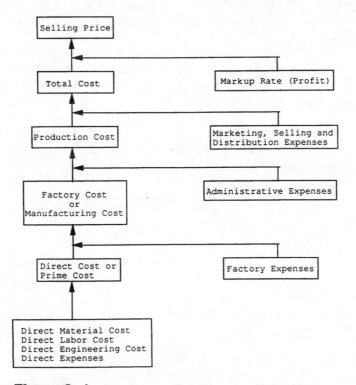

Figure 3-1   Cost diagram illustrating cost relationships among cost terms.

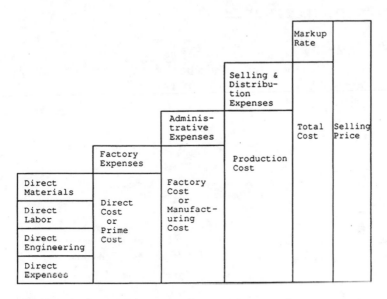

Figure 3-2 Cost ladder illustrating cost relationships among cost terms. (Adapted from *Product Design and Process Engineering* by Niebel & Draper, p. 38. Copyright 1974 by McGraw-Hill. Reproduced with permission).

the terms prime cost, factory cost, production cost, total cost and selling price. Some terms have more than one name; for example, the prime cost is frequently called the direct cost. These relationships can be expressed in equation form as:

$$
\begin{aligned}
\text{Prime Cost} \;=\; & \text{Direct Material Cost} + \\
\text{(Direct Cost)} \quad & \text{Direct Labor Cost} + \text{Direct Expenses} + \\
& \text{Direct Engineering Cost} \qquad\qquad\qquad (3\text{-}1)
\end{aligned}
$$

$$
\begin{aligned}
\text{Factory Cost} \;=\; & \text{Prime Cost} + \text{Factory Expenses} \\
\text{(Manufacturing Cost)} & \qquad\qquad\qquad\qquad\qquad\qquad (3\text{-}2)
\end{aligned}
$$

$$
\text{Production Cost} \;=\; \text{Factory Cost} + \text{Administrative Expenses} \qquad (3\text{-}3)
$$

$$
\begin{aligned}
\text{Total Cost} \;=\; & \text{Production Cost} + \text{Marketing, Selling,} \\
& \text{and Distribution Expense} \qquad\qquad\qquad (3\text{-}4)
\end{aligned}
$$

$$
\text{Selling Price} \;=\; \text{Total Cost} + \text{Markup (Profit)} \qquad\qquad (3\text{-}5)
$$

ILLUSTRATIVE EXAMPLE PROBLEMS

Example Problem 3-1

Calculate the prime cost, factory cost, production cost, total cost, and selling price per item from the data given in Table 3-1 for the year 1990:
Solution:

$$
\begin{aligned}
\text{Direct Material Used} &= \text{Stock on Hand 12/31/89} + \\
&\quad \text{Raw Materials Purchased in 1990} \\
&\quad - \text{Stock on Hand 12/31/90} \\
&= \$\,25,000 + \$\,40,000 - \$\,15,000 \\
&= \$\,50,000
\end{aligned}
$$

$$
\begin{aligned}
\text{Prime Cost} &= \begin{array}{llll} \text{Direct} & + \text{Direct} & + \text{Direct} & + \text{Direct} \\ \text{Material} & \text{Labor} & \text{Engineering} & \text{Burden} \end{array} \\
&= \$\,50,000 + \$\,8,000 + \$\,6,000 \quad + \$\,1,000 \\
&= \$65,000
\end{aligned}
$$

$$
\begin{aligned}
\text{Factory Cost} &= \text{Prime Cost} + \text{Factory Expense} \\
&= \$\,65,000 + \$\,9,750 \\
&= \$\,74,750
\end{aligned}
$$

Table 3-1 Data for Example Problem 3-1

Item	Value
Raw Materials Inventory 12/31/89	$ 25,000
Raw Materials Purchased 1990	40,000
Raw Materials Inventory 12/31/90	15,000
Direct Labor Cost	8,000
Direct Engineering Costs	6,000
Direct Burden Costs	1,000
Factory Expense	9,750
Administrative Expense	6,500
Selling & Distribution Expense	3,250
Markup Rate 10%	
Number of Units Produced 650	

Production Cost = Factory Cost + Administrative Expense
                  = $ 74,750 + $ 6,500
                  = $ 81,250

Total Cost = Production Cost + Selling Expense
           = $ 81,250 + $ 3,250
           = $ 84,500

Selling Price = Total Cost + Markup (10%)
             = $ 84,500 + (.10 × $ 84,500)
             = $ 84,500 + $ 8,450
             = $ 92,950

Total Cost/Unit = Total Cost / Number of Units
                = $ 84,500 / 650
                = $ 130 / Unit

Selling Price/Unit = Total Selling Price / Number of Units
                  = $ 92,950 / 650
                  = $ 143 / Unit

Example Problem 3-2

From the data in Table 3-2 for a small robotic manufacturer, prepare a statement showing the prime cost, factory cost, production cost, total cost, and profit. Solution:

Material Cost = Value on 12/31/88 +
                Materials purchased in 1989 −
                Value on 12/31/89
             = $ 25,000 + 274,000 − $ 35,000
             = $ 264,000

Prime Cost = Material Cost + Labor Cost +
              Engineering Cost + Direct Expense
          = $ 264,000 + $ 120,000 + $ 15,000 + $ 1,500
          = $ 400,500

Table 3–2   Data for Example Problem 3–2

Item	Value
Value of stock on 12/31/88	$ 25,000
Materials purchased 1989	274,000
Value of stock on 12/31/89	35,000
Labor Cost	120,000
Engineering Cost	15,000
Depreciation of plant and machinery	18,000
Depreciation of office equipment	2,000
Rent, taxes, and insurance for factory	6,000
General administration expense	3,400
Factory utilities	6,600
Office utilities	4,500
Direct expenses	1,500
Sales commission	8,000
Plant manager's salary	60,000
Office staff salary	20,000
Sales income	550,000

Factory Overhead

Rent, taxes, and insurance for factory	$ 6,000
Depreciation of plant and machinery	18,000
Factory utilities	6,600
Plant managers salary	60,000
Total	$ 90,600

Factory cost = $ 90,600 + $ 400,500 = $ 491,100

Administrative Expense

Depreciation of office equipment	$ 2,000
General administrative expense	3,400
Office utilities	4,500
Office staff salary	20,000
Total	$ 29,900

Production cost = $ 491,100 + $ 29,900 = $ 521,000

Sales Expense	
Sales commission	$ 8,000
Total	$ 8,000

Total Cost = $ 521,000 + $ 8,000 = $ 529,000

$$Profit = Sales\ Income\ -\ Total\ Cost$$
$$= \$\ 550,000\ \ \ -\ \$\ 529,000$$
$$= \$\ 21,000$$

SUMMARY AND CONCLUSIONS

Costing is a process of recording expenses after they have occured in the production of a product. The data obtained from costing is necessary to form accurate data bases for the development of cost estimates. Costing is used to evaluate the accuracy of the cost estimate. The profitability of products can be determined accurately only if a good costing system is in place.

Table 3-3 Manufacturing Data for Problem 3 of Evaluative Questions

Item	Value
Raw Material Cost	$ 1,500,000
Direct Labor	500,000
Direct expenses	40,000
Plant manager & staff	130,000
Plant utilities	8,000
Plant and equipment depreciation	25,000
Storage expenses(warehouse)	10,000
Office utilities	1,500
Office depreciation	2,500
Engineer's salary(plant)	5,500
Engineering expenses(plant)	2,500
Administrative staff salaries	15,000
Sales staff salaries and commissions	12,000

Number of pumps made 250
Percent markup 15%

EVALUATIVE QUESTIONS

1. What are the four elements of cost? List them and give an example of each element of cost.
2. Explain the terms prime cost, factory cost, total cost, and selling price. Show the relationships between these terms.
3. From the monthly data of a pump manufacturer in Table 3–3, calculate the production cost and selling price per pump.

BIBLIOGRAPHY

1. Adithan, M., and Pabla, B.S., *Production Engineering, Estimating, and Costing*, Konark Publishers Pvt. Ltd., Dehli, India pp. 104–114.
2. *Standard Cost Engineering Terminology—AACE Standard No. 10S-90.* American Association of Cost Engineers, Morgantown, WV. p. 72.

4
Analysis of Overhead Expenses

INTRODUCTION

Overhead expenses are those costs which are incurred by the manufacturer but cannot be identified and charged directly to any order or product. Overhead expenses include all expenditures incurred by the manufacturer on the product except the direct costs, that is, direct material, direct labor, direct engineering, and direct expenses.

In most manufacturing organizations the overhead expenses are the greatest single item, more than direct labor or direct material. Administrative and selling expenses are part of the overhead expenses and thus the total overhead costs are frequently 200 to 300 percent of the direct labor cost. The overhead expenses are usually divided into the three categories of factory overhead, administrative overhead, and selling overhead. If one considers only the factory overhead, it is about 30 percent of the factory cost. The emphasis will be upon the determination of the factory overhead, but consideration of the administrative and selling overheads will be discussed.

FACTORY OVERHEAD

The factory overhead is frequently subdivided into indirect labor, indirect materials, indirect engineering, and other indirect expenses. A major problem is the distribution of the overhead expenses to the products, and several different methods will be presented.

Indirect Material Expense

Indirect materials are those materials which are consumed in the operations and processes in the factory but cannot be identified as part of a product. These materials do not form a part of the final product, but are consumed in the process of conversion of raw material into the finished product. These indirect material expenses include the cost of oils, grease, lubricants, sand binders, cleaning materials such as grinding wheels and shot blast, die lubricants for forming, cutting fluids in machining, etc. Some direct materials, such as screws and bolts, nails, fasteners, etc., which are low in cost and used in small quantities, are charged as indirect materials to reduce recordkeeping expenses.

Indirect Labor Expense

Indirect labor is that labor which is not employed in the direct manufacturing of the product, but whose services are used in an indirect manner. The indirect labor includes supervisors, foremen, repair and maintenance staff, crane operators, sweepers, and other factory staff. Sometimes administrative staff, sales staff and distribution staff are included as indirect labor, but most frequently they are included as administrative overhead and as sales and distribution overhead. Salaries and wages paid to indirect labor need to be distributed to the products manufactured.

Indirect Engineering Expense

Indirect engineering expenses include software packages, computer supplies, computer printers and other devices to assist in the design and production of the product. This can include equipment for engineering tests for product development, product and process design, and process control. The indirect engineering expenses are higher for the high technology products which require sophisticated tests for performance evaluation.

Burden (Other Indirect Expense)

The last category of the factory overhead expense is the burden or other indirect expense. It includes all factory expenses not included in any of the other groups. It usually includes depreciation for machinery, factory building expenses and utilities, factory taxes, etc. The administrative expenses of corporate staff, research and development staff, and sales, advertising, marketing, and distribution are usually kept separate as administrative expense and as sales and distribution expense. Attempts to keep track of these expenses by product should be made if possible, but it is usually extremely difficult to do so and usually is not done.

DISTRIBUTION OF OVERHEAD COSTS

The distribution of overhead costs has become one of the most critical issues in cost estimation and cost management (2,3). If only a single product is produced, the total overhead costs may be simply divided by the number of items produced. When there are two or more items produced, the distribution of overheads is a significantly more complicated task. It is a critical task as products are selected for production by the ability to produce a profit, and if the overhead costs are not properly assigned, incorrect decisions about product manufacture can be made. One issue is the separation of product costs from poor capacity utilization and demand costs (3). To illustrate the problems in overhead distribution, various approaches will be presented. The approaches will include single parameter methods, multiple parameter methods, and unused capacity costs. The most common method used for assigning overheads is probably predetermined allocation. That is, the percentage overhead has been determined for a previous period and is applied on that basis in future periods.

To illustrate these approaches, an example problem is given using two products, product R and product C, and the data is presented in Table 4–1 and Table 4–2.

Single Parameter Analysis

Several methods are used for the allocation of overhead costs to the different products and the choice of method depends upon the organization. None of the methods is best for all organizations, so it is important for the company to select the best method for its products. The data from Tables 4–1 and 4–2 will

Table 4–1 Production Data for Example Problem for Overhead Analysis

Production item	Product R	Product C
Production Quantity	1000	2000
Machine Hours	60	40
Direct Labor Hours	300	400
Production Floor Space	100	40

Table 4–2 Data Base for Evaluation of Different Methods for Overhead Analysis

Part A Cost data for determining product costs

Item	Labor rate ($/hr)	Labor amount (hours)	Material rate ($/unit)	Material amount (units)	Cost ($)
Product R					
Direct Labor	10.00	300			3,000
Direct Material			2.00	1,000	2,000
Product C					
Direct Labor	6.00	400			2,400
Direct Material			5.00	2,000	10,000

Part B Product costs, indirect expenses, and total costs for cost items

Cost Item	Product R	Product C	Indirect expenses			Total cost
			Factory	Administrative	Sales & Distrib.	
Direct Labor	$ 3,000	$ 2,400				$ 5,400
Indirect Labor			$ 1,600			1,600
Direct Material	2,000	10,000				12,000
Indirect Mat'l.			4,000			4,000
Direct Engr.	700	1,200				1,900
Indirect Engr.			1,000			1,000
Direct Expense	600	1,000				1,600
Other Factory			1,200			1,200
Adm. Expense				$ 4,400		4,400
Sales & Dist.:						
Direct	700	600				1,300
Indirect					$ 1,800	1,800
Total	7,000	15,200	7,800	4,400	1,800	36,200

be used as an example and the overhead distribution and unit costs will be calculated by the methods commonly used. One should be aware of the effect of the overhead distribution used upon the total unit cost.

Allocation by Direct Cost Proportioning

In this method the amount of overhead is distributed in proportion to the ratio of the direct cost of the product of concern to the total direct cost.

$$\text{Overhead Amount to Product R} = \frac{\text{Direct Cost of Product R}}{\text{Total Direct Costs}} \times \text{Total Overhead Cost}$$

$$= \frac{\$\,7,000}{\$\,22,200} \times \$\,14,000$$

$$= \$\,4,414$$

$$\text{Unit Cost for Product R} = \frac{\text{Direct Cost + Overhead}}{\text{Number of Units Produced}}$$

$$= \frac{\$\,7,000 + \$\,4,414}{1000}$$

$$= \$\,11.41$$

Similarly,

$$\text{Overhead Amount to Product C} = \frac{\text{Direct Cost of Product C}}{\text{Total Direct Cost}} \times \text{Total Overhead Cost}$$

$$= \$\,\frac{15,200}{22,200} \times \$\,14,000$$

$$= \$\,9,586$$

$$\text{Unit Cost for Product C} = \frac{\text{Direct Cost + Overhead}}{\text{Number of Units Produced}}$$

$$= \frac{\$\,15,200 + \$\,9,586}{2000}$$

$$= \$\,12.39$$

Allocation by Direct Labor Cost Proportioning

In this method the amount of overhead is distributed in proportion to the ratio of the direct labor cost of the product of concern to the total direct labor cost.

$$\text{Overhead Amount to Product R} = \frac{\text{Direct Labor Cost of Product R}}{\text{Total Direct Labor Cost}} \times \text{Total Overhead Cost}$$

$$= \frac{\$ 3,000}{\$ 5,400} \times \$ 14,000$$

$$= \$ 7,778$$

$$\text{Unit Cost for Product R} = \frac{\text{Direct Cost + Overhead}}{\text{Number of Units Produced}}$$

$$= \frac{\$ 7,000 + \$ 7,778}{1000}$$

$$= \$ 14.78$$

Since only two products are involved, the amount of overhead to the second product, Product C, is equal to the total overhead minus the overhead allocated to product R.

$$\text{Overhead Amount to Product C} = \text{Total Overhead} - \text{Overhead Amount to Product R}$$

$$= \$ 14,000 \quad - \$ 7,778$$

$$= \$ 6,222$$

$$\text{Unit Cost for Product C} = \frac{\$ 15,200 + \$ 6,222}{2000}$$

$$= \$ 10.71$$

Allocation by Direct Material Cost Proportioning

In this method the amount of overhead is distributed in proportion to the ratio of the direct material cost of the product of concern to the total direct material costs. The calculations will be made only for one product, but the results will be given for the other.

$$\text{Overhead Amount to Product R} = \frac{\text{Direct Material Cost of Product R}}{\text{Total Direct Material Costs}} \times \text{Total Overhead Cost}$$

$$= \frac{\$ 2,000}{\$12,000} \times \$ 14,000$$

$$= \$ 2,333$$

$$\text{Unit Cost for Product R} = \frac{\text{Direct Cost} + \text{Overhead}}{\text{Number of Units Produced}}$$

$$= \frac{\$7,000 + \$2,333}{1,000}$$

$$= \$9.33$$

Similarly,

Overhead Amount = $11,667
to Product C

and

Unit Cost for Product C = $13.43

Allocation by Direct Labor Hour Proportioning

In this method, the amount of overhead is distributed in proportion to the ratio of the direct labor hours of the product of concern to the total direct labor hours for the time period.

Overhead
Amount to
Product R

$$= \frac{\text{Direct Labor Hours} - \text{Product R}}{\text{Total Direct Labor Hours}} \times \text{Total Overhead Cost}$$

$$= \frac{300}{700} \times \$14,000$$

$$= \$6,000$$

$$\text{Unit Cost for Product R} = \frac{\$7,000 + \$6,000}{1000}$$

$$= \$13.00$$

Similarly,

Overhead Amount = $8,000
to Product C

and

Unit Cost for Product C = $11.60

Allocation by Machine Hour Proportioning

In this method the amount of overhead is distributed in proportion to the ratio of the machine hours used for the product in question to the total machine hours used in the time period.

$$\text{Overhead Amount to Product R} = \frac{\text{Machine hours of Product R}}{\text{Total Machine Hours}} \times \text{Total Overhead Cost}$$

$$= \frac{60}{100} \times \$ 14,000$$

$$= \$ 8,400$$

$$\text{Unit Cost for Product R} = \frac{\text{Direct Cost} + \text{Overhead}}{\text{Number of Units Produced}}$$

$$= \frac{\$ 7,000 + \$ 8,400}{1000}$$

$$= \$ 15.40$$

Similarly,

$$\text{Overhead Amount to Product C} = \$ 5,600$$

and

$$\text{Unit Cost for Product C} = \$ 10.40$$

Allocation by Production Quantity Proportioning

In this method the amount of overhead is distributed in proportion to the ratio of the production quantity of the product of concern to the total production of all products.

$$\text{Overhead Amount to Product R} = \frac{\text{Production Quantity of Product R}}{\text{Total Production Quantity}} \times \text{Total Overhead Cost}$$

$$= \frac{1000}{3000} \times \$ 14,000$$

$$= \$ 4,667$$

Unit Cost for Product R $= \dfrac{\text{Direct Cost} + \text{Overhead}}{\text{Number of Units Produced}}$

$= \dfrac{\$\,7,000 + \$\,4,667}{1000}$

$= \$\,11.67$

Similarly,

Overhead Amount $= \$\,9,333$
to Product C

and

Unit Cost for Product C $= \$\,12.27$

Production Floor Area

In this method the amount of overhead is distributed in proportion to the ratio of the production space used for the product of concern to the total production floor space for all products.

Overhead Amount to Product R $= \dfrac{\text{Production Floor Area for Product R}}{\text{Total Floor Area}} \times$ Total Overhead Cost

$= \dfrac{100}{140} \times \$\,14,000$

$= \$\,10,000$

Unit Cost for Product R $= \dfrac{\text{Direct Cost} + \text{Overhead}}{\text{Number of Units Produced}}$

$= \dfrac{\$\,7,000 + \$\,10,000}{1,000}$

$= \$\,17.00$

Similarly,

Overhead Amount $= \$\,4,000$
to Product C

and

Unit Cost for Product C $= \$\,9.60$

Predetermined Allocation Base

If the data presented in Tables 4–1, 4–2, and 4–3 represented all the production for a specific time period, such as one month, then the overhead could be allocated on a direct hour basis. The allocation base would then be direct labor hours. Another allocation base frequently used is machine hours. For example, the total overhead costs are $ 14,000 and the total direct labor hours were 700 hours, then the overhead rate could be determined as:

$$\text{Overhead Rate per Direct Labor Hour} = \frac{\$\ 14,000}{700}$$

$$= \$\ 20.00/hr$$

The unit cost for the two products based upon this rate would be:

$$\text{Unit Cost for Product R} = \frac{\text{Direct Cost of Product R} + \text{Overhead Amount}}{\text{Number of Units}}$$

$$= \frac{(\$\ 7,000 + 300 \text{ hrs} \times \$\ 20.00/hr)}{1000 \text{ units}}$$

$$= \$\ 13.00$$

Similarly, the unit cost for product C can be evaluated to be $ 11.60. Note that these are the same values as determined by the direct labor hour proportioning method. However, in the future the overhead rates would be based upon the same rate of $ 20.00/hr, even if the actual costs changed. The importance of the value of $ 20.00/hr is that it permits one to estimate the costs in the future rather than wait until after the expenses have occurred.

The use of single parameter analysis gives significantly different results depending upon the allocation parameter used. From the example data, the overhead costs for product R varied from $ 2,333 to $ 8,400 depending upon

Table 4–3 Multiple Parameter Analysis Example Data

Item	Product R	Product C	Total
Prime Cost	$ 6,300	$ 14,600	$ 20,900
Sales Direct Expense	$ 700	$ 600	$ 1,300
Total Direct Expense	$ 7,000	$ 15,200	$ 22,200
Total Production Quantity	1,000	2,000	3,000
Direct Labor Hours	300	400	700
Machine Hours	60	40	100

the allocation parameter selected. This led to a variation in the unit cost of $ 6.07, or a 65 percent increase above the lowest unit cost. This indicated the importance of determining the allocation method which best represents the actual distribution of costs.

Calculation Consistency

The total cost of $ 36,200 must be recovered by the two parts, so the sum of the products of the unit costs and the production quantities must equal $ 36,200. For example, if overhead was allocated by direct labor hours, the total allocated costs would be:

$$
\begin{aligned}
\text{Allocated Costs} &= \text{Units of R} \times \text{Unit Cost of R} + \\
&\quad\ \ \text{Units of C} \times \text{Unit Cost of C} \\
&= 1000 \text{ units} \times 13.00 \text{ \$/unit} + \\
&\quad\ \ 2000 \text{ units} \times 11.60 \text{ \$/unit} \\
&= \$ 13,000 + \$ 23,200 \\
&= \$ 36,200
\end{aligned}
$$

Multiple Parameter Analysis

The example presented gives significantly different results for unit costs depending upon the allocation parameter being used. The use of multiple allocation parameters (2,3) is an attempt for a better distribution of the overheads to the products. The overheads for the three areas, factory, administrative, and sales, may be assigned to different parameters rather than all being allocated in the same manner. For example, the factory expense may best be represented by the direct labor hours, the administrative expense by the prime cost, and the sales expense by the production quantity. The data in Table 4–3 summarizes some of the information from the other tables for use in the multiple parameter analysis.

Using the data in Table 4–3 for allocation of overhead and the determination of unit costs, the values are:

$$
\begin{aligned}
\text{Overhead for} \atop \text{Product R} \ \ &= \ \frac{300}{700} \times \$ 7,800 + \frac{6,300}{20,900} \times \$ 4,400 + \\
&\quad\ \ \frac{1,000}{3,000} \times \$ 1,800 \\
&= \$ 3,343 + \$ 1,326 + \$ 600 \\
&= \$ 5,269
\end{aligned}
$$

Unit Cost for Product R $= \dfrac{\$\,7,000 + \$\,5,269}{1000}$

$\qquad\qquad\qquad\qquad = \$\,12.27$

Similarly,

Overhead Amount $= \$\,8,731$
    for Product C

and

Unit Cost for Product C $= \$\,11.97$

The use of multiple parameter allocation for overheads has the possibility of preventing some of the wrong decisions that would have been made regarding the profitability of products. It is important that the correct overheads be applied so the costs, and therefore profitability, can be properly determined for the individual products.

ADMINISTRATIVE AND SELLING OVERHEADS

The administrative and selling expenses can amount to more than 20 percent of the total operating cost. Some of the items of administrative expense as listed by Adithan and Pabla are salaries of office and administrative staff; office building rent and utilities; legal and accounting expenses; administrative travel and entertainment expenses; and research and development laboratory expenses (1). The AACE recommended practice estimates these expenses as 60 percent of the total labor costs (4). The selling expenses include the wages, commissions, and bonuses of the sales staff; travel and entertainment allowances for the sales staff; advertising and marketing expenses; packing, delivery, and shipping expenses; warehousing and storage expenses; customer service; and etc. The AACE recommended practice estimates these expenses as 10 percent of the total sales value (4). These costs, administrative and sales expenses, are a large portion of the total cost, and cost control must be maintained in these areas as well as in the factory.

PRODUCT CAPACITY UTILIZATION AND DEMAND EFFECTS

If the capacity of a facility is not fully used, the idle labor (3) and machine costs should not be attributed to a specific product. For example, if it takes only six hours for the direct labor for a task and no additional work is available, often the product will be assigned eight hours of effort even though only six hours of work is performed. This gives an inflated cost to the product and may thus give it the appearance of being not profitable when in fact it is profitable. The unused time should be classified as idle time and its costs should not be attributed to a specific product and falsely inflate the cost of that product. The unused time can be used as a measure of management performance; the better management performs, the less unused or idle time will occur. Management through its planning and scheduling, should be able to plan for occurrences when materials are not ready, and have productive work ready at all times.

SUMMARY

Overhead costs are a major contributor to the total cost of a product and there are numerous methods used to allocate these overhead costs to specific products. Although most companies use one of the single parameter allocation methods, serious consideration should be given to the development of multiple parameter allocation methods to provide a more accurate method of overhead allocation.

EVALUATIVE QUESTIONS

1. Calculate the overhead amounts and unit costs of product C for the methods not done in detail but where the results were given; that is for the direct material proportioning, direct labor hour proportioning, machine hour proportioning, and production quantity proportioning methods.
2. What would be the unit cost for products R and C for the multiple parameter analysis if the factory expense is best represented by the factory prime cost, the administrative expense by the direct labor hours, and the sales expense by the production quantity?
3. Change the indirect material cost in Table 4–2 from $ 4,000 to $ 2,000 and reevaluate the unit costs of products R and C by the single parameter allocation methods of:
   a. Direct Cost Proportioning
   b. Direct Labor Cost Proportioning
   c. Direct Material Cost Proportioning
   d. Direct Labor Hour Proportioning
   e. Machine Hour Proportioning
   f. Production Quantity Proportioning
   g. Production Floor Area
4. If the predetermined allocation base was machine hours instead of direct labor hours, determine the overhead rate per machine hour. Use

this overhead rate and then determine the unit costs for product R and product C. Compare these unit costs with those determined by machine hour proportioning.

BIBLIOGRAPHY

1. Adithan, M., and Pabla, B. S., *Production Engineering, Estimating, and Costing*, Konark Publishers Pvt. Ltd., Delhi, India, pp. 104–126.
2. Koons, F. J., "Manufacturing Cost Management", *Cost Engineering*, May 1990, pp. 9–15.
3. Moore, L. Ted, and Creese, R. C., "Manufacturing Cost Estimation", *Cost Engineering*, May 1990, pp. 17–21.
4. *Conducting Technical and Economic Evaluations in the Process and Utility Industries*, AACE Recommended Practice No. 16R-90, American Association of Cost Engineers, Morgantown, WV 1990, pp. 1–84.

5
Break-Even Analysis

INTRODUCTION

Break-even analysis is one of the most commonly used techniques for decision making in economic evaluations. It is used for different types of evaluations, a few of which are:

1. For comparison of different processes, and to decide which process is most economical at different levels of production.
2. To determine sales price necessary for a product to be profitable at a given level of production.
3. To determine the break-even point, i.e., the level of production at which the revenue equals total cost.

Although break-even analysis is a rather simple methodology, it does give a good first analysis for evaluating alternatives. Though the emphasis in cost analysis is in comparing alternatives and in determining break-even production levels on a cost comparison, it is also extremely useful for evaluating sales prices. The break-even analysis does become more complex when evaluating the shutdown point or evaluating the break-even point when taxes are considered.

FIXED AND VARIABLE COSTS

The two main items needed for a break-even analysis are the fixed and variable costs for the product or process of concern. Fixed costs are the items of expenditure which remain constant over time, regardless of the production level. Some examples of fixed costs are depreciation of plant and buildings, administrative salaries, property taxes, janitorial services, clerical staff and supervisory salaries.

Variable costs are items of expenditure which vary with the level of production. Some of these items are the direct material costs, direct labor costs, utilities used for production, storage and inventory costs, and other items which can be tied to the level of production. Sometimes the costs do not vary in a perfect linear fashion, but may increase in a stepwise fashion, and these tend to be called semi-variable costs. For example, if production exceeds the normal scheduled capacity, some overtime work may be needed and the wage rates would then increase for this excess production, or an additional crane operator may be needed. The costs would not increase uniformly at these levels and thus these costs are called semi-variable. The results of semi-variable costs are therefore usually step increases in variable costs or the change in slope of the variable cost curve.

BREAK-EVEN ANALYSIS FOR THE COMPARISON OF ALTERNATIVES

The basic equation for break-even cost analysis is:

$$TC = FC + VC \times X \qquad (5\text{--}1)$$

where

TC = Total Cost for production quantity X units
FC = Total Fixed Costs over time period in which X units are produced
VC = Variable Cost per unit produced
X = Quantity of units produced or level of production

In the comparison of two alternatives on a cost basis, the break-even point is that level of production at which the total costs for the two alternatives are equal. For example, if one compares process A and process B, then

$$TC(A) = TC(B)$$
$$FC(A) + VC(A) \times X = FC(B) + VC(B) \times X$$

Solving for the value of X at which the two costs are equal gives the break-even point, symbolized by BE(X):

$$BE(X) = \frac{\{FC(B) - FC(A)\}}{\{VC(A) - VC(B)\}} \qquad (5\text{--}2)$$

The alternative with the lower fixed cost has the lower total cost until the break-even point is reached. Beyond the break-even level, the alternative with the lower variable cost has the lower total cost.

Example Problem 5-1

From the data in Table 5-1, determine the break-even point between alternative A and alternative B.
Solution:

$$
\begin{aligned}
BE(X) &= \frac{\{\$\,500 - \$1,000\}}{\{\$4.00\ /unit - 6.00\ /unit\}} \\
&= \frac{-\,500}{\$-2.00/unit} \\
&= 250\ units
\end{aligned}
$$

This means that alternative B, the low fixed cost alternative, has a lower total cost than alternative A until a production quantity of 250 is reached. At production levels above 250 units, alternative A, the low variable cost alternative, has a lower total cost than alternative B. This is shown in Figure 5-1, which is a break-even chart. Note that the difference in fixed costs was a negative number and the difference in variable costs was also a negative number, so the answer is a positive number. In most instances, one considers alternative A to be the high fixed cost alternative (with the corresponding low variable cost), but it is not necessary to do this. The break-even point is the intersection of the two total cost curves as illustrated in Figure 5-1. Note that the intersection of the total cost curves with the total cost axis at zero production is the total fixed cost for that total cost curve.

Table 5–1 Break-Even Analysis Data For Example Problem 5-1

Expenditure item description	Cost (fixed or variable)		A	B
			Alternative	
Material Cost	V	$/unit	2.00	2.00
Labor Cost	V	$/unit	1.25	2.35
Energy Cost	V	$/unit	0.75	1.65
Maintenance Cost	F	$	500	200
Depreciation	F	$	500	300
Total Variable Costs	V	$/unit	4.00	6.00
Total Fixed Costs	F	$	1,000	500

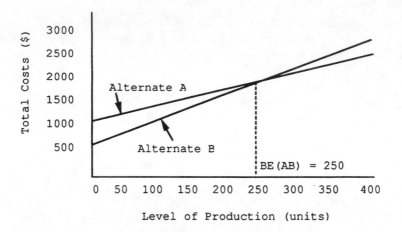

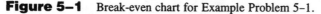

Figure 5–1   Break-even chart for Example Problem 5-1.

BREAK-EVEN ANALYSIS FOR PRODUCT PROFITABILITY

The second main use of break-even analysis is with respect to sales revenue versus product cost. In this analysis the total revenue is equal to the total cost at the break-even point. Therefore,

$$\text{Total Revenue} = \text{Total Cost}$$
$$S \times X = FC + (VC \times X) \tag{5-3}$$

where

S = Selling Price per unit ($/unit)
FC = Fixed Costs in producing product ($)
VC = Variable Costs in producing product ($/unit)
X = Level of production or quantity produced

At the break-even point,

$$BE(X) = FC / (S - VC) \tag{5-4}$$

Where $BE(X)$ is the break-even point in terms of the production quantity X. At production levels greater than the break-even point, revenues exceed costs and a profit is made. When the production level is less than the break-even point, costs exceed revenue and a loss is incurred.

Example Problem 5-2

Use the data in Table 5-2 and determine the break-even point where revenues equal costs.

Solution:

The break-even point can be calculated by using Equation 5-4 and the results are:

$$BE(X) = \$\,2,750 \,/\, (\$5.00\,/\text{unit} - \$3.00\,/\text{unit})$$
$$= 1,375\ \text{units}$$

This implies that 1,375 units must be sold before the costs are recovered or before any profit can be made. If the sales level is less than 1,375 units, the costs will exceed the revenues and a loss will incur. Figure 5-2 illustrates the break-even point and the production level at which a profit or a loss will be obtained.

Example Problem 5-3

Determine what sales price is necessary if the break-even point is to be 1000 units? Use the data in Table 5-2.

Solution:

In this case Equation 5-4 can be solved for the selling price (S) which results in:

$$S = [FC/BE(X)] + VC \qquad (5\text{-}5)$$

Table 5-2 Break-Even Analysis Data For Example Problem 5-2

Item description	Item classification		Item value
Material Cost	V	$/unit	2.50
Labor Cost	V	$/unit	0.50
Depreciation	F	$	1,500
Administrative Overhead	F	$	750
Sales & Distribution OH	F	$	500
Sales Price	V	$/unit	5.00
Total Variable Costs	V	$/unit	3.00
Total Fixed Costs	F	$	2,750
Total Revenue per Unit	V	$/unit	5.00

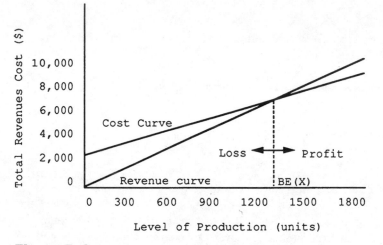

Figure 5–2   Break-even chart for Example Problem 5-2.

For the data in Table 5-2, the sales price necessary for a break-even point of 1000 units would be:

S = $ 2,750 / 1,000 units + $ 3.00/unit
  = $ 5.75 / unit

Since the break-even point is lower than the original value of 1,375 units, the selling price must be greater to overcome the fixed costs. This makes the slope of the revenue curve greater so the intersection can occur at a lower production quantity.

BREAK-EVEN ANALYSIS FOR MULTIPLE ALTERNATIVES

In the comparison of alternatives, there can often be more than two alternatives for comparison and this will lead to multiple break-even points. All of the break-even points will not be critical, but they need to be evaluated to determine if they are critical. A critical break-even point is one that involves the minimum total cost for that production level whereas a noncritical break-even point is at a higher cost than one or more of the other alternatives. The number of break-even points can be calculated from the number of alternatives using the binominial distribution; that is

$$N(BE) = \frac{N!}{2! \times (N-2)!} \tag{5-6}$$

where

N(BE) = Number of Break-Even points
  N = Number of alternatives considered

Example Problem 5-4

What is the number of break-even points if there are four alternatives?
Solution:

$$N(BE) = \frac{4!}{2! \times (4-2)!}$$
$$= 6 \text{ break-even points}$$

To the data of Example 1, a third alternative (alternative C) has been added
to illustrate multiple break-even points. If one applies Equation 5-6, the
number of break-even points is 3. The extended data is shown in Table 5-3.
The break-even point between alternatives A and B was previously calculated
to be 250 units. It is left as an exercise to show that the break-even point
between alternatives A and C is 400 units and that the break-even point
between alternatives B and C is 100 units. Figure 5-3 is a plot of the total cost
lines for the three alternatives and indicates the three break-even points. It is
apparent from the Figure 5-3 that the break-even point between alternatives A
and B is not critical; both of these alternatives have a cost higher than alternative C. That is:

TC(A) = $ 1,000 + 250 × $ 4.00 = $ 2,000
TC(B) = $ 500 + 250 × $ 6.00 = $ 2,000
TC(C) = $ 600 + 250 × $ 5.00 = $ 1,850

Table 5-3 Break-Even Analysis Data for Multiple Break-Even Points

Expenditure description	Cost		Alternative		
	(F or V)		A	B	C
Material Cost	V	$/unit	2.00	2.00	2.00
Labor Cost	V	$/unit	1.25	2.35	1.45
Energy Cost	V	$/unit	.75	1.65	1.55
Maintenance Cost	F	$	500	200	400
Depreciation	F	$	500	300	200
Total Variable Cost	V	$/unit	4.00	6.00	5.00
Total Fixed Costs	F	$	1,000	500	600

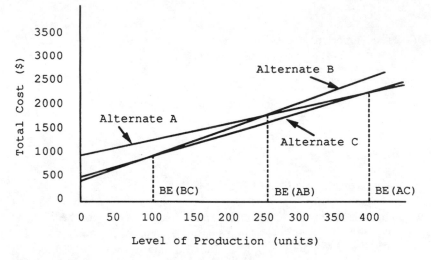

Figure 5–3   Break-even chart for multiple alternatives A, B, and C.

The results of the break-even points can be interpreted that for the lowest cost, alternative B should be used for a level of production from zero to 100 units, alternative C should be used if the level of production is between 100 and 400 units, and alternative A should be used if the level of production is over 400 units. Note that the break-even point of 250 units is not used for the lowest cost and is therefore a noncritical break-even point.

BREAK-EVEN ANALYSIS WITH SEMI-VARIABLE COSTS

Costs often cannot be classified as either fixed or variable in a linear fashion with production, but may increase in a stepwise fashion (Type 1), a variable slope change (Type 2), or may be the sum of a fixed and a variable cost (Type 3). The Type 1 changes are usually considered to occur at a specific production level and the net effect is that the cost curve no longer has a constant continuous slope. There may be more than one break-even point and it is advisable to use a graphical display to help understand the meaning of the break-even points. One common item that causes the break-even curve to have a slope change (type 2) is income taxes on profit; the tax doesn't start until a profit is being made, which starts at the break-even point. Table 5–4 contains the data for Example Problem 5–5 to illustrate the effect of semi-variable costs.

Example Problem 5–5

Use the data in Table 5–4 and determine the break-even points. This problem incorporates both Type 1 and Type 2 changes. Which of the break-even points is the actual break-even point of concern?

Solution:

The first break-even calculation will be made in the range of zero to 400 units. The break-even point is:

$$BE(X) = \frac{\$800}{(\$5.00/\text{unit} - \$2.50/\text{unit})}$$
$$= 320 \text{ units}$$

This means that from zero to 320 units, the costs exceed the revenues and from 320 to 400 units the revenue exceeds the cost. This is shown in Figure 5–4. The second calculation, from 400 to 500 units, is more difficult because a change has occurred in the variable rate. An adjustment must be made to Equation 5–4 to account for the change which results in adjusting the fixed cost as indicated in Equation 5–7:

$$BE(X) = \frac{[FC + L(1) \times (VC1 - VC2)]}{[S - VC2]} \qquad (5-7)$$

Table 5–4 Break-Even Analysis Data for Semi-variable Cost Problem

		Cost	Production	Item
Item description		(F or V)	range (units)	value
Material Cost	V	$/unit	all	2.00
Labor Cost	V	$/unit	0–400	0.50
	V	$/unit	401–800	1.00
Depreciation	F	$	all	500
Factory Overhead	F	$	0–500	300
	F	$	500–1000	900
Sales Price	V	$/unit	all	5.00
Total Variable Costs	V	$/unit	0–400	2.50
			401–800	3.00
Total Fixed Costs	F	$	0–500	800
	F	$	501–1000	1400
Total Revenue per Unit	V	$/unit	all	5.00

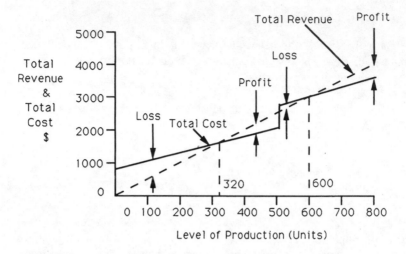

Figure 5–4 Break-even analysis with semi-variable costs.

where

    L(1) = Production Limit for variable cost 1
    VC1 = Variable unit Cost 1
    VC2 = Variable Unit Cost 2
     FC = Fixed Cost
      S = Selling Price per Unit

For this example,

$$BE(X) = \frac{[\$ \ 800 + 400 \ \text{units} \times (2.50 \ \$/\text{unit} - 3.00 \ \$/\text{unit})]}{[\ 5.00 \ \$/\text{unit} - 3.00 \ \$/\text{unit}]}$$

$$= 300 \ \text{units}$$

Since this is below the minimum value of the range of 400 to 500 units, this implies that a profit will be made when the production level is in this range. The third range, from 500 to 800 units, since 800 is the maximum unit for which there is labor cost data, also uses Equation 5-6 and the new fixed cost and the result is:

$$BE(X) = \frac{[\$ \ 1400 + 400 \times (2.50 \ \$/\text{unit} - 3.00 \ \$/\text{unit})]}{(\ 5.00 \ \$/\text{unit} - 3.00 \ \$/\text{unit})}$$

$$= 600 \ \text{units}$$

This indicates that in the range of 501 to 800 units, a profit is made when the production is above 600. Figure 5-4 indicates that profit is made between 300 and 500 units and above 600 units. When the fixed costs have step increases, the occurrence of more than one break-even point is very possible. Thus the break-even point of concern is 320 if production is less than 500, and the break-even point of concern is 600 if production is greater than 500 units. The break-even points and the two regions of profit are illustrated in Figure 5-4. The step increase in costs at 500 units was more than the profits at that level and thus a second break-even point will occur.

The third type of semi-variable cost can be represented as the sum of a fixed and variable cost. This approach, as illustrated by Humphreys and Katell (3), can lead the determination of another type of break-even point, called the shutdown point (4). An example of a Type 3 semi-variable cost is maintenance costs; there is a fixed cost to staff the maintenance department and as production increases, maintenance costs also tend to increase in a linear fashion. The shutdown point is when the sales revenue is equal to the revenue of the variable and the semi-variable costs. When production is below this level, the plant should shutdown and stop production as it is not recovering its variable costs, let alone the fixed costs.

$$BE(SD) = \frac{FC(SVC)}{[S - [TVC + VC(SVC)]]} \tag{5-8}$$

where

$$BE(SD) = \text{Break-Even at Shutdown}$$
$$FC(SVC) = \text{Fixed Cost portion of the Total Semi-Variable Costs}$$
$$S = \text{Selling Price per Unit}$$
$$TVC = \text{Total of the Variable Costs}$$
$$VC(SVC) = \text{Variable Cost portion of the Total Semi-Variable Costs}$$

Example Problem 5-6

Determine the shutdown and break-even production levels for the data presented in Table 5-5.
Solution:

The shutdown point can be found by using Equation 5-8 and the data of Table 5-5 which results in:

$$BE(SD) = \frac{\$ 1000}{[\$ 10.00/\text{unit} - (\$ 5.00/\text{unit} + \$ 1.00/\text{unit})]}$$
$$= 250 \text{ units}$$

Table 5–5 Break-Even Analysis Data for Type 3 Semi-Variable Cost for
Determination of Shutdown and Break-Even Points

Cost item	Cost type	Cost value		
		($/unit)	or	($)
Materials	Variable	$ 2.50/unit		
Labor	Variable	$ 0.50/unit		
Tooling	Fixed			$ 2,000
Maintenance	Semi-variable	$ 1.00/unit	and	$ 1,000
Overhead	Variable	$ 2.00/unit		
Cost Summary				
Total Variable		$ 5.00/unit		
Total Fixed				$ 2,000
Total Semi-variable		$ 1.00/unit	and	$ 1,000
Revenue				
Sales Revenue	Variable	$ 10.00/unit		

The break-even point can be found by using Equation 5–4 and using the sum
of all the fixed costs and fixed semi-variable costs and the sum of all the variable costs and variable semi-variable costs which results in:

$$BE = \frac{[\$\ 1,000 + \$\ 2,000]}{[\$\ 10.00/unit - (\$5.00/unit + \$\ 1.00/unit)]}$$
$$= 750\ Units$$

These results are illustrated in Figure 5–5. Note the variable costs are plot-
ted first, then the semi-variable costs are added to the variable costs, and then
then fixed costs are added to obtain the total cost curve. The intersection of the
variable and semi-variable cost total with the total revenue is the shutdown
point.

BREAK-EVEN ANALYSIS WITH REQUIRED RETURN
AND INCOME TAX

Required return is the amount of return on investment that the company wants
to earn for the risk and cost of investing capital for equipment. This is often
treated as a fixed expense, but it is viewed as a profit by most tax collectors
and taxes must be paid on profits. To illustrate the break-even analysis prob-

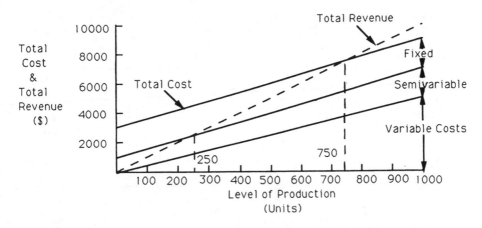

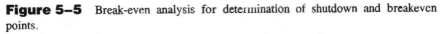

Figure 5–5 Break-even analysis for determination of shutdown and breakeven points.

lems when required return and taxes are involved, an example problem with taxes is presented.

Example Problem 5-6

Determine the break-even point with no required return and with a required return of $ 200 when the tax rate is 30 percent. Use the data in Table 5–6.
Solution:

The break-even point at cost, with no required return and no taxes is calculated by:

BE(Cost) = Total Fixed Costs/(Sales Revenue − Total Variable Cost)
= ($ 500 + $ 300) / ($4.50 /unit − $2.50 /unit)
= 400 units

The second break-even point of interest is that after which the required return has been obtained. The problem is that the taxes start after the first 400 units have been produced and is on the profit. The method used to determine the break-even point is to equate the total revenues to the total expenses including required return and taxes. This is expressed as:

Total Revenue = Total Cost (fixed and variable) +
                Required Return + Taxes
$4.50 × BE(RR) = $ 800. + 2.50 × BE(RR) + $ 200
                + 0.30 × (4.50 − 2.50) × (BE(RR) − 400)

Table 5–6 Break-Even Analysis Data for Required Return and Taxes Problem

Item description	Variable or fixed	Units	Value
Material Cost	V	$/unit	2.00
Labor Cost	V	$/unit	0.50
Depreciation	F	$	500
Required Return	F	$	200
Factory Overhead	F	$	300
Tax Rate 30%	V	Tax $/Profit $	0.30
Sales Revenue	V	$/unit	4.50

which results in

BE(RR) = 543 units

The taxes of 30 percent are on the unit profit, which is the difference between revenues at \$4.50/unit and variable costs at \$2.50/unit, for those units above the cost break-even point of 400 units. The calculation procedure for verifying the break-even point at required return after taxes of 543 units is demonstrated in Table 5–7. Figure 5–6 illustrates the two break-even points, the first being the break-even point at cost, BE(Cost), and the second is the break-even at required return after taxes, BE(RR). After the second break-even point of 543 units, the product would be making profit in excess of that required for the investment.

Table 5–7 Calculation Procedure for Verifying Break-Even Point of 543 Units with Required Return of $ 200

Line	Description and calculation	$ Value
A	Revenues 4.50 $/unit × 543 units	= 2444
B	Variable Costs 2.50 $/unit × 543 units	= 1358
C	Fixed Costs	= 800
D	Gross Profit = A − B − C	= 286
E	Taxes = 0.30 × D	= 86
F	Net Profit = D − E	= 200
G	Required Return	= 200
H	Net Profit − Required Return = F − G	= 0

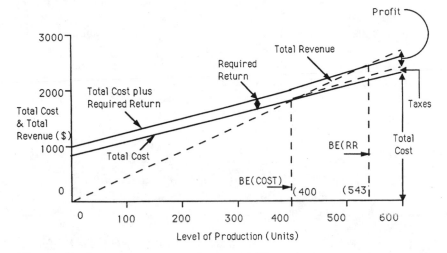

Figure 5–6 Break-even analysis curves with required return and tax considerations.

SUMMARY

Break-even analysis is a tool which is extremely helpful in making decisions concerning alternatives. The tool is used for a wide variety of situations, including alternative comparisons and the determination of the production levels needed for profitability. The effect of the various types of semi-variable costs upon the break-even points indicates the importance of knowing how the costs vary. The taxes make the calculation of the break-even point more difficult, but the need to determine the effect of taxes is sometimes critical.

EVALUATIVE QUESTIONS

1. Explain the following terms: Fixed Costs, Variable Costs, Profit, and Break-even Point.
2. Change the labor rate for alternative A in Table 5–1 from $ 1.25 to $ 1.75 per unit and determine the break-even point. Compare this value with the one previously calculated and explain the difference.
3. Change the sales price for the item in Table 5–2 from $ 5.00 to $ 7.00 and calculate the new break-even point. Compare this value with the one previously calculated for this problem and explain the difference.
4. If five alternatives are being compared, what is the maximum number of break-even points to be considered?

5. Change the depreciation of alternative A in Table 5-3 from $ 500 to $ 300 and calculate the effect on the break-even points between alternatives A and C, A and B, and B and C. One break-even point does not change; give an explanation for this effect.

6. Change the tax rate in the data in Table 5-6 from 30 to 40 percent and calculate the effect on the break-even point at cost, BE(Cost), and the break-even point at the required return, BE(RR). If taxes increase, what is the general effect upon the two break-even points?

BIBLIOGRAPHY

1. Adithan, M., and Pabla, B. S., *Production Engineering, Estimating, and Costing*, Konark Publishers Pvt. Ltd., Delhi, India, pp. 135–144.
2. Park, W. R., and Jackson, D. E., *Cost Engineering Analysis*, 2nd Edition, 1984, Wiley Interscience, pp. 237–251
3. Humphreys, K. K. and Katell, S., *Basic Cost Engineering*, 1981, Marcel Dekker, New York, pp. 36–40.
4. *Standard Cost Engineering Terminology*, AACE Standard No. 10S-90, American Association of Cost Engineers, Morgantown, WV, 1990, 102 pp.

6

Depreciation, Taxes, Cash Flow, and Time Value of Money Considerations

INTRODUCTION

The key to the success of a company is its ability to make a profit. In determining the profit of a product, it is not only necessary to determine the direct costs, but also to include the effects of depreciation and taxes. The cash flow analysis is another method for evaluating investments, and the time value of money is both an engineering and financial tool used to evaluate the effect of timing upon income and disbursements in profit evaluation. These are important tools which are introduced at a basic level to indicate their effect upon cost estimating decisions.

DEPRECIATION

Depreciation is the method used for recovering the original cost of a capital investment (asset) through a series of annual deductions distributed over the economic life of the product when the product life is greater than one year. If the product life is less than a year, the product is treated as a current expense. Depreciation has a significant effect upon income taxes and the cash flow for the capital investment. Depreciation represents the reduction in value of the capital asset due to wear or technical obsolescence. Other causes of equipment failure may be due to accidents or the lack of repairs and/or maintenance, but these are premature failures and usually are handled in a different manner.

The viewpoint of depreciation is slightly different between accountants and cost engineers. Accountants are interested in depreciation of equipment already in service with an emphasis upon tax-deductible expenses. Cost

with a viewpoint of capital recovery. Cost engineers are more concerned about the time value of money and how the money is recovered, whereas accountants are more interested in the actual expenses incurred. Both accountants and cost engineers generally want to depreciate capital investments as rapidly as possible, not only for the tax advantages but to recover the capital investment as rapidly as possible.

There are numerous methods for calculating depreciation, but only a few of the most common methods are presented. These methods are:

1. Straight-Line Depreciation Method
2. Declining Balance Method
3. Modified Accelerated Cost Recovery System (MACRS)
4. Production-Based Depreciation Method

Equipment Life

The investment life or asset life is the period during which the equipment is expected to be economically usable. The equipment becomes uneconomically usable because of excessive costs or reduced profitability. In the United States, the Internal Revenue Service (IRS), which is the federal tax collecting agency, has established the ranges and lives permitted for various types of assets. Some of the values are presented in Table 6–1 (1).

More recently, in 1987, the IRS instituted the Modified Accelerated Cost Recovery System (MACRS). This system establishes various classes of assets which are based upon the midpoint value of the former Class Life Asset Depreciation Range system as illustrated in Table 6–1. The asset lives are classified into two groups based upon the ADR value. It is noted that the MACRS recovery period is generally shorter than the alternative methods. Table 6–2 indicates the types of property in the MACRS property classes.

Table 6–1 Class Life and Recovery Periods

Asset Class	Asset Description	Class Life (years)	Recovery Period MACRS (years)	Recovery Period Alternate MACRS* (years)
00.11	Office Furniture	10	7	10
00.12	Information Systems (computers, etc.)	6	5	5
00.22	Automobiles, Taxis	3	5	5
33.2	Mfg. of Primary Nonferrous Metals	14	7	14
33.3	Mfg. of Foundry Products	14	7	14
34.0	Mfg. of Fabricated Metal Products	12	7	12
37.11	Mfg. of Motor Vehicles	12	7	12
37.2	Mfg. of Aerospace Products	10	7	10

*Alternate MACRS is also ADS, alternate depreciation system. From Ref. 9, pp. 55–65.

Table 6-2 MACRS Property Classes and Types of Property

Property Class	Types of Property
3-Year Property	Trailer units for use over-the-road Special tools for: manufacture of motor vehicles, fabricated metal products, glass products, rubber products.
5-Year Property	Automobiles, taxis, buses, light trucks; information systems–computers and peripherals; construction; manufacture of apparel; cutting of timber; manufacture of chemicals and allied products; special tools in mfg. of nonferrous metals; manufacture of electronic components, products and systems.
7-Year Property	Equipment for the manufacture of cement; glass products; primary ferrous Metals; foundry products; fabricated metal products; aerospace products; electrical and nonelectrical machinery, motor vehicles; ship and boat building. Office furniture and Fixtures.
10-Year Property	Petroleum refining equipment; equipment for the manufacture of grain and grain mill products, ship and boat building dry docks.
15-Year Property	Pipeline transportation; telephone distribution equipment; electrical utility Nuclear Plant; Municipal Waste Water Treatment.
20-Year Property	Electrical utility steam production; gas utility production plants; water utilities; municipal sewer.
Residential Rental Property	Rental structures (depreciated over 27.5 years)
Nonresidential Property	Buildings (depreciated over 31.5 years)

From Ref. 9, pp. 55–65.

Straight-Line Depreciation Method

The straight-line method of depreciation provides for a fixed amount of depreciation during the life of the investment. It is the easiest method to understand and is the method used for residential and commercial property listed in Table 6–2. The amount of depreciation is calculated by:

$$D(t) = \frac{(I - S)}{L} \qquad (6-1)$$

where

D(t) = Depreciation of asset for year t
I = Initial installed cost
S = Salvage value of asset
L = Total investment life

and

$$B(t) = I - [t \times (I - S) / L] \qquad (6-2)$$

where

B(t) = Book Value of asset in year t
t = Year of concern but $\leqslant$ L

The IRS has now developed tables for straight line depreciation which use a midyear convention. The midyear convention allows for only a half-year's depreciation in the first year and the last half-year will be obtained in the year after the class life is over. However for the sample problems, the standard formulas are used.

Example Problem 6–1

In a foundry a new molding machine was installed for $ 420,000 with an expected ADR life of 14 years. The molding machine is expected to make 25,000,000 molds over its life. The salvage value is zero. Determine the annual depreciation amount and the book value of the molding machine after four years.

Solution:

Using Equations 6–1 and 6–2, one obtains:

D(t) = ($ 420,000 − 0) / 14
    = $ 30,000 (this is the same for all values of t)

and

$$B(4) = \$ 420,000 - 4 \times (420,000 - 0) / 14$$
$$= \$ 420,000 - \$ 120,000$$
$$= \$ 300,000$$

These values will be compared with the values obtained by other methods of calculating depreciation.

Declining Balance Method

The declining balance method assumes that an asset decreases by a fixed percentage rather than a fixed value or amount as in the straight line method. This results in a greater depreciation in the earlier years and less in the later years. This method is actually the basis of MACRS and is a part of it and is rarely used as a separate method. The method has a drawback; the amount depreciated is a percentage of the previous book value and does not go to zero, and this is handled by reverting to the straight-line method at a critical point. The percentage used is usually a multiple of the straight-line depreciation percentage.

The equations for the declining balance method are:

$$D(t) = P \times (1.00 - P)^{(t-1)} \times I \qquad\qquad (6\text{--}3)$$

where

$D(t)$ = Depreciation of asset for year t
  P = Decimal value of depreciation rate Percentage
  t = Year of concern but $\leqslant L$
  I = Initial installed cost

and

$$B(t) = (1.00 - P)^t \times I \qquad\qquad (6\text{--}4)$$

where

$B(t)$ = Book value of asset in year t

Although the IRS now has tables for declining balance depreciation and uses the midyear convention, the standard formulas will be used for the problems.

Example Problem 6–2

Use the data from Example Problem 6–1 and determine the depreciation and book value for the eighth year when the depreciation rate is double or 200 percent of the straight-line depreciation rate. Compare the first year depreciation

of the double declining balance method versus the straight-line method.
Solution:

The depreciation amount for the straight-line method as a percentage is determined by:

$$P(SL) = D(t) / I$$
$$= \$ 30,000 / \$ 420,000$$
$$= 0.0714 \text{ or } 7.14\% \tag{6-5}$$

Note that $D(t)/I$ is equivalent to the expression $1/L$. The percentage used for the declining balance method is usually 150 or 200 percent that of the straight-line method. Thus, the percentage for the double declining balance method (that is 200 percent of the straight-line method) is 14.29 percent or 0.1429 as a decimal fraction for P. Therefore, $D(8)$ is calculated by

$$D(4) = 0.1429 \times (1.00 - 0.1429)^{(4-1)} \times \$ 420,000$$
$$= \$ 37,800$$

and

$$B(4) = (1.00 - 0.1429)^4 \times \$ 420,000$$
$$= \$ 226,700$$

Also, for comparison purposes, $D(1)$ is:

$$D(1) = 0.1429 \times \$ 420,000$$
$$= \$ 60,000 \text{ or double the straight-line value for } D(1)$$

Thus one can observe that the declining balance method gives more depreciation in the earlier years and less in the later years. For the first year the depreciation was $ 60,000 and in the fourth year it was only $ 37,800, which is slightly more than the straight-line value of $ 30,000. The book value by the double declining balance method was $ 226,700 or nearly $ 73,300 less than that by the straight-line method. The declining balance method gives nearly $ 73,300 more depreciation over the first four years than the straight-line method.

Modified Accelerated Cost Recovery System (MACRS) Method

There are different methods for calculating the depreciation based upon when the equipment was put into service. For the sake of simplicity, the half-year convention will be used with the double declining balance basis. There are also mid-quarter rates, an optional 150 percent with half-year convention, and optional straight-line convention. The depreciation rates for the three, five, seven, and ten year class properties are presented in Table 6–3.

Since the values assume that the asset was purchased in midyear, the depreciation is spread over the class life plus one year. For example, a five year class life property is depreciated over six years. The equations for the MACRS system are:

$$D(t) = P(c,t) \times I \qquad (6\text{--}6)$$

where

$D(t)$ = Depreciation of asset for year t
$P(c,t)$ = Decimal value of Percentage rate Depreciation for depreciation class c in year t
I = Initial installed cost

and

$$B(t) = I \times (1.00 - \text{sum of all depreciation percentages on a decimal basis up to t }) \qquad (6\text{--}7)$$

Example Problem 6–3

Use the data from Example Problem 6–1 and determine the MACRS depreciation amount and book value for the fourth year. Assume the class life is 14

Table 6–3   MACRS Half-Year Depreciation Percentages

Recovery year	3-year class	5-year class	7-year class	10-year class
1	33.33	20.00	14.29	10.00
2	44.45	32.00	24.49	18.00
3	14.81	19.20	17.49	14.40
4	7.41	11.52	12.49	11.52
5		11.52	8.93	9.22
6		5.76	8.92	7.37
7			8.93	6.56
8			4.46	6.55
9				6.55
10				6.55
11				3.28

From Ref. 9, p. 25.

years; this implies a 7-year property life. Also determine the depreciation for the first year and compare this amount with the amount determined by the straight-line method.

Solution:

Using the appropriate values from Table 6-3 in Equations 6-6 and 6-7, one obtains:

$$D(4) = P(7\text{-yr}, 4) \times I$$
$$= .1249 \times \$\,420,000$$
$$= \$\,52,458$$

and

$$B(4) = \$\,420,000 \times [1.00 - (.1429 + .2449 + .1749 + .1249]$$
$$= \$\,420,000 \times (1.00 - 0.6876)$$
$$= \$131,208$$

Also for the first year,

$$D(1) = P(7\text{-yr}, 1) \times I$$
$$= 0.1429 \times \$\,420,000$$
$$= \$\,62,118$$

The MACRS system greatly increases the amount depreciated and correspondingly reduces the book value in comparison with the other two time-based methods. The book value of $131,208 is much less than $300,000 obtained by the straight-line method and $226,700 obtained by the double declining balance method. This is primarily due to the greatly reduced asset life of the MACRS method. The first year depreciation is $ 52,458 and this is considerably larger than the straight-line value and only slightly lower than the double declining balance value of $ 60,000. It must also be noted that with the mid-year convention, the first year depreciation for the straight-line method would be only $ 15,000 and for the double declining balance only $ 30,000, or half the calculated values. Thus the MACRS method, with its rapid depreciation, is the method most frequently used in the United States.

Production-Based Depreciation Method

In some cases depreciation is apportioned over the production quantity rather than over a time basis. In this case the depreciation is per unit quantity rather than per unit time. The method of depreciation is a straight-line method, but is based on a production quantity life rather than a time-based life.

Example Problem 6–4

The foundry molding machine problem of Example Problem 6–1 is analyzed with respect to mold life and the following additional data is obtained. Approximately 10,000,000 molds have been produced with the molding machine over its eight year life, with 1,500,000 produced in the last year. What is the depreciation and book value if the initial cost was $ 420,000 and expected life of 25,000,000 molds?
Solution:
The depreciation amount would be calculated by:

$$D(t) = \frac{(I - S) \times Q(t)}{Q(l)} \qquad (6\text{-}8)$$

where

$D(t)$ = Depreciation of asset for year t
I = Initial installed cost
S = Salvage value of asset
$Q(t)$ = Quantity produced in year t
$Q(l)$ = Estimated Quantity produced in asset lifetime

and

$$B(t) = (I - S) \times [1.00 - \text{total production units to date}/Q(l)] \qquad (6\text{-}9)$$

where

$B(t)$ = Book value of asset in year t

For the example, the numerical values are:

$$D(4) = (\$\,420{,}000 - 0) \times (1{,}500{,}000\,/\,25{,}000{,}000)$$
$$= \$\,25{,}200$$

$$B(4) = (\$\,420{,}000 - 0) \times [1.00 - (10{,}000{,}000\,/\,25{,}000{,}000)]$$
$$= \$\,252{,}000$$

One advantage of the production-based method is that the investment asset costs can be more directly related to the unit of production and unit cost. The cost is a direct cost rather than an overhead type cost. The disadvantage of the method is that if production is low, then the depreciation rate will also be low. This method of depreciation is generally not used in the United States.

Other Methods of Depreciation

There are other methods of depreciation used, such as the depletion method for the removal of coal, timber, stone, oil, and other natural resources. The description and use of these methods can be found in engineering economy books (5–8).

TAXES AND CASH FLOW

Taxes are the primary sources of income for governments to provide services for their people. People demand various services and the governments must collect the revenues through taxes.

Corporation taxes are based upon profits, and different depreciation amounts will result in different taxes. However, if the total depreciation over the life of the investment is the same, then the total taxes would be the same if all other items are equivalent. Thus the net effect of depreciation is not on the amount of taxes, but when the taxes are paid. If rapid depreciation occurs, then the taxes are lower in the initial periods and higher later for that asset. The advantage of rapid depreciation and lower initial taxes is important when the time value of money is considered.

The cash flow represents the net funds available for investment in projects, dividends, debt repayment, etc. It is not the same as profits; for the typical industrial investment it is expressed as:

$$CF = (1.00 - T) \times (R - C - D) + D \qquad (6\text{-}10)$$

where

CF = Cash Flow
T = Tax Rate on a decimal basis
R = Revenues generated by asset
C = Expenses operating asset
D = Depreciation of asset

On the other hand, the net profit would be

$$NP = (1.00 - T) \times (R - C - D) \qquad (6\text{-}11)$$

where

NP = Net Profit

Example Problem 6.5

In Table 6–4 data is presented for two years on revenues and expenses. Two different depreciation amounts are presented. If the tax rate is 40 percent, ver-

Table 6-4 Cash Flow and Net Profit Data for Example Problem 6-5

Year	Revenue	Expenses	Depreci- ation-I	Depreci- ation-2	Gross profit-1	Gross profit-2
1	$ 10,000	$ 6,000	$ 3,000	$ 2,000	$ 1,000	$ 2,000
2	$ 15,000	$ 8,000	$ 2,000	$ 3,000	$ 5,000	$ 4,000
Total	$ 25,000	$ 14,000	$ 5,000	$ 5,000	$ 6,000	$ 6,000

Year	Taxes-1 (0.40)	Taxes-2 (0.40)	Net-1 profit	Net-2 profit	Cash flow-1	Cash flow-2
1	$ 400	$ 800	$ 600	$ 1,200	$ 3,600	$ 3,200
2	$ 2,000	$ 1,600	$ 3,000	$ 2,400	$ 5,000	$ 5,400
Total	$ 2,400	$ 2,400	$ 3,600	$ 3,600	$ 8,600	$ 8,600

ify that the gross profits, taxes, net profits, and cash flow amounts are correct. Also determine the total amounts after the two year life.

Solution:

Use Equations 6-10 and 6-11 to calculate the net profits and cash flow values. Follow the procedure in Table 5-7 to calculate the gross profit and taxes.

From the results in Table 6-4 it is apparent that the total gross profits, total depreciation amounts, total taxes, total net profits, and total cash flows are equivalent. The net profits are higher for depreciation method 2 in the first year, but if there are no time value of money concerns, the methods can be considered as equivalent. If time value of money is considered, then the methods will not be equivalent and method 2 will be the preferred method.

TIME VALUE OF MONEY

The time value of money deals with the concept that a dollar now is worth more than a dollar in the future. This is also implied in the saying "A bird in the hand is worth two in the bush." The problem is trying to determine how much more a dollar now is worth versus a dollar in the future, which leads to the concept of rate of return, also called required rate of return, return on investment (ROI), and internal rate of return. The rate of return includes not only the interest one would earn on investing but also a risk factor as the investment may fail, a factor for inflation, a factor for profits, etc.

Managers and engineers consider that this return is needed to make the investment attractive, whereas accountants are interested only in the expenses actually incurred. Accountants view rate of return as the cost of what you would pay if you borrowed the money, which does not include all the risk factors. Thus managers and engineers desire rates of return of 15–50 percent whereas accountants look at actual costs and have lower expectations, that is in the 5–25 percent range.

The primary expression from engineering economy that relates the present value and future worth of an asset investment is given by:

$$PW = FW / (1.00 + RR)^n \qquad\qquad (6\text{--}12)$$

where

PW = Present Worth of investment
FW = Future Worth of investment after n periods
RR = Rate of Return per period (expressed in decimal fraction)
  n = number of periods

Example Problem 6–6

Calculate the present worth values of the net profits for the two depreciation methods in Table 6–4. The rate of return to be considered for this problem is 20 percent.

Solution: A flow diagram of the net profits for each of the two depreciation methods is illustrated in Figure 6–1. The calculations for the present worth values for the two depreciation methods are:

$$
\begin{aligned}
PW(NP,D\!:\!1) &= \$\,600/(1.00 + 0.20)^1 + \$\,3{,}000/(1.00 + 0.20)^2 \\
&= \$\,500 + \$\,2{,}083 \\
&= \$\,2{,}583 \\
PW(NP,D\!:\!2) &= \$\,1{,}200/(1.00 + 0.20)^1 + \$2{,}400/(1.00 + 0.20)^2 \\
&= \$\,1{,}000 + \$\,1{,}667 \\
&= \$\,2{,}667
\end{aligned}
$$

PW(NP,D:1) represents the present worth of the net profits with depreciation method 1 being used and PW(NP,D:2) represents the present worth of the net profits with depreciation method 2 being used.

The calculations indicate that the present worth of the net profits is $ 2,583 for depreciation method 1 and $ 2,667 for depreciation method 2. Note that the present worth values are both less than the total net profits of $ 3,600 calculated without consideration of the time value of money. The calculations indicate that depreciation method 2 is worth $ 84 more than depreciation method 1 when the rate of return is 20 percent. When the time value of money is used, the net profits are decreased by approximately $ 1,000 as per the present worth analysis; that is, the total net profits distributed over the two

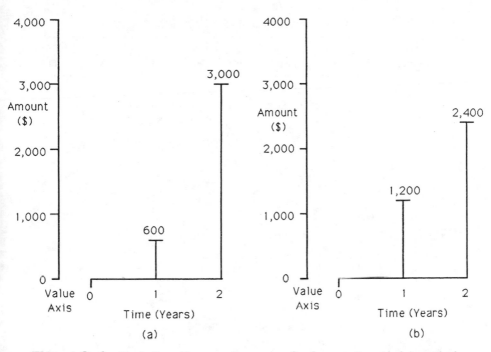

Figure 6–1 Fund flow diagrams for net profits for two depreciation methods from data in Table 6–4. (a) Fund flow diagram of net profits for first depreciation method. (b) Fund flow diagram of net profits for second depreciation method.

year period is worth $ 1,000 less at time zero (present worth) if the rate of return is 20 percent. On the other hand, if one does a present worth analysis of the cash flows, the result will be that the present worth of the cash flow generated by method 1 will be greater than that generated by depreciation method 2. This illustrates that profits and cash flows are not the same and often do not agree on recommendations. Cash flows are important from the viewpoint of having money available to prevent short-term cash problems whereas profits are necessary for the long-term security of the company.

Example Problem 6–7

A $ 10,000 investment is to be evaluated with respect to cash flows and net profits. The anticipated revenues, expenses, and depreciation values are presented in Table 6–5. The tax rate is 40 percent and the required return desired is 20 percent. The fund flow diagrams for cash flows and net profits are presented in Figure 6–2. Does the investment meet the 20 percent required return on a cash flow basis and on a net profit basis?

Table 6–5 Data for Investment Analysis for Example Problem 6–7

Year	Invest-ment	Revenue	Expenses	Depre-ciation	Gross profit	Taxes (0.40)	Net profit	Cash flow
0	$10,000	—	—	—	—	—	—	$ –10,000
1	-	$ 10,000	$ 4,000	$ 5,000	$ 1,000	$ 400	$ 600	$ 5,600
2	-	$ 15,000	$ 6,000	$ 5,000	$ 4,000	$ 1,600	$ 2,400	$ 7,400

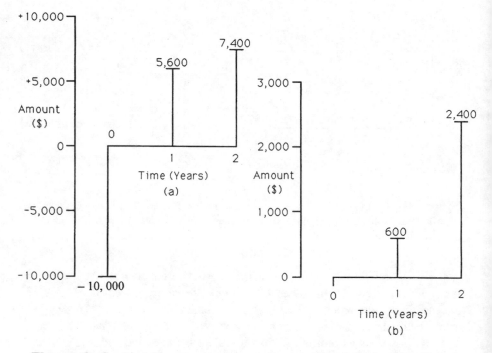

Figure 6–2 Fund flow diagrams for cash flows and net profits for Example Problem 6–7. (a) Fund flow diagram for cash flows. (b) Fund flow diagram for net profits.

Solution:

As one calculates the present worth of the cash flows, the initial investment will appear as a negative cash flow at time zero as indicated in Figure 6–2.

$$
\begin{aligned}
PW(CF) &= -\$10,000 + \$5,600/(1.00 + .2)^1 + \$7,400/(1.00 + .2)^2 \\
&= -\$10,000 + \$4,667 + \$5,139 \\
&= -\$194.
\end{aligned}
$$

This means that the discounted cash flow is less than the investment by $ 194 over the two year time period with a rate of return of 20 percent. Thus the present worth of the cash flows indicates that a 20 percent required return on the cash flows is not attained. The present worth of the net profits is:

$$PW(NP) = [\$ 600 / (1.00 + 0.20)^1 + [\$ 2,400 / (1.00 + 0.20)^2]$$
$$= \$ 500 + \$ 1,667$$
$$= \$ 2,167$$

If the discounted net profit is divided by the investment, a rate of return on the investment is 21.67 percent, which exceeds the desired rate of return of 20 percent. Thus this investment would meet a profitability return of 20 percent and not have a discount cash flow of 20 percent. For further investigation of required return and discount cash flows, references such as those listed in the bibliography should be studied.

One of the problems with accelerated depreciation for cost estimating is in the amount to be charged in the overhead rate. When straight line depreciation is used, the depreciation amount is the same per year, whereas if accelerated depreciation is used, the depreciation amount varies per year and this would cause the costs also to be changed. It is useful, therefore, to account for the depreciation differences over time and develop a meaningful average value which includes time value of money considerations. This requires the introduction of the present worth factor equation to determine the equal payments for depreciation under accelerated depreciation conditions. The factor is:

$$A = \frac{PW \times RR \times [1.0 + RR]^n}{[(1.0 + RR)^n - 1.0]} \tag{6-13}$$

where

A = Annual equivalent depreciation amount
PW = Present Worth of accelerated depreciation amounts
RR = Rate of Return
n = Number of annual time periods

Example Problem 6–7

Table 6–6 gives depreciation amounts for a $ 10,000 investment with a three year class life property. The required return is 20 percent and the present worth of the annual depreciation amounts are also presented in Table 6–6. What is the average annual equivalent depreciation amount if the required return is 20 percent?

Table 6–6 Data for Calculation of Equivalent Annual Depreciation Values from Accelerated Depreciation Schedule with Required Return of 20 percent and 3 Year Class Property

Year	Invest-ment $	Accelerated depreciation rate %	Accelerated depreciation amount $	Present worth of accelerated depreciation $
0	10,000			
1		33.33	3,333	2,777.50
2		44.45	4,445	3,086.80
3		14.81	1,481	857.10
4		7.41	741	357.30
Total		100.00	10,000	7,078.70

Solution:

Use Equation 6–13 to determine the annual equivalent depreciation amount:

$$A = \$ 7{,}078.7 \times 0.20 \times (1.00 + 0.20)^4 / \{(1.00 + 0.20)^4 - 1.0\}$$
$$= \$ 1415.74 \times 2.0736 / (2.0736 - 1.0)$$
$$= \$ 2{,}734.4$$

This means that the annual depreciation should be $ 2,734 because of accelerated depreciation instead of the expected average of $ 2,500. If the required rate of return was zero, then the annual depreciation would have been $ 2,500. The effect of accelerated depreciation with a positive rate of return is to increase the annual depreciation. This indicates that an overhead rate slightly higher than that used for straight line depreciation should be used when accelerated depreciation is applied.

SUMMARY

Depreciation, taxes, cash flows and the required rate of return for the time value of money are important factors in the investment of capital for assets. Accelerated depreciation results in the faster recovery of assets, but it also results in higher overhead rates than would result from straight line depreciation. Profits tend to be increased by accelerated depreciation whereas cash flows tend to decrease when time value of money considerations are used.

EVALUATIVE QUESTIONS

1. A new computer is purchased for the plant and the installed cost is $ 8,000 with an expected salvage value of $ 2,000. Calculate the depreciation schedule using an ADR life of six years by the following methods:
   a. Straight Line
   b. Declining Balance-200 % (i.e.Double-declining balance method)
   c. MACRS
2. Change the revenues for year 1 and 2 in Table 6–4 to $ 12,000 and $ 18,000 respectively and then recalculate for both depreciation methods the following: gross profits, taxes, net profits, and cash flows.
3. Calculate the present worth of the following annual payments if the rate of return is 25 percent:

Year	Payment
0	$ − 10,000
1	$ 5,000
2	$ 7,000
3	$ 6,000

4. Calculate the present worth of the cash flows in Table 6–5 if the required rate of return is 25 percent.
5. Verify the calculation of the present worth of accelerated depreciation values given in Table 6–6.
6. Calculate the equivalent annual depreciation amount from the sample problem in Table 6–6 if the required rate of return is 25 percent instead of 20 percent.

BIBLIOGRAPHY

1. Thuesen, G. J., and Fabrycky, W. J., *Engineering Economy*, 7th Edition, Prentice-Hall,1989, pp. 363–402.
2. *J. K. Lasser's Your 1990 Income Tax*, J. K. Lasser Institute, New York, Simon & Schuster, Inc, 1990, pp. 422–438.
3. Adithan, M., and Pabla, B. S., *Production Engineering, Estimating, and Costing*, Konark Publishers Pvt. Ltd., Dehli, India, 1989, pp. 125–131.
4. Park, W. R., and Jackson, D. E., *Cost Engineering Analysis*, 2nd Edition, Wiley Interscience, 1984, pp. 237–251.

5. Ostwald, P. F., *Cost Estimating*, 2nd Edition, Prentice-Hall, 1984, p. 541.
6. Couper, J. R. and Rader, W. H., *Applied Finance and Economic Analysis for Scientists and Engineers*, Van Nostrand Reinhold Co., 1986, New York, p. 434.
7. DeGarmo, E. P., Sullivan, W. G., and Canada, J. R., *Engineering Economy*, 7th Edition, 1984, p. 669.
8. Fleischer, G. A., *Engineering Economy*, Brooks/Cole Engineering Division, Monterey, California, 1984, p. 521.
9. IRS Publication 534, *Depreciation*, Department of the Treasury, U.S. Government Printing Office 1991-285-562, pp. 8, 25, 55-65.

7
Costing for Materials with Design Considerations

INTRODUCTION

In the early 1900s direct labor costs were the primary costs of manufacturing products, and the industrial engineers primarily focused their efforts on methods to reduce labor costs. But in the late 1900s, the predominant cost item in the manufacturing is the material cost. The total manufacturing cost breakdown for a typical high technology, large equipment manufacturing company (1) is:

Item	Cost(%)
Material	64
Factory Labor	8
Factory Overhead	16
Manufacturing Overhead	12
Total	100

Other studies have also indicated that the largest prime cost item is the direct material cost, and a major problem is how to reduce the material costs. One approach to the problem is to work with the designer in the selection of a cost-effective material for the product. A second approach is to accurately cost the scrap to determine where to improve operations with a maximum impact upon product costs.

The selection of the material can effect the process operations required to obtain the desired material shape, so a total cost analysis is needed to obtain the overall cost benefit of a material. For example, a material may cost less for the desired shape, but if the scrap rates are higher, the final material cost may be higher. If different equipment is used, then the higher processing costs may offset the materials savings. The methods presented in this chapter will assist the designer, cost engineer, and production manager in analyzing material costs and evaluating alternative materials.

PERFORMANCE BASED MATERIAL COST SELECTION SYSTEM

The selection of a material in a performance based system implies that the material must meet the desired performance requirements set by the designer. It is useful to work with the designer in this process as the designer can determine the critical design requirements for evaluation. Since the different materials have different engineering design properties, the cross-sectional area will be different for the different materials in order to meet the same performance requirements. References 2 and 3 have more details on the development of specific expressions and are recommended for further reading. Charles and Crane list 28 different formulas for the evaluation of stress limited and deflection limited designs for different components and loadings. Only a few will be used to illustrate their importance. Since most materials are costed on a dollar/weight basis, such as dollars/kg or dollars/lb, the total cost can be represented as:

$$C(u) = C(r) \times M \tag{7-1}$$

where

$C(u)$ = Total Unit Cost in dollars
$C(r)$ = Material Cost in \$/kg (\$/lb)
M = Material weight in kg (lb) per unit

The material weight can be expressed in terms of the material density, which is a material property, and the volume of material required, so Equation 7-1 becomes:

$$C(u) = C(r) \times \rho \times V \tag{7-2}$$

where

ρ = Material Density in kg/m^3 (lb/in^3)
V = Material Volume in meters^3 (inches^3)

The volume of material can be expressed in terms of the cross-sectional area and length, and these parameters are frequently involved in the basic design relationships. Equation 7-2 becomes:

$$C(u) = C(r) \times \rho \times A \times L \qquad (7\text{-}3)$$

where

A = Design cross-sectional Area in m^2 (in^2
L = Design Length in m (in)

The cross-sectional area and design length are values that are either specified or calculated from basic strength of materials and design relationships. Table 7-1 lists the basic design relationships used for the structural cross-sections.

The relationships in Table 7-1 can use the material properties relating to the strength of the material and to the modulus of elasticity. These relationships can be used to solve for the design parameter of interest namely, the cross-sectional area. The new relationships are presented in Table 7-2 and Table 7-3 lists the nomenclature.

From the expressions developed, the material properties of interest are the yield strength, modulus of elasticity, density, and also the cost of the material. Table 7-4 includes these properties for different materials in both the metric and English (or US) units. Some example problems will be presented showing how to use the formulas and interpret the results obtained.

Example Problem 7-1

Which material in Table 7-4 is the best to construct a solid bar to support a load of 178 kN (40,000 pounds) over a length of 25.4 centimeters (0.254 m or 10 inches)?

Table 7-1 Design Relationships for Basic Structural Cross-sections

Structural cross-section shape	Loading type	Design relationship for	
		stress	deflection
Solid Bar, Rod, or Cylinder	Tension, Compression	S = P/A	$\delta = PL/AE$
Solid Cylinder	Bending (center load)	S = mc/I	$\delta = PL^3/48EI$
Solid Rectangular Plate	Bending (center load)	S = mc/I	$\delta = PL^3/48EI$

Table 7-2 Design and Cost Relationships for Strength and Deflection

Structural Cross-Section Shape	Loading Type	Design Area	Design Equation for Area for Condition of:		General Material Relationship for:		General Cost Performance Relationship for:	
			Strength	Deflection	Strength	Deflection	Strength	Deflection
1. Solid Bar, Rod or Cylinder	Tension or Compression	A	P/S	PL/(δE)	1/S	1/E	ρ×C(r)/S	ρ×C(r)/E
2. Solid Bar	Bending	A						
a) Circular Section	(Single Load)	(πD²/4)	[PL(π).5/S]^{2/3}	[PL³/3δE]^{1/2}	[1/S]^{2/3}	[1/E]^{1/2}	ρ×C(r)/S^{2/3}	ρ×C(r)/E^{1/2}
b) Rectangular Section (w fixed, h Variable)	(Single Load)	(wxh)	[3PLw/2S]^{1/2}	[PL³w²/4δE]^{1/3}	[1/S]^{1/2}	[1/E]^{1/3}	ρ×C(r)/S^{1/2}	ρ×C(r)/E^{1/3}

Table 7–3 Nomenclature for Relationships in Tables 7-2 and 7-4

Symbol	Definition, Metric Unit (English unit)
S	= Material yield strength, MPa (psi)
A	= Cross-sectional area, square meter (square inches)
E	= Material Modulus of elasticity, GPa (psi)
L	= Length of part, meter (inch)
P	= Applied load, kN (pounds)
m	= Applied moment, Newton-meter (inch-pounds)
c	= Distance from neutral axis to outer fibers, meter (inch)
I	= Moment of inertia, meter^4 (inch^4)
C(r)	= Cost dollars/kg (dollars/lb)
ρ	= Material density, kg/m^3 (lb/in^3)
π	= 3.141692
δ	= Deflection, meter (inches)
Dia	= Diameter(variable) of circular section, meter (inch)
w	= Width (fixed) of rectangular section, meter (inch)
h	= Thickness (variable) of rectangular section, meter (inch)

Solution:

If best means the lowest cost material which will meet the strength requirements, then the general cost relationship for strength in Table 7-2 is to be used for the materials. This means the values for the expression $\{\rho \times C(r)\}/S$ must be calculated for each material and the lowest value would be the best material. To make the numbers easier to interpret, each is multiplied by 1,000,000 for both the metric and English systems and the values are in Table 7-5. The units of the ratios are not critical, as only the values are being compared. However, the same units must be used for each material in the comparison.

This indicates that ductile iron has the lowest cost in this comparison. The actual cost is determined from Equation 7-3, but the cross-sectional area needs to be determined first, and from Table 7-2 it would be P/S which is:

$$P/S = 178 \text{ kN} / 345 \text{ MPa}$$
$$= 0.000516 \text{ m}^2 \ (0.80 \text{ in}^2)$$

Therefore,

$$C(u) = \$ 0.55/\text{kg} \times 6935 \text{ kg/m}^3 \times 0.00516 \text{ m}^2 \times 0.254 \text{ m}$$
$$= \$ 0.50/\text{unit}$$

Table 7-4 Material Property (6) and Cost Data

Material Description Metal/Alloy	Yield Strength S (MPa)	(kpsi)	Density ρ (kg/m³)	(lb/in³)	Elastic Modulus E (GPa)	(Mpsi)	Material Cost C(r) ($/kg)	($/lb)
Magnesium								
AS91C-T6	145	(21)	1831	(.066)	44.8	(6.5)	4.40	(2.00)
AK60A-T5	283	(41)	1831	(.066)	44.8	(6.5)	4.84	(2.20)
Aluminum								
2024-T861	455	(66)	2774	(.100)	72.4	(10.5)	2.20	(1.00)
3003-H18	200	(29)	2746	(.099)	70.3	(10.2)	1.98	(.90)
7175-T66	524	(76)	2802	(.101)	71.7	(10.4)	2.75	(1.25)
Titanium								
Ti-6Al-6V-2Sn	965	(140)	4531	(.165)	110	(16.0)	13.20	(6.00)
Ti-13V-11Cr-3Al	1103	(160)	4854	(.175)	110	(16.0)	13.75	(6.25)
Steels								
1015	345	(50)	7905	(.285)	207	(30.0)	.66	(.30)
4140 Q&T	1738	(252)	7905	(.285)	207	(30.0)	2.75	(1.25)
304 Stainless Steel	586	(85)	7961	(.287)	193	(28.0)	4.40	(2.00)
Cast Iron								
Gray Cast Iron	138	(20)	6935	(.250)	103	(15.0)	.44	(.20)
Ductile Iron	345	(50)	6935	(.250)	207	(30.0)	.55	(.25)

All cost values are estimates.

1 kpsi = 1,000 psi   1 MPa = 1,000,000 Pa

1 Mpsi = 1,000,000 psi   1 GPa = 1,000,000,000 Pa

Material Property Data adapted from *ASM Metals Handbook*, 9th Edition, Volumes 1, 2, and 3. Reprinted with the permission of ASM.

Table 7–5 General Cost Performance Relationship for Strength Evaluated for Materials with Properties and Costs Presented in Table 7–4

Material		Strength Cost Performance Ratio* $[\rho \times C(r)/S] \times 1,000,000$	
		(Metric)	(English)
Magnesium	- AS91C-T6	55.6	6.28
	- AK60A-T5	31.3	3.54
Aluminum	- 2024-T861	13.4	1.52
	- 3003-H18	27.1	3.07
	- 7175-T66	14.7	1.66
Titanium	- Ti-6Al-6V-2Sn	62.6	7.07
	- Ti-13V-11Cr-3Al	60.5	6.83
Steel	- 1015	15.1	1.71
	- 4140 Q&T	12.5	1.41
	- 304 Stainless	59.8	6.75
Cast Iron	Gray Cast Iron	22.1	2.50
	- Ductile Iron	11.1	1.25

*Ratio is multiplied by 1,000,000 so typical values will be between 1 and 100.

The next lowest cost material is the 4140 Q&T steel and its cost can be determined by:

$$P/S = 178 \text{ kN} / 1,738 \text{ MPa}$$
$$= 1.024 \times 10^{-4} \text{ m}^2 \ (0.159 \text{ in}^2)$$

Therefore,

$$C(u) = \$ 2.75/\text{kg} \times 7905 \text{ kg/m}^3 \times 1.024 \times 10^{-4} \text{ m}^2 \times 0.254 \text{ m}$$
$$= \$ 0.57/\text{unit}$$

If one wants the minimum material volume, one would select the material with the lowest 1/S value, which leads to the material with the highest yield strength. From the list, that would be the 4140 Q&T steel; the volume is obtained from:

$$V = A \times L$$
$$= 1.024 \times 10^{-4} \text{ m}^2 \times 0.254 \text{ m}$$
$$= 2.60 \times 10^{-5} \text{ m}^3 \ (1.59 \text{ in}^3)$$

The weight is the product of the density and volume, and is

$$M = 7905 \text{ kg/m}^3 \times 2.60 \times 10^{-5} \text{ m}^3$$
$$= 0.206 \text{ kg } (0.453 \text{ lb})$$

If one wants the minimum material weight, one would select the material with the lowest ρ/S value, or conversely, the highest S/ρ ratio. From the materials in Table 7-4, the lowest ρ/S ratio is 4.40 for the Ti-13V-11Cr-3Al alloy. The minimum weight is given by:

$$M = \rho \times A \times L \qquad (7\text{-}5)$$

where the cross-sectional area is determined from P/S, and

$$M = 4854 \text{ kg/m}^3 \times (178 \text{ kN } / 1103 \text{ MPa }) \times 0.254 \text{ m}$$
$$= 0.199 \text{ kg } (0.438 \text{ lb})$$

Thus from this example, it can be seen that the material selection depends upon what is best; the lowest cost was ductile iron, the lowest volume was 4140 Q&T steel, and the lowest weight was the Ti-13V-11Cr-3Al alloy. Due to the complexity of the relationships and conditions to be considered, it is advised that the cost engineer or manager work with the designer in decisions involving material selection.

To indicate some additional complexity that may be involved in the material selection, let us modify Example Problem 7-1 and restrict the materials considered in Example Problem 7-2.

Example Problem 7-2

Which of the three materials, 7175 Al, 4140 Q&T Steel, or Ti-13V-11Cr-3Al, is the best (lowest cost) to construct a solid bar to support a load of 178 kN (40,000 lb) and have a maximum extension of 2 mm (0.002 m or 0.08 inches) over a length of 0.254 m (10 inches)?
Solution:

The first step is to calculate the cross-sectional area for each of the two conditions and take the maximum area. The area value calculations and results are presented in Table 7-6 for the three materials selected.

These results indicate that the load is critical for the aluminum whereas the extension is the critical factor for the steel and titanium alloys. Thus the cost for the required materials according to Equation 7-3, and using the maximum area value for that material in Table 7-6 results in:

Table 7-6 Cross-Sectional Area Calculations for Load and Extension Conditions for Three Materials for Example Problem 7-2

	Cross-sectional area based upon:	
Material	Load $A = P/S$	Extension $A = PL/\delta E$
7175 Al	178kN/524MPa $A = 3.4 \times 10^{-4}\ m^2\ (.526\ in^2)$	(178kN × .254m)/(.002m × 71.7GPa) $A = 3.15 \times 10^{-4}\ m^2\ (.488\ in^2)$
4140 Steel	178kN/1738MPa $A = 1.02 \times 10^{-4}\ m^2\ (.159\ in^2)$	(178kN × .254m)/(.002m × 207GPa) $A = 1.09 \times 10^{-4}\ m^2\ (.169\ in^2)$
Ti-13V -11Cr-3Al	178kN/1103MPa $A = 1.61 \times 10^{-4}\ m^2\ (.250\ in^2)$	(178kN × .254m)/(.002m × 110GPa) $A = 2.06 \times 10^{-4}\ m^2\ (.319\ in^2)$

Note: The results include the following unit conversions in the calculations to arrive at the answers given:
1 kN   = 1000 N
1 MPa = 1,000,000 Pa
1 GPa = 1,000,000,000 Pa

$$C(u)\ for\ Al = \$\ 2.75/kg \times 2802\ kg/m^3 \times 3.4 \times 10^{-4}\ m^2 \times 0.254m$$
$$= \$\ 0.665/unit$$
$$C(u)\ for\ Steel = \$\ 2.75/kg \times 7905kg/m^3 \times 1.09 \times 10^{-4}\ m^2 \times 0.254m$$
$$= \$\ .602/unit$$
$$C(u)\ for\ Ti = \$\ 13.75/kg \times 4854kg/m^3 \times 2.06 \times 10^{-4}\ m^2 \times 0.254m$$
$$= \$\ 3.49/unit$$

The aluminum and steel costs are rather close, with the steel having a slight advantage. This competitiveness between steel and aluminum occurs in practice, and when there is more than one critical design factor, each factor needs to be evaluated, as the load was critical for the aluminum, whereas the extension was the critical factor for the steel.

The factors are more complex for the bending conditions as indicated in Table 7-2. The general cost relationships have fractional exponents, such as 1/2, 1/3, and 2/3. These relations do permit quick comparisons of two materials for a general case as illustrated in Example 7-3.

Example Problem 7-3

Which material, 2024 Al or 4140 Q&T, is the most economical for a solid plate in bending to support 30 kN load over a span length of 1 meter and a width of 0.20 meters?

Solution:

Use the data in Table 7–4 to calculate the value of the general cost performance relationship for strength for a solid plate with a rectangular cross-section in Table 7–2; that is

General Cost Performance $= \rho \times C(r) / S^{1/2}$
Relationship for Strength

The evaluation of this expression for the two materials gives the following results:

For 2024 Al $= (2774 \text{ kg/m}^3) \times (2.20 \text{ \$/kg}) / (455\text{MPa})^{1/2}$
$= 286$

For the 4140 Q&T Steel $= (7905 \text{ kg/m}^3) \times (2.75 \text{ \$/kg}) / (1738\text{MPa})^{1/2}$
$= 521$

These values indicate that the 2024 Al is more economical for this application as it has the lower value of the ratios. To find the actual cost, the cross-sectional area must be calculated from the design equation for area in Table 7–2, and then Equation 7–3 must be applied to determine the cost.

Cross-sectional $= [3PLw/2S]^{1/2}$ (From Table 7–2)
Area Equation
2024 Al Area $= [3 \times 30\text{kN} \times 1\text{m} \times 0.20\text{m} / (2 \times 455\text{MPa})]^{1/2}$
$= 0.00444 \text{ m}^2 \ (6.89 \text{ in}^2)$

(The conversion of kN to N and of MPa to Pa must be made to obtain the answer given)
The thickness, h, of the beam would be:

$h = 0.00444 \text{ m}^2 / 0.2 \text{ m}$
$= 0.0222 \text{ m or } 22.2 \text{ mm}$

Similarly, the values for the steel are:

4140 steel Area $= [3 \times 30\text{kN} \times 1\text{m} \times 0.20\text{m}/(2 \times 1738\text{MPa})]^{1/2}$
$= 0.00227 \text{ m}^2 \ (3.53 \text{ in}^2)$

The thickness, h, for the steel would be:

h $=$ 0.00227 m^2 / 0.20 m

$=$ 0.0114 m or 11.4 mm

From Equation 7–3, the cost values would be:

2024 Al
C(u) $=$ \$ 2.20/kg $\times$ 2774 kg/m^3 $\times$ 0.00444 m^2 $\times$ 1 m

$=$ \$ 27.10/unit

4140 Q&T Steel
C(u) $=$ \$ 2.75/kg $\times$ 7905 kg/m^3 $\times$ 0.00227 m^2 $\times$ 1 m

$=$ \$ 49.35/unit

The 2024 aluminum is a much better material than the 4140 steel for this problem, but in Example Problem 7–1 the 4140 steel was better than the aluminum. This illustrates the difficult problem in materials selection for many non-engineers and engineers alike. The materials selection is very much dependent upon the particular application and one material is not always better than another; what is limiting for one material may not be the critical constraint for a second material.

THE EFFECT OF SCRAP RATES AND OPERATION COSTS UPON UNIT COST

The effect of scrap costs upon the total cost of a product is usually larger than most managers expect. The benefits of quality control and statistical process control in reducing scrap costs have resulted in higher benefits than most engineers and managers expected. The development of expressions for the operation scrap costs and total scrap costs has been presented by Creese (5). Thus not only has quality been improved, but in many cases the costs have decreased due to the reduced scrap.

The total operation cost can be represented as the sum of the operation cost and the operation scrap cost. This can be represented as Equation 7–6:

Total Operation Cost $=$ Operation Cost $+$ Operation Scrap Cost   (7–6)

The operation scrap cost can be calculated from the operation yield, cumulative operation cost, and operation cost as indicated by Equation 7–7:

Operation $=$ [(100 $-$ Yield) / Yield] $\times$
Scrap Cost   [Cumulative Total Unit Cost $+$ Current Operation Cost]

(7–7)

where

    Yield = process yield in percent
            = 100 − operation scrap rate in percent

and

                            Total cumulative operation
Cumulative Total Unit Cost = cost of all prior operations
                            excluding the current operation

Example Problem 7-4

A raw material is being processed in three operations—casting, machining, and plating. The unit material cost, unit operation costs, and process scrap rates are presented in Table 7-7. Determine the unit scrap costs, total unit scrap cost, and cumulative total unit cost.
Solution:

    The solution is obtained by applying Equations 7-7 and 7-6 to the data in Table 7-7. The cumulative total unit cost for the raw material calculation would be zero as it is the first step. The total operation cost and the cumulative total unit cost values are the same for the first step. The total unit scrap cost is $ 1.7397, the cumulative total operation cost is $ 8.7397, and the operation unit scrap costs are in Table 7-7.

    When one examines the results of the sample problem, the scrap cost represents almost 20 percent of the total cost. This cost is larger than two of the three unit operation costs, and if there are a large number of operations the scrap costs can be 40–50 percent of the total cost. The result of a process improvement can have a larger effect than expected; for example, if a process improvement is made in the casting operation to reduce the scrap from 10 to 8 percent, what is the effect on the total unit cost? This can be observed by

Table 7-7 Scrap Cost and Total Cost Analysis

Item Description	Operation or Material Cost ($/unit)	Operation Scrap (%)	Operation Yield (%)	Unit Scrap Cost ($)	Total Operation Unit Cost ($)	Cumulative Total Unit Cost ($)
Raw Material	2.00	1	99	0.0202	2.0202	2.0202
Metal Casting	2.50	10	90	0.5022	3.0022	5.0224
Machining	1.50	5	95	0.3433	1.8433	6.8657
Plating	1.00	10	90	0.8740	1.8740	8.7397
Total	7.00			1.7397		8.7397

repeating the calculations of Table 7–7 and the results are presented in Table 7–8.

Note that in addition to a lowering of the scrap costs in the metal casting operation, the scrap costs were lowered in the machining and plating operations as a result of the lower unit cost when the product came out of the casting department. This resulted in a $ 0.1277 total savings per unit or approximately a 1.5 percent total savings from a 2 percent scrap reduction in a single operation. The 2 percent scrap reduction in the casting department lead to a 3.6 percent cost reduction in the casting department. The savings in the casting department of $ 0.1091 resulted in the total savings of $ 0.1277 via compounding; that is, the lower cost of the casting lead to lower scrap and operation costs in the departments which had operations after the casting operation.

SUMMARY

Significant savings can occur in the selection of the proper material and in the reduction of process scrap. The material cost is usually the highest cost item in the total manufacturing cost. The selection of materials based upon performance criteria depends upon the particular design relationship which is critical and should be done with the consent of the design engineer, as the designer determines which relationship is critical. The examples shown indicate that which material is best depends not only upon the cost but also upon the design criteria which is critical.

The example problems illustrate the high cost of scrap as a portion of the total unit cost and the potential effects of scrap reduction through process improvement. Improved cost performance in one operation leads to reduced costs in the following operations and quality improvement programs will frequently lead to higher benefits than initially expected because of the compounding effect.

Table 7–8 Effect of Casting Scrap Reduction from 10 to 8 Percent

Item Description	Operation or Material Cost ($/unit)	Operation Scrap (%)	Operation Yield (%)	Unit Scrap Cost ($)	Total Operation Unit Cost ($)	Cumulative Total Unit Cost ($)
Raw Material	2.00	1	99	.0202	2.0202	2.0202
Metal Casting	2.50	8	92	.3931	2.8931	4.9133
Machining	1.50	5	95	.3375	1.8375	6.7508
Plating	1.00	10	90	.8612	1.8612	8.6120
Total	7.00			1.6120		8.6120

EVALUATIVE QUESTIONS

1. In Example Problem 7-1, the load was 178 kN (40,000 lb) and the length was 0.254 m (10 inches), and ductile iron was the best material. If the load changes to 200 kN and the length increases to 0.300 m, which material is the best material? What would be the new unit cost?
2. Evaluate the 1015 steel for the conditions in Example Problem 7-2 and calculate its unit cost and compare it with the other three materials.
3. Evaluate the 1015 steel for the conditions in Example Problem 7-3 and calculate its unit cost and compare it with the 2024 Al and 4140 Q&T steel.
4. In Example Problem 7-4, show that the effect of reducing scrap in the plating operation from 10 to 8 percent results in a reduction of the total unit cost by $ 0.1900. Why is this greater than the reduction from 10 to 8 percent in the metal casting operation?

BIBLIOGRAPHY

1. *Industrial Engineering*, February 1984, p. 64
2. Dieter, G. E., *Engineering Design*, 1983, McGraw-Hill, pp. 178–181.
3. *Metals Handbook-Volume 1*, 8th Edition, 1961, American Society for Metals, Metals Park, Ohio, pp. 179–188.
4. Charles, J. A. and Crane, F. A. A., *Selection and Use of Engineering Materials*, Second Edition, 1989, Butterworth & Co., pp. 4–5.
5. Creese, R. C., How Much Does Scrap Really Cost?, *Cost Engineering*, Vol. 30, No. 7, July 1988, pp. 15–19.
6. *ASM Metals Handbook*, Ninth Edition, Vol. 1, 2, & 3.

8
Conceptual Cost Estimating Techniques

INTRODUCTION

Conceptual cost estimating, as discussed in Chapter 2, is estimating during the conceptual design stage. In the conceptual design stage the geometry and materials have not been specified, unless they dictate essential product functions. In the conceptual design stage, the costs associated with a change in the design are low, and the possibilities of such a change to influence other costs are numerous, but little is known about the product (1). In the conceptual design stage, the incurred costs are only 5–7 percent of the total cost whereas the committed costs are 75–85 percent of the total cost.

The accuracy of the conceptual cost estimate depends upon the accuracy of the data base and the expressions developed. For example, the use of an expression developed from general data in the literature would have an average accuracy range much larger than the −30 to +50 percent, but the use of an expression developed from internal company data (2) was −20 to +20 percent, with an average of plus 7.1 percent over 4400 estimates. Over 50 percent of the estimates were in the +5 to +10 percent range.

The importance of accurate conceptual cost estimation cannot be overemphasized as it is at the conceptual design stage where the significant cost savings can occur. The method of estimating is a top-down approach where costs are in aggregated form and derived statistically instead of the bottom-up approach where individual work elements, scheduling, materials, and yields are known (3). The conceptual cost estimating methods include expert opinion, analogy methods, and formula based methods. The emphasis of this chapter is on the formula based methods.

CONCEPTUAL METHODS BASED ON EXPERT OPINION AND ANALOGY

Occasionally the only basis for a cost estimate is expert opinion, because backup and/or historical data are scarce or nonexistent. The disadvantages of estimates based on expert opinion are great and some of them are: the estimate is subject to bias; the estimate cannot be substantiated or quantified; the estimate may not reflect increased program complexity; and the estimate generally does not lead to an information base that can be developed for future estimates (3). Despite these disadvantages, the expert opinion is useful not only when data is nonexistent, but also as a verification method for the other methods of conceptual estimating.

Analogy estimating (3) derives the cost of a new product from data on past costs of similar products. This technique frequently involves incremental or marginal cost estimating. Cost adjustments can be made based upon the differences between the new and previous system. The cost adjustments frequently take the form of mathematical expressions and may be considered a formula based method. Analogy estimating requires that the products be analogous and may be limited to products built by a particular facility. One limitation is that the estimates tend to be based upon a static technology, and if the facility technology changes the analogy estimating relationships would need to be modified to reflect the technology changes. A second limitation (3) is that analogy estimates often lack important details that make costs considerably higher than the original cost estimates.

CONCEPTUAL METHODS BASED ON FORMULAS

There are four formula methods that are primarily used in the conceptual costing stage. These methods are the factor method, the material cost method, the function method, and cost-size relationships. These methods, sometimes referred to as global cost estimation methods, often use only one factor, but in most cases more than one factor is needed to provide the necessary accuracy. Wierda (1,5,6) has done a rather extensive survey of these methods and much of the information presented is from his works.

The Factor Method

The factor method is one of the simplest methods, but it can in many instances give fairly reliable estimates if the data are kept current. The factor method can either be on a relative basis or on a specific reference. An example of the relative basis (4) is that for equipment. Equipment can be divided into three broad categories:

1. Functional—automobile, grader, pipelayer
2. Mechanical/Electrical—small kitchen appliances, small electrical equipment
3. Precision—cameras, electronic testing equipment

The equipment in each category costs about the same on a weight basis, and the cost between categories increases by a factor of approximately ten. That is, a precision piece of equipment is approximately 10 times the cost of a mechanical/electrical piece of equipment which is about 10 times the cost of a functional piece of equipment. For example, an automobile is approximately five dollars per pound, a portable telephone or sophisticated blender/mixer is about 50 dollars per pound, and an automatic focusing camera is about 500 dollars per pound. These ranges are coarse, so they can be refined, but a system could be developed for classifying many types of equipment to give quick and relatively reliable estimates.

One problem is that there may be many additions to the basic functional piece of equipment which significantly increases the cost. Automobiles have a cost range of about 10, from the low cost subcompact car to the high cost luxury car, and the weight factor does not change by ten. Thus other factors must be taken into account for more detailed estimates.

Example Problem 8-1

What is the expected cost of an automobile if the weight is 1,800 pounds and a camera at 1.5 pounds?
Solution:
The basic expression, from Equation 2-1, is:

$$C = F \times AM \tag{8-1}$$

where

C = Estimated Cost
F = Factor for total cost estimate
AM = Amount of Major cost item

Therefore

$$C(\text{automobile}) = \$\ 5/\text{lb.} \times 1800\ \text{lb.} = \$\ 9{,}000$$

and

$$C(\text{camera}) = \$\ 500/\text{lb.} \times 1.5\ \text{lb.} = \$\ 750$$

This method has been very successful with estimating in the construction industries, where factors have been obtained for cost per mile of highway and cost per square foot of livable space in home construction.

A more extended form of the factor method is to include a sum of factors and amounts. For example for n items;

$$C = F(1) \times AM(1) + F(2) \times AM(2) + \cdots + F(n) \times AM(n) \qquad (8\text{-}2)$$

where

$F(1)$ = Factor for item 1
$AM(1)$ = Amount of item 1
$F(n)$ = Factor for item n
$AM(n)$ = Amount of item n

In the home construction problem, the factors could be for lighting/wiring, piping, painting, duct work, and cabinets. The units for wiring, piping, duct-work, and cabinets may be per linear foot whereas painting would be on a square foot basis.

Previously the cost of metal castings could be predicted rather accurately on a per pound basis, but the new molding methods and environmental disposal problems have restricted the application of the earlier formulae. This also indicates the importance of keeping the relationships up to date as inflation and environmental, legal, and social concerns tend to cause an increase in costs.

The Material Cost Method

The material cost method has been somewhat justified since the material cost is the largest cost item in the prime cost of many manufacturing companies; in one reported instance the material cost was 64 percent of the total prime cost.

There are three variations to the material cost methods. The first method was presented in Chapter 2 where:

$$C = MC/MCS \qquad (8\text{-}3)$$

where

C = Estimated Cost of item
MC = Material Cost of item being estimated
MCS = Material Cost Share of item being estimated (decimal)

The material cost share of various items are listed in Table 8-1, as well as the share classification.

Table 8–1 Material Cost Shares For Various Items

Item description	Material cost share (%)	Share classification
Automobile	70	large
Railway Freight Car	68	large
Chemical Plant	64	large
Railway Passenger Car	58	large
Construction Equip.	54	large
Diesel Engines	50	large
Machine Tools	48	large
Amplifiers	45	large
Clocks, Watches	25	medium
Electrical Inst.	25	medium
Measuring Tools	20	medium
Glass Products	14	small
China Products	7	small

Adapted from Refs. 6 and 7.

Example Problem 8–2

What is the total cost of a measuring tool if the material cost is $ 2.00?
Solution:
From Table 8–1, the material cost share for measuring instruments is 20 percent. Therefore, the total cost would be:

$$C = \$ 2.00 / .20$$
$$= \$ 10.00$$

Another approach to the material cost share is a result of an analysis breakdown of production costs for some 20 manufacturing industry groups. The largest cost is the direct materials portion (4), and the material cost share for the industry groups is in Table 8–2.

Example Problem 8–3

If the cost of the raw materials to make a ton of steel is $ 150.00, what would be the expected selling price per ton of steel?

Table 8–2   Direct Material Cost Share of Total Annual Sales

SIC* code	Industry group description	Direct materials	Direct labor	Indirect payroll	All other
20	Beverages	0.65	0.08	0.05	0.22
21	Tobacco	0.55	0.07	0.02	0.36
22	Textile Mill Prod.	0.56	0.20	0.05	0.19
23	Apparel	0.48	0.23	0.07	0.22
24	Wood Products	0.52	0.21	0.05	0.22
25	Furniture, Fixtures	0.45	0.24	0.09	0.22
26	Paper Products	0.51	0.17	0.07	0.25
27	Printing, Publish.	0.33	0.20	0.16	0.31
28	Chemicals	0.43	0.09	0.07	0.41
29	Petroleum Products	0.75	0.04	0.02	0.19
30	Rubber and Plastics	0.45	0.20	0.08	0.27
31	Leather	0.46	0.25	0.07	0.22
32	Stone, Clay, and Glass	0.41	0.21	0.08	0.30
33	Primary Metals	0.56	0.17	0.06	0.21
34	Fabricated Metal	0.46	0.21	0.09	0.24
35	Nonelectrical Mach.	0.42	0.21	0.12	0.25
36	Electrical Equip.	0.42	0.19	0.14	0.25
37	Transportation Eq.	0.57	0.15	0.08	0.20
38	Instruments	0.34	0.17	0.14	0.35
39	Miscellaneous Mfg.	0.44	0.21	0.10	0.25
Average for all Manufacturing Industries		0.51	0.16	0.10	0.23

*SIC = Standard Industrial Classification
Adapted from Ref. 4.

Solution:

From Table 8–2, the material cost share in the primary metals industry is 0.56 or 56%; therefore the selling price would be:

$$C = \$ 150.00/0.56$$
$$= \$ 267.86/ton$$

A third approach to the material cost method is the one–three–nine rule for product cost estimation suggested by H. F. Rondeau (9). The one represents the material cost, the three represents the manufacturing cost, and the nine represents the selling price. The material cost includes a 10 percent scrap factor as well as a 10 percent tooling cost, so the material cost is actually the raw material value of the part with a 20 percent addition for scrap and tooling costs.

Example Problem 8–4

If a part is made from aluminum which costs $ 3.00 per kilogram and weighs 2 kilograms, what is the estimated material cost, part cost, and selling price?
Solution:

Using the one–three–nine rule and the 10 percent allowances for scrap and tooling, the material cost would be:

$$MC = 1.2 \times \text{material cost(\$/kg)} \times \text{part weight(kg)}$$
$$MC = 1.2 \times \$ 3.00 \times 2$$
$$= \$ 7.20$$

The part cost (PC) is then:

$$PC = 3 \times \$ 7.20$$
$$= \$ 21.60$$

Finally, the selling price(SP) would be:

$$SP = 3 \times \$ 21.60$$
$$= \$ 64.80$$

The material cost share method should be used only for complex objects which include many parts and many operations (8,10); it should not be used for estimating operation costs. The method does account somewhat for inflation as the material costs are subject to inflation in a manner similar to the other cost items.

The Function Method

The function method is similar to the factor method, but more variables are used and the expressions are often nonlinear. The function is basically a mathematical expression with constants and variables that provides a cost estimate for the variable levels specified. There are a wide variety of expressions used, and two illustrative examples will be provided to indicate typical expressions and applications.

An example expression for the turbofan engine cost given by Dieter (11) is:

$$C = 0.13937 \times a^{0.7435} \times b^{0.0775} \tag{8-4}$$

Where

$C =$ Cost of turbofan engine development, in million dollars a = Maximum engine thrust in pounds

b = Number of engines produced.

Example Problem 8–5

If the engine thrust is 15,000 pounds and the number of engines to be produced is 100, what is the development cost?
Solution:

$$C = 0.13937 \times 15,000^{0.7435} \times 100^{0.0775}$$
$$= \$ 254 \text{ million}$$

The problem with such formulae is that the range limitations of the expression are not presented with the formulae; that is, there is a range of thrust for which the expression is applicable; and 100,000 pounds may be outside the range of data used to develop the formula. The development of such formulae allow predictions to be made in situations for new developments and new technology.

A rather complex model for evaluating costs at the design stage was developed by Mahmoud and Pugh (11) for turned components. The costing equation was developed for turned components produced by a variety of machines and is based upon the time taken for turning and the material cost. The complex expression developed has several variables and several factors are needed to make adjustments for shape, materials, and machine capability. The accuracy of the formula was such that the values calculated were within plus or minus 10 percent for 90 percent of the components considered. The system was restricted to parts with a mean diameter range of two to 50 inches. The expression developed for the turned components costing model is:

$$C = (R \times N_d / 60) \times [(K_c \times L \times D_m / 4.77) + S_t / (X \times Q)] + M \quad (8\text{–}5)$$

where

C = Cost of turned component, \$/unit

R = Hourly labor plus overhead Rate, \$/hr.

N_d = Component complexity factor

K_c = Machine–material complexity factor = $K_1 \times K_2 \times K_{mat}$

K_1 = Machining factor

K_2 = Machine type factor

K_{mat} = Material type factor

L = Total machined Length, inches

D_m = Mean Diameter, inches

S_t = Machine Set-up time, minutes

X = Machine tooling capacity (maximum number of tools)

Q = Batch size (number of units)

M = Material cost per unit, including estimated scrap losses, $

The value of the component complexity factor, or discontinuity factor, N_d, represents the sum of the number of set-ups plus the nature and the number of discontinuities of the machined surface. The discontinuity ratings for the turned parts are presented in Table 8–3. The discontinuity factor is the sum of the products of the number of the discontinuities times the rating of that discontinuity. Thus, if a surface had two one inch recesses, it would have a factor of six for those two recesses, plus all other contributions.

The machining factor, K_1, is dependent upon the surface finish and the tolerance. The values for the machining factor are in Table 8–4.

The Machine Type Factor, K_2 represents the differences by which machines manipulate the tools and handle the various machine movements. The factors developed for the particular machines in the data base are in Table 8–5.

The material type factor, K_{mat} is based on an index related to the metal removal rate per unit horsepower. The factors used for the different materials are listed in Table 8–6.

Table 8–3 Component Description and Rating Factors Used To Compute the Discontinuity Factor for the Turned Components Costing Model

Component description	Rating factor
Number of Set-ups (usually 1 or 2)	≥ 1
Unmachined Surfaces	0
Machined Surfaces	1
Threaded Portions–not previously machined	1
Threaded Portions–previously machined once	2
Threaded Portions–previously machined twice	3
Shoulders or Faces < 1/16 inch	0
Shoulders or Faces ≥ 1/16 inch	1
Chamfers < 1/8 inch	0
Chamfers ≥ 1/8 inch	1
Radii < 1/8 inch	0
Radii ≥ 1/8 inch	1
Drilled Holes	1
Reamed Holes	1
Bored Holes	1
Recesses ≤ 1/4 inch	1
Recesses > 1/4 inch	3

Adapted from Ref. 12.

Table 8—4   Machining Factor for Tolerance-Surface Finish Conditions for the Turned Components Costing Model

Machining factor, K_1	Tolerance range (inches)	Finish Type
1.0	>0.010	rough
1.5	0.005<x<0.010	medium
2.0	<0.005	fine, threading

Adapted from Ref. 12.

Table 8—5   Machine Type and Machine Tooling Capacity Factors for the Turned Components Costing Model

Machining type factor, K_2	Machine description	Machine tooling capacity, X
1.00	Center Lathe	7
0.75	Capstan 2S,4S	11,12
0.80	Combination Turret	14
0.33	N.C. Lathe	12

Adapted from Ref. 12.

Table 8—6   Material Type Factors for the Turned Components Costing Model

Material type factor, K_{mat}	Material
1.00	Mild Steel
0.60	Duralumin
0.35	Cast Brass
0.70	Cast Iron
0.50	Die Cast Aluminum
0.60	Bronze

Adapted from Ref. 12.

The machine tooling capacity, X, represents the number of tools that can be loaded onto the machine. These factors have been included in Table 8-5. The mean diameter was the average of the final turned diameters and the length was the total machined length, including all chamfers, shoulders, radii, and faces of 1/8 inch or more.

Example Problem 8-6

The mild steel part shown in Figure 8-1 is to be rough turned and produced on a Capstan 4S lathe. The labor and overhead rate, various factors, set-up time, batch size and material cost data are presented in Table 8-7. Determine the unit cost of the turned component.

Solution:

From Figure 8-1 and the data in Tables 8-3 through 8-7, the mean diameter, total machined length, component complexity factor, and machine-material complexity factor can be calculated as:

$$D_m = (1 + 3/4 + 2) / 3 = 1.25 \text{ inches}$$
$$L = \text{length} + \text{face} + \text{internal}$$
$$L = (2 + 1 + 3) + (1 + 2) + 2 = 11 \text{ inches}$$
$$N_d = 1 \times 2 \text{ set-ups (surfaces d,e)} + 1 \times 1 \text{ hole(f)} +$$
$$\qquad 1 \times 2 \text{ machined surfaces (a,c)} + 3 \times 1 \text{ recess (b)}$$
$$= 8$$
$$K_c = 1.00 \times 0.75 \times 1.00 = 0.75$$

Therefore

$$C = (\$ 30.00 \times 8 / 60) \times [(0.75 \times 11.0 \times 1.25 / 4.77)$$
$$\qquad + 45 / (12 \times 200)] + \$ 3.80$$
$$= \$ 4.00 \times [2.162 + 0.019] + \$ 3.80$$
$$= \$ 8.72 + \$ 3.80$$
$$= \$ 12.52$$

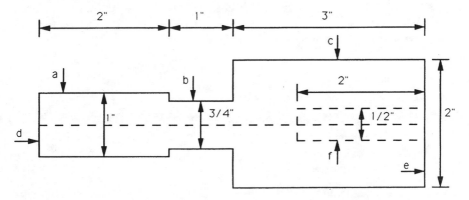

Figure 8-1 Mild steel component rough turned on Capstan 4S lathe.

Table 8–7 Data for Mild Steel Component Rough Turned on Capstan 4S Lathe for Example Problem 8-6, using the Turned Components Costing Model

Data Description	Data Value
Labor plus Overhead Rate	$ 30.00/hr.
Machining Factor K_1	
(tolerances and Finish)	1.0
Machine Type Factor K_2	0.75
Tooling Capacity Factor, X	12
Material Factor K_{mat} (mild steel)	1.00
Machine Set-Up Time S_t	45 minutes
Batch Size	200 units
Material Cost (including scrap)	$ 3.80/unit

This formula is more detailed than expected for the conceptual design stage because it does require knowledge about the material and the product dimensions. If, however, the exact dimensions for surfaces a, b, and c were not known, except for the total length, the result would have been the same.

Cost-Size Relationships

Another approach to the determination of conceptual costing is via the unit size (13–16). In this approach one can compare the cost of different designs on a relative basis or on an actual cost basis. Expressions have been developed from data on investment castings (13) and for machined parts (14–16). These relationships follow the cost-capacity relationship, which indicates that as the size of a piece of equipment increases or as the plant capacity increases, the costs increase at a rate less than linear. These cost-capacity relationships are used frequently in the chemical processing industries, but have not been developed or used in the basic manufacturing industries. The general form of the cost-size relationship is:

$$C = A \times V^B \tag{8-6}$$

where

    C = Unit cost of part of size V in $/unit
    V = Size of part
    B = Cost-size exponent
    A = Cost-size constant

From an examination of the data of Michaels and Wood (13), the following relative cost expression for an investment casting was developed:

$$RC = 5.0V^{0.6} \tag{8-7}$$

where

RC = Relative Cost of investment casting
 V = Investment casting Volume, cubic inches
 B = 0.6, size cost exponent for investment casting
5.0 = Relative cost of a one cubic inch investment casting

Example Problem 8-7

If one wanted to double the volume of an investment casting turbine blade from four to eight cubic inches, what would be the increase in cost? What would be the cost of an eight cubic inch turbine blade compared to the cost of a one cubic inch turbine blade?
Solution:

Using Equation 8-6 and the turbine blade sizes of eight and four cubic inches, the cost increase would be:

$$RC(8) - RC(4) \times (8/4)^{0.6}$$
$$= RC(4) \times 1.5$$

The cost is 1.5 times the reference cost; that is, the cost would increase by 50 percent when the volume of the investment casting is doubled. This relationship was developed for a volume range of 0.1 to 10 cubic inches. If one compares the cost of the eight cubic inch casting to the one cubic inch reference casting, the cost would be:

$$RC(8) = 8^{0.6}$$
$$= 3.5$$

This implies the cost of an eight cubic inch investment casting is 3.5 times the cost of a one cubic inch investment casting, or that the cost has increased by 250 percent.

Such relationships can be developed for other casting processes from the curves presented by Michaels and Wood (13). The exponent of 0.6 is the value commonly used in the chemical processing industries and is frequently called "the six-tenths rule".

Some very interesting work on machined component cost estimates has been done at the University of Rhode Island by Boothroyd and his associates (14,15,16). One of his graduate students, Radovanovic, developed approximate cost estimating relationships for machined components with different surfaces (14). The results were in terms of $/finished volume as function of the finished volume of the part. If these curves are multiplied by the product volume, then unit costs can be obtained. The values obtained would be conceptual estimates. The relationships developed from Radovanovic's data (14) are presented in Table 8-8. These relationships have numerous assumptions incorporated in them, such as 55 percent of the initial volume is removed, the part is medium carbon steel, batche size is 200 units. The specific labor and overhead rates and material cost value used were not specified. The cost data does appear to be typical of the 1989 time period when the thesis was written.

The equations have rather small exponents for parts of small volume, that is, less than 20 cubic inches. This is because for small parts the material cost is not the dominant cost; the nonproductive costs are over 50 percent of the total cost. For large parts, the material cost is the dominant cost, and is over 60 percent of the total part cost. Thus for the large parts, the size cost exponent approaches unity. From the formulas developed, as the shape complexity increases, the cost-size constant increases.

Example Problem 8-8

The component in Figure 8-1 is to be evaluated using the relationships in Table 8-8. The part is primarily rotational with a secondary operation. What is the estimated unit cost?

Table 8-8 Conceptual Cost-Size Estimating Expressions for Machined Components as a Function of Product Shape Category and Product Volume

| | Part Volume Range | |
Shape Category	0.1–20 Cubic Inches	20–400 Cubic Inches
1. Primary Rotational	$C = 4 \times V^{0.33}$	$C = 0.7 \times V^{0.89}$
2. Primary Rotational with Secondary	$C = 5 \times V^{0.33}$	$C = 0.9 \times V^{0.86}$
3. Primary Planar	$C = 8 \times V^{0.33}$	$C = 2 \times V^{0.81}$
4. Primary Rotational and Primary Planar		
5. Primary Rotational, Primary Planar, and Secondary		
6. Primary Planar with Secondary	$C = 9 \times V^{0.40}$	$C = 4 \times V^{0.70}$

Note: Groups 3, 4, and 5 curves were approximately equal and only one expression was developed for these 3 shape categories.

Solution:

The volume of the part must be calculated. The volume can be considered as a series of cylinders and the volume would be:

$$V = (\pi/4) \times [(1^2 \times 2) + (3/4)^2 \times 1 + 2^2 \times 3 - (1/2)^2 \times 2]$$
$$= 11.0 \text{ cubic inches}$$

Therefore, using the cost-size relationship for primarily rotational parts with secondary operations for the appropriate part volume range, the unit cost is:

$$C = 5 \times (11.0)^{0.33}$$
$$= \$ 11.03 / \text{unit}$$

This value is in good agreement, from a conceptual estimate range of -30 percent to $+50$ percent, with the $ 12.52 value obtained by the turned components costing system in Example Problem 8-6.

SUMMARY

The estimating formulae for manufacturing are rather sparse when compared to those available for the construction and chemical process industries. Care must be used when applying conceptual formulae as they need to be updated and they should be documented as to the range of applicability, or as to the constraints on the formula. These formulae are generally for the factory cost and do not represent the total cost or selling price. The development of cost-size relationships for conceptual estimating in manufacturing does appear to be a promising area of activity.

EVALUATIVE QUESTIONS

1. If the material cost for a lathe is $ 1,500, what is the expected factory cost using the material cost share method?
2. In the one-three-nine rule, what does the three represent?
3. Which industry has the largest portion of its cost in direct materials? Which industry has the largest portion of its cost in indirect costs?
4. Estimate the development cost of a lot of 50 turbofan engines with 5,000 pounds thrust? What is the cost if only 10 engines are in the lot?
5. Redo Example Problem 8-6 using cast iron instead of mild steel and in a batch size of 100 units. The material cost remains $3.80.
6. A second recess is added to the component in Figure 8-1. Determine the cost of machining the part from brass. The material cost is increased to $4.50 for the brass.

7. Determine the cost of a part with a primarily planar with secondary operations shape category and a volume of 25 cubic inches.

BIBLIOGRAPHY

1. Wierda, L., Private Communication, Ph.D. Dissertation Notes, p.13.
2. Apgar, H. E. and Daschbach, J. M., "Analysis of Design Through Parametric Cost Estimation Techniques", *International Conference on Engineering Design-Proceedings*, Boston, MA, 17–20 Aug., 1987, pp. 759–766.
3. Micheals, J. V. and Wood, W. P., *Design to Cost*, 1989, Wiley Interscience, New York, pp. 280–295.
4. Park, W. R., and Jackson, D. E., *Cost Engineering Analysis*, 2nd. Edition, 1984, Wiley Interscience, pp. 133, 139.
5. Wierda, L. *Kosteninformatie voor ontwerpers*, Jan., 1986, Report K134, Delft University of Technology, The Netherlands, p. 74.
6. Wierda, L. "Product Cost-Estimation by the Designer", *Engineering Costs and Production Economics*, Vol. 13, 1988, pp. 189–198.
7. Hubka, V., "Bewerten und Entscheiden beim Konstruieren", *Konstruktionsmethoden-Reading*, Heurista WDK-8, 1982, p. 164.
8. Wierda, L. *Detailed Cost Estimation Concept and Database Structure for DIDACOE*, Aug., 1988, Report K177, Delft University of Technology, The Netherlands, p. 122.
9. Rondeau, Herbert F., "The 1–3–9 Rule for Product Cost Estimation", *Machine Design*, August 21, 1975, pp. 50–53.
10. "Technisch-Wirtschaftliches Konstruieren" *VDI: Verein Deutscher Ingenieure*, VEI Richtlinie 2225, VDI-Verlag, Dusseldorf, 1977.
11. Dieter, G. E., *Engineering Design*, McGraw-Hill, 1983, p. 330.
12. Mahmoud, M. A. M., and Pugh, S., "The Costing of Turned Components at the Design Stage", *Information for Designers*, 4th. International Symposium, University of Southhampton, July 1979, pp. 37–42.
13. Michaels, J. V., and Wood, W. P., *Design to Cost*, 1989, Wiley Interscience, New York, pp. 177–179.
14. Radovanovic, P., *Approximate Cost Estimating for Machined Components*, University of Rhode Island, MS Thesis, Department of Industrial and Manufacturing Engineering, 1989, p. 140.
15. Boothroyd, G. and Knight, W. A. *Fundamentals of Machining and Machine Tools*, 2nd. Edition, 1989, Marcel Dekker, pp. 438–463.
16. Boothroyd, G. and Reynolds, C. *Approximate Machining Cost Estimates*, Report # 17, 1987, Department of Industrial and Manufacturing Engineering, University of Rhode Island, p. 33.

9
Basic Costing for Machining Processes

INTRODUCTION

The most costly of the basic forming processes, machining, casting, and deformation processing, is generally the machining process. However, it is rather fast, the equipment is flexible, and the surfaces generated are usually better than those generated by other processing methods. Many books have been written about machining operations and machining economics, and some of the general references used for this section are those by Adithan (1), Boothroyd (2), and Ostwald (3). Most frequently the casting and deformation processing operations form a near net shape which is completed by machining to obtain the final dimensions and the necessary finish. Machining processes are generally considered to be the most important of the basic forming processes with regard to obtaining the desired shape, but tend to be more costly than the other basic forming processes. The amount of material removed for a typical light machining operation is 62 percent of the initial material (2), and thus the machining costs and material costs for machined parts tend to be high.

COMPONENTS OF MACHINING TIME

The determination of the total machining time is the initial step in determining the machining costs. The time data can be broken into elements (1) which are independent of the number of pieces and into elements which can be directly related to each piece. The piece related elements can be classified (2) into productive elements, that is elements in which the piece is being cut, and non-productive elements, which are necessary but do not involve metal cutting.

The elements which will be considered are setup time, handling time, machining time, teardown time, down time, and allowances.

Fixed Time Elements (Independent of Production Level)

1. Setup Time—This is the time taken to prepare the machine for operation and includes: time to study the drawing (print); time to obtain the correct tool; time to install the tools, align the fixtures, jigs, and stops; and the time to produce and inspect the first piece to make certain they are correct. The setup time occurs only once per batch or production lot.
2. Teardown time—This is the time taken to remove the tools, jigs, and fixtures from the machine and to clean the machine and tools after a batch has been made. The teardown time occurs only once per batch or production lot.
3. Down Time—This is the time wasted due to lack of operator, machine breakdown, lack of materials, delay in getting tools, and other interruptions preventing production.

Piece Related Elements

Nonproductive elements

Handling Time—The time taken by the operator for loading and unloading the part.

Tool Return Time—Time to return tool to the beginning of the cut. This is often included as part of the handling time.

Unit Tool Changing Time—The time needed to change the worn tools. This can be calculated directly if the tool life is known for the cutting conditions, or it can be considered as part of the allowances. It will be considered as part of the allowances in the calculations presented, as the number of pieces produced per unit tool is not known prior to production. The decision to change the tool is usually made by the operator during the cutting operation.

Allowances—Allowances for personal needs, fatigue, inspection, and other items that are not included in the normal operation cycle. The allowances are often a percentage of the normal operation time.

Productive element

Machining time is the time the machine works on the component, that is, the time from when the tool touches the work until the time the operation is complete and the tool leaves the component. This is the most important element and will be presented in more detail.

PRIMARY METAL CUTTING VARIABLES

The primary variables in the metal cutting operation are the depth of cut, the feed, and the cutting speed. The product of these three variables results in the metal removal rate, and generally a high metal removal rate is desirable. However, the tool costs and tool changing costs increase as the three variables increase, so there is an optimal set of parameter levels for the three variables. The general situation is to first select the depth of cut, then the feed, and finally the cutting speed as this is the typical increasing order of importance for tool life. Usually the depth of cut is determined by the part dimensions and machine power requirements, the feed is controlled by the surface finish or machine power, and the cutting speed is controlled by the economical or production requirements. Economic cutting models (4,5) are used to determine optimal cutting speeds to minimize total unit cutting costs. These primary cutting variables are indicated in Figure 9-1. Some definitions by Drozda and Wicks (6) of these terms are:

Depth of Cut—The depth of cut, also known as back engagement or undeformed chip thickness, is the thickness of the layer of material removed from the previous workpiece surface to the new workpiece surface. The units are usually expressed as thousandths of an inch or in millimeters.

Feed—The feed rate as defined by Boothroyd (2) is the displacement of the tool along the workpiece in the direction of the feed motion, and is expressed as a length per stroke or per revolution of the workpiece or tool. The units are usually expressed as thousandths of an inch per stroke or per revolution.

Cutting Speed—The cutting speed is the rate at which the workpiece surface moves past the cutting tool. It is usually expressed in surface feet per minute or meters per second.

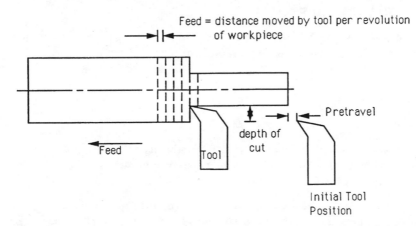

Figure 9-1   Depth of cut and feed illustrated for turning operation.

All three variables depend upon the cutting tool material, the workpiece material, the cutting fluids (if used), the type of machining operation, the machine capabilities, and the surface finish desired. These variables are important for determining the machining times as well as for estimating the power requirements.

APPROACHES FOR ESTIMATING MACHINING TIME

There are three major approaches to the determination of machining time. The first approach is the determination of the machining time based upon the specific machining operations and the details of the machining process. This is the traditional approach and requires a detailed knowledge of the specific machines and the primary cutting variables; the variable of emphasis is the feed rate. The second major approach is the estimation of the machining time from the cutting path length and the cutting velocity. The cutting path length is the path the tool travels with respect to the part surface. The major variable of emphasis is the cutting speed, and this method permits optimization of the cutting costs. The third approach is a hybrid approach (10) between the parametric approach of the conceptual methods and the detail process approaches of the previous two methods. This third approach, referred to as the approximate method (10), can also be described as a feature based approach. This method characterizes the part by the basic shape and then has a general formula for the machining time of parts of that shape category. Each of the three approaches will be presented in detail, with the major emphasis upon the traditional or feed based approach as more information is available on that approach.

THE FEED BASED APPROACH

The feed based approach is based upon the feed rate and the length of cut for the process. The approach will be presented for the basic machining processes of turning, drilling, milling, and shaping. The overall expression is:

$$T = L / F \qquad\qquad (9\text{--}1)$$

where

    T = Machining Time in minutes, also referred to as cutting time
    L = Length of cut in feed direction, in inches or millimeters
    F = Feed rate in inches/minute or millimeters/minute

The length of cut is the total distance traveled by the tool at the feed rate on the workpiece plus any pretravel and overtravel for the tool to clear the workpiece. That is,

L = length of workpiece to be machined + pretravel (also called approach length) + overtravel

The feed rate is the product of the feed and the rotational rate of the tool or workpiece, that is:

$$F = f \times N \tag{9-2}$$

where

   F = Feed rate in inches/minute or millimeters/minute
   f = Feed rate in inches/revolution (ipr) and in inches/stroke or in millimeters/revolution (mm/rev) and millimeters/stroke
   N = Rotational rate in revolutions/minute (rpm) and in strokes/minute

In the milling operation, the feed rate, f, in inches/revolution (millimeters/revolution), is calculated from:

$$f = f_t \times n_t \tag{9-3}$$

where

   f_t = Feed per tooth in inches/tooth or millimeters/tooth
   n_t = Number of teeth per revolution of the cutter

The cutting speed and revolutions per minute are related, so the rpm can be determined from the cutting speed for operations with a rotating tool (drilling or milling) or a rotating workpiece (turning) in U.S. units by:

$$V = \pi \times D \times N / 12 \tag{9-4}$$

where

   V = Cutting speed in feet/minute
   π = 3.1416
   D = Diameter of tool or average diameter of workpiece in inches
   N = Revolutions per minute, rpm

When metric units are used, Equation 9-4 becomes:

$$V = \pi \times D \times N / 1000 \tag{9-4a}$$

where

   V = Cutting speed in meters/minute
   π = 3.1416
   D = Diameter of tool or average diameter of workpiece in millimeters
   N = Revolutions per minute, rpm

Some of the parameters which need to be specified and the calculated parameters for the primary metal cutting processes are presented in Table 9–1.

Estimating Operation Times for Turning Operations

In order to demonstrate how to apply the relations in Table 9-1, example problems will be presented in both U.S. and metric units.

Table 9–1 Specified Process Parameters and Parameter Calculations for Turning, Drilling, Milling, and Shaping

Parameters Selected	Units US (ISO)	Symbol	Process Turning	Drilling	Milling	Shaping
Workpiece						
Diameter, ave.	in (mm)	D_{av}	D_{av}	-	-	-
Length *	in (mm)	L_p	L_p	L_p	L_p	L_p
Width	in (mm)	W	-	-	W	W
Cutter						
Diameter	in (mm)	D_c	-	D_c	D_c	-
Width	in (mm)	W_c	-	-	W_c	-
No. of teeth	-	n_t	-	-	n_t	-
Cutting Speed	ft/min (m/min)	V	V	V	V	V
Depth of Cut	in (mm)	d	d	-	d	d
Feed per revol.	ipr (mm/rev)	f_r	f_r	f_r	f_r	-
Feed per tooth	in/tooth (mm/tooth)	f_t	-	-	f_t	-
Feed per stroke	in/stroke (mm/stroke)	f_s	-	-	-	f_s
Return/Cutting Speed Ratio	-	R	-	-	-	R
Calculated Unit Parameters						
Rev. per min	rpm	N	$12V/\pi D_{av}$ $(1000V/\pi D_{av})$	$12V/\pi D_c$ $(1000V/\pi D_c)$	$12V/\pi D_c$ $(1000V/\pi D_c)$	
Strokes/min	min⁻¹	n_s				$12V/[L(1+1/R)]$ $1000V/[L(1+1/R)]$
Feed rate	in/min (mm/min)	F	Nf_r	Nf_r	Nf_r	$n_s f_s$
Feed	in/rev (mm/rev)	f_r	-	-	$n_t f_t$	-
Cutting time	min.	T	L/F	L/F	L/F	W/F
Metal Removal Rate	in³/min mm³/min	Q	$\pi D_{av} dF$	$\pi D_c^2 F/4$	WdF or $W_c dF$**	$L_p\, dF$
Cutting Path Length	ft (m)	Z	$\pi D_{av}L/12f$ $(\pi D_{av}L/1000f)$	$\pi D_c L/12f_r$ $(\pi D_c L/1000f_r)$	$\pi D_c L/12f_r$ $(\pi D_c L/1000f_r)$	$L(1+1/R)W/12f_s$ $(L(1+1/R)W/1000f_s)$
Cutting Fraction of Tool Path	-	Y	L_p/L	L_p/L	0-0.5	$L_p R/L(R+1)$

* The length used for calculating, L, is the length of the workpiece, L_p, plus pretravel, lead, and overtravel.

** The Metal removal rate for milling depends upon what ever is smaller, that is W or W_c.

Example Problem 9–1

Calculate the machining time to turn the dimensions shown in Figure 9–2 starting with a 3 inch diameter bar. The diameter is reduced to 2.5 inches and then to 1.5 inches, with each length being two inches. The material is mild steel and the recommended cutting speed, feed rate, and depth of cut for turning are presented in Table 9–2.

Solution:

The first step is to determine the number of passes needed to turn the part from 3.0 inches to 2.5 inches and then from 2.5 inches to 1.5 inches.

Number of Passes = Depth of Material to be
Removed / Depth of Cut

Depth of Material to be Removed = (Large Dia. — Small Dia.) / 2

(Note: One divides by 2 since in turning the depth of cut is off the radius and thus twice the depth of cut is removed from the diameter.)

Depth of Material to be removed = (3.0 − 2.5) / 2
= 0.250 inches

If the cut is rough cut, the maximum depth of cut allowed is 0.150 inches. (Table 9–2).

Number of Passes = 0.250 / 0.150 = 1.67

which means that two passes are needed. (One rounds the answer up to the next largest integer if the answer is not an integer.) The total depth of material

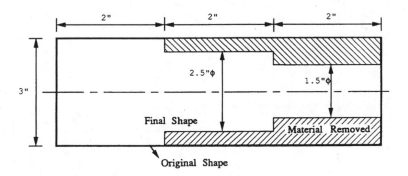

Figure 9–2   Part drawing for Example Problem 9–1.

Table 9-2 Cutting Speeds, Feed Rates, and Depth of Cuts for Turning Various Materials

A Cutting speed and feed rate data

Material	Cutting speed tool materials				Feed rate range	
	HSS		Carbide			
	rough	finish	rough	finish	rough	finish
Mild Steel	130* (40)*	200 (60)	300 (90)	600 (180)	0.025-0.080* (0.65-2.0)*	0.005-0.030 (.125-0.75)
Cast Steel	50 (15)	80 (24)	150 (45)	325 (100)	0.020-0.050 (0.5-1.25)	0.005-0.020 (0.125-0.5)
Stainless Steel	50 (15)	60 (18)	90 (27)	150 (45)	0.020-0.040 (0.5-1.0)	0.003-0.008 (0.075-0.175)
Gray Cast Iron	60 (18)	90 (27)	200 (60)	325 (100)	0.015-0.100 (0.4-2.5)	0.0075-0.040 (0.2-1.0)
Aluminum	300 (90)	500 (150)	800 (240)	1200 (360)	0.004-0.020 (0.1-0.5)	0.003-0.010 (0.075-0.25)
Brass	250 (75)	325 (100)	600 (180)	900 (270)	0.015-0.080 (0.375-2.0)	0.003-0.050 (0.02-1.25)
Phosphor Bronze	60 (18)	120 (36)	400 (120)	600 (180)	0.015-0.030 (0.375-0.75)	0.005-0.020 (0.125-0.5)

B Depth of cut data for rough and finishing cuts

Units for depth of cut	Type of Cut	
	rough	finish
U.S.(inches)	0.150	0.025
Metric (millimeters)	4.0	0.60

*Units are ft/min and (m/min) for cutting speeds, and in/rev and (mm/rev) for the feed rate values.

Adapted from Ref. 1

to be removed is split between the two passes, i.e. depth of cut / pass = 0.125 inches.

If the tool is a high speed steel, and the cut is a roughing cut, the recommended speed from Table 9-2 is 130 ft/min and the recommended feed range is 0.025 to 0.080 in/rev for rough turning and 0.005 to 0.030 in/rev for finish turning. If one takes the value of 0.030 in/rev, as it could be used for either rough or finish turning, the revolutions per minute can be calculated from the formula in Table 9-1 for turning as:

$$N = 12V / \pi D_{av}$$

For the first pass, the average diameter is the outside diameter minus the depth of cut for that pass, that is;

$$D_{av} = 3.0 - 0.125 = 2.875 \text{ inches}$$

$$\text{Thus } N(\text{pass 1}) = 12 \times 130 / 3.1416 \times 2.875$$
$$= 172.7 \text{ or } 175 \text{ rpm}$$

For the second pass the diameter is

$$3.0 - 2 \times 0.125 = 2.75 \text{ inches and}$$
$$D_{av} = 2.75 - 0.125 = 2.625 \text{ inches}$$

$$N \text{ (pass 2)} = 12 \times 130 / 3.1416 \times 2.625$$
$$= 189 \text{ or } 190 \text{ rpm}$$

Although one would save time by using the 190 rpm, most frequently the operator would use 175 rpm for both passes as it may take more time to change the machine to the new rpm than to use the same rpm for both passes. If the machine had a variable speed motor, the operator would change the speed for each pass as it can be done quickly.

The cutting time, from the formulas in Table 9-1 for turning is:

$$T = L / F$$

The length of cut is the total length over both 2 inch sections, i.e. for a total of 4 inches plus any pretravel or overtravel. The pretravel and overtravel can be assumed to be small, each approximately 1/4 of an inch. (Note: there is no overtravel involved in this case.)

$$T = (2 + 2 + 1/4) / (0.030 \times 175)$$
$$= 0.810 \text{ minutes per pass}$$

Thus the time for both passes would be:

$T = 2 \times 0.810 = 1.620$ minutes

The next step is to turn the end 2 inches of the 2.5 inch diameter section to 1.5 inches. The calculation procedure is similar to the previous one and the results are:

Depth of Material to be removed $= (2.5 - 1.5) / 2$
$= 0.500$ inches
Number of Passes $= 0.500/0.150 = 3.33$

which means that four passes must be used and the depth of cut used would be $0.500 / 4 = 0.125$ inches per pass. In this case, it is recommended to change the rpm after the first two passes. The average diameter used for the first calculation will be the average diameter of the first pass which is:

$D_{av} = 2.50 - 0.125 = 2.375$ inches and

$N(\text{pass 1 and 2}) = 12 \times 130 / (3.1416 \times 2.375)$
$= 209$ or 210 rpm

$T = L / F = (2.0 + 1/4) / (210 \times 0.030)$
$= 0.357$ minutes per pass
$= 0.714$ minutes for the first two passes on the second part

The average diameter for the third pass is:

$D_{av} = 2.00 - 0.125 = 1.875$ inches, and

$N(\text{pass 3 and 4}) = 12 \times 130 / 3.1416 \times 1.875$
$= 264.8$ or 265 rpm

$T = L / F = (2.0 + 1/4) / (265 \times 0.030)$
$= 0.283$ minutes per pass
$= 0.566$ minutes for the second two passes on the second section

The total cutting time would be the sum of all three times, that is;

$T = 0.566 + 0.714 + 1.620 = 2.900$ minutes

This time refers to the time for the cutting cycle only, it does not include the handling time or setup time. The handling time can be estimated from a data base such as that by Ostwald (3) or Boothroyd and Knight (2). Some of the handling time data is in Table 9–3.

Thus, if this machine was a lathe with a universal chuck, the unit handling time would be 0.39 minutes and the unit piece time, without considering setup time would be:

$$T = 2.900 + 0.39$$
$$= 3.290 \text{ minutes per piece}$$

Allowances

The allowances for personal needs, fatigue, inspection, and other items that are not included in the normal production cycle must be added to determine production standards. The allowances are divided into two types, those which apply to machine controlled work and those which apply to human controlled work. The human controlled work includes all allowances, whereas the machine controlled work does not include fatigue allowances. Table 9–4 lists typical allowances for most manufacturing operations.

If the allowances are applied, the nine percent would apply to the machining time and the 15 percent would apply to the handling time. Thus;

$$T = 1.09 \times 2.900 + 1.15 \times 0.39$$
$$= 3.161 + 0.449$$
$$= 3.610 \text{ min}$$

Table 9–3 Basic Loading and Unloading Times (in minutes) For Various Work Holding Devices and for Different Workpiece Weights

Work holding device	Loading and unloading times per piece for workpiece weight ranges	
	0–10 lbs	10–30 lbs
Between Centers (no dog)	0.30 min	0.40 min
Between Centers (with dog)	0.67 min	0.96 min
Universal Chuck	0.39 min	0.53 min
Independent Chuck	0.69 min	0.83 min
V Block	0.50 min	0.59 min
Vice	0.30 min	0.40 min

From Ref. 2.

Table 9-4 Typical Allowances for Manufacturing Operations

Allowance description	Manufacturing operation is controlled by	
	machine (%)	operator (%)
Personal	5	5
Fatigue	—	6
Delays, Interruptions	4	4
Total	9	15

That is, 3.61 minutes would be allowed to produce a unit. This does not include setup time.

Setup Time

The setup times are difficult to estimate, but Ostwald (6) does give a wide variety of values for machining operations. Some of the values for cutting operations are presented in Table 9-5 as a starting point. The total setup time would be approximately 150 percent of the basic times of Table 9-5.

Thus, the setup time for the piece being turned in Figure 9-2, since it was in a chuck, would be 29 minutes according to the values in Table 9-5. The total setup time would be 150 percent, or 43.5 minutes. If the lot consisted of 100 pieces, the time to do the job would be:

$$\begin{aligned} \text{Total Time} &= \text{Setup Time} + 100 \times \text{Piece Time} \\ &= 43.5 + 100 \times 3.61 \\ &= 404.5 \text{ minutes or } 6.74 \text{ hours for the lot} \\ &= 4.045 \text{ min/piece} \end{aligned}$$

This example illustrates the large amount of information and details needed to make a time estimate; it does not include other important cost items such as the material cost, the labor and overhead rates, the tooling costs, and etc. Items such as allowances can vary considerably from one workplace to another and this is why it is essential for companies to develop their own databases for their equipment and processes for accurate cost estimating.

Estimating Operation Times for Milling

The basic formulas for milling are in Table 9-1 and the data in Tables 9-3, 9-4, and 9-5 can also be used for milling operations. The speeds and feeds are

Table 9–5   Setup Times for Basic Machining Operations

Operation description	Holding device	Setup	Time (min)	
Turning		1 tool	2 tools	
Engine Lathe or	Collet	20	28	
NC Lathe	Chuck	29	34	
	Fixture	31	38	
Milling		1 tool		
Plane Surface	Vice	69		
	Collet or Chuck	75		
Saw Slab, Profiles	Vice	69		
	Collet or Chuck	75		
Slot-Profile	Vice	87		
	Collet or Chuck	93		
Slot-Peripheral	Vice	99		
	Collet or Chuck	103		
		Number of Spindles		
Drilling		1	2	3
Sensitive	Table or Vice	10	15	20
	Parallels, V-Block	11	16	21
Radial	Table or Vice	17		
	Fixture	24		
		1 tool		
Shaping	Parallels	11		

Adapted from Ref. 3. Reprinted with permission of *American Machinist*.

different for milling when compared to turning. Table 9–6 shows some average speed and feed ranges for milling. Note that the feed for milling is in inches or millimeters per tooth instead of inches or millimeters per revolution, as in turning.

Example Problem 9–2

A carbon steel plate is to be face milled using a high speed steel cutter. The plate is 50 millimeters by 200 millimeters, the cut is a rough cut with a depth of cut of 2.5 millimeters, and the high speed cutter is 75 millimeters in diameter and has 8 teeth. An illustration of the cutter and workpiece is shown in Figure 9–3. What is the time to surface a batch of 40 pieces?

Solution:

From Table 9–5, the setup time for a plane surface for milling is 69 minutes, and with a 150 percent adjustment, the total setup time would be:

Table 9–6 Feeds and Cutting Speeds for Milling Operations for Different Work Materials

Work material	Feed/Tooth general range		Cutting speed average value	
	in/tooth	(mm/tooth)	ft/min HSS	(m/min) Carbide
Carbon Steel	0.003–0.015	(0.075–0.381)	150(45)	600(180)
Cast Iron	0.005–0.030	(0.130–0.750)	125(40)	300 (90)
Stainless Steel	0.002–0.030	(0.050–0.750)	100(30)	550(170)
Aluminum Alloys	0.003–0.030	(0.075–0.750)	750 (230)	2500 (760)
Copper/Copper Alloys	0.005–0.030	(0.130–0.750)	225(70)	800(250)

Note: Low feeds and high speeds are used for finish cuts.
Adapted from Ref. 7.

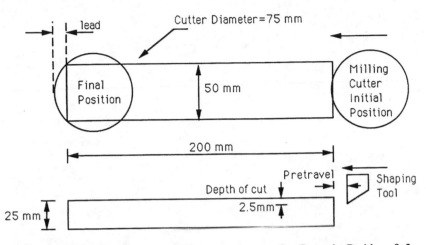

Figure 9–3 Illustration of workpiece and cutter for Example Problem 9–2 and for Example Problem 9–3.

T(setup) = 69 × 1.5 = 103.5 minutes

Since the material is carbon steel, Table 9–6 recommends a cutting speed for HSS tool as 45 m/min for a rough cut and an average feed value would be 0.25mm/tooth. Since this is a rough cut and tool marks from the leading edge are acceptable, the lead can be calculated by:

Lead = D / 2 − 1 / 2 × $(D^2 − W^2)^{1/2}$

where

D = Cutter Diameter = 75 millimeters
W = Piece Width   = 50 millimeters

Lead = 37.5 − 1/2 $(5625−2500)^{1/2}$
     = 9.549 mm or 9.5 mm

The total length of cut is:

L = piece length + lead + pretravel and overtravel
  = 200 + 9.5 + 6 (normal)
  = 215.5 millimeters

The value for the rpm can be calculated from the formulas in Table 9–1 as:

$$N = 1000 \, V / \pi \, D_c = 1000 \times 45 / (3.1416 \times 75)$$
$$= 191 \text{ rpm}$$

Therefore the cutting time per piece can be calculated from L / F, but the feed must be calculated by:

$$F = N \times f_t \times n_t$$
$$= 191 \times 0.25 \times 8$$
$$= 382 \text{ millimeters/minute}$$

The cutting time is therefore:

$$T = \frac{215.5 \text{mm}}{382 \text{mm/min}}$$
$$= 0.56 \text{ minutes}$$

The loading and unloading time, from Table 9–3, and by using a vice, would be 0.30 minutes. The time per piece, if the allowances are applied, would be:

$$T = 1.09 \times 0.56 + 1.15 \times 0.30$$
$$= 0.955 \text{ minutes/piece}$$

The setup time, for milling a plane surface, from Table 9–5, is 69 minutes and with the adjustment factor of 150 percent, the total setup time would be 103.5 minutes. The total time for 40 pieces would be:

$$\text{Total Time} = \text{Setup Time} + 40 \times \text{Time/Piece}$$
$$= 103.5 + 40 \times 0.955$$
$$= 103.5 + 36.50$$
$$= 140.00 \text{ minutes or } 2.333 \text{ hours}$$

It is important to note that the setup time is much larger than the actual machining time and this does frequently occur when small lots are made.

Estimating Operation Times for Shaping

The basic formulas for shaping are in Table 9–1 and the data in Tables 9–3, 9–4, and 9–5 also apply to shaping. The cutting speeds and feeds for shaping are presented in Table 9–7. Note that the feeds are in inches or millimeters per stroke, and not inches or millimeters per revolution or per tooth.

Table 9-7 Cutting Speeds and Feeds for Shaping, Planing, and Slotting

	Tool material							
	HSS (High Speed Steel)				Carbide			
	speed		feed/stroke		speed		feed/stroke	
Work material	ft/min	m/min	in	mm	ft/min	m/min	in	mm
Steel-hard	25	8	0.04	1.00	140	40	0.035	0.9
Steel-medium	65	20	0.03	0.75	210	65	0.05	1.25
Steel-soft	80	25	0.06	1.50	235	70	0.05	1.25
Cast Steel	40	12	0.05	1.25	140	40	0.04	1.00
Cast Iron-hard	40	12	0.06	1.50	150	45	0.05	1.25
Cast Iron-soft	65	20	0.12	3.00	165	50	0.05	1.25
Malleable Iron	70	21	0.09	2.25	200	60	0.04	1.00
Brass	200	60	0.05	1.25				
Bronze	45	15	0.08	2.00	210	65	0.05	1.25
Aluminum	250	75	0.04	1.00				

in/s* = inches/stroke
mm/s* = millimeters/stroke
Other data for shaping, planing, and slotting:
Return to Cutting Speed Ratio for Shapers
  Hydraulic Shaper R = 2.0
  Mechanical Shaper R = 1.6
Typical depth of cut
  routh cut 0.15 in (4mm)
  finish cut 0.002 in (0.05 mm)
Adapted from Ref. 1.

Example Problem 9-3

The surface generated in problem 9-2 can also be generated by shaping, so Example Problem 9-2 will be resolved for the shaping process. The tool will be a high speed steel single point tool and the feeds and speeds in Table 9-7 will be used in the solution.
Solution:

If the carbon steel is equivalent to the soft steel, the recommended cutting speed is 25 m/min and the feed is 1.5 mm per stroke. For a shaper the return velocity is greater than the cutting velocity, and a mechanical shaper will be used with a R value of 1.6 as listed in Table 9-7.

The setup time can be estimated from Table 9-5 where the time for shaping is assumed to be equal to that of a drill press with parallels, which is 11 minutes. If the 150 percent adjustment is applied, the total setup time would be 16.5 minutes.

The length of cut is the piece length plus some pretravel and overtravel, the pretravel being about 5 mm and the overtravel set at 15 mm. The total length for the cut is thus:

$$L = \text{piece length} + \text{pretravel} + \text{overtravel}$$
$$= 200 + 5 + 15$$
$$= 220 \text{ mm}$$

The feed rate, from Table 9-1, is the product of the number of strokes per minute and the feed per stroke. The number of strokes per minute, from Table 9-1 and using the metric formula is:

$$n_s = 1000\,V / [L\,(1 + \frac{1}{R})]$$
$$= 1000 \times 25 / [(220(1 + \frac{1}{1.6})]$$
$$= 69.9 \text{ strokes/minute or } 70 \text{ strokes/minute}$$

The feed rate is the product of n_s and f_s which is:

$$F = n_s \times f_s$$
$$= 70 \times 1.5$$
$$= 105 \text{ millimeters/minute}$$

The cutting time for the shaper operation, as found in Table 9-1, is:

T = W / F = 60 millimeters / 105 millimeters/minute (5 mm is added to
each side for pretravel and overtravel clearance of the width
being cut, so the total width across which the feed occurs is
50 + (2 × 5) or 60 mm)

= 0.57 minutes/piece

The loading and unloading time, from Table 9–3, and by using a vice,
would be 0.30 minutes. The time per piece, if the allowances are applied,
would be:

T = 1.09 × 0.57 + 1.15 × 0.30

= 0.966 minutes/piece

The total time for the batch of 40 pieces would be:

Total Time = Setup Time + 40 × Time/Piece

= 16.5 + 40 × 0.966

= 16.5 + 38.6

= 55.1 minutes or 0.919 hours

For the example presented, the setup time for shaping was considerably
shorter than that for milling and since the cutting times were nearly equal, the
total time for shaping was less than that for milling the same part. The cutting
times for milling are usually shorter than those for shaping, especially when
large amounts of metal are to be removed.

Estimating Operation Times for Drilling

The basic equations for drilling are presented in Table 9–1 and the data in
Tables 9–3, 9–4, and 9–5 also apply to drilling. The feeds and speeds for drilling are presented in Table 9–8. The feed rates are in inches per revolution.

Example Problem 9–4

A four by four inch square plate, one inch thick, is to have four 1/2 inch diameter holes drilled and a 1 inch diameter hole as illustrated in Figure 9–4. The
work material is aluminum and the drill material is high speed steel. The drill
press used is a sensitive drill press with two spindles and a lot of 50 pieces is
to be processed.

Table 9–8 Feeds and Speeds for Drilling in Various Materials using High Speed Drills

	A Cutting speeds and feed classes for various materials		
	Cutting speed		Feed class
Work material	ft/min	m/min	
Soft Cast Iron	150	45	1
Medium Cast Iron	80	25	2
Mild Steel	90	27	2
Alloy Steel	60	18	3
Tool Steel	50	15	3
Brass and Bronze	200	60	1
Copper	150	45	1
Aluminum and Magnesium Alloys	350	105	1

B Feed rates as a function of feed class		
Feed class	General material description	Feed rate**
1	Free Machining Materials	0.02 D*
2	Tough or Hard Materials	0.01 D
3	Very Hard Materials	0.005 D

*represents the diameter of the drill, in either inches or millimeters
**The feed rate is in inches per revolution, if the drill diameter is in inches, or in millimeters per revolution, if the drill diameter is in millimeters.
Feed data adapted from *Introduction to Manufacturing Processes*, J. A. Schey, 1987 McGraw-Hill. Reprinted with permission. Ref. 8.
Cutting speeds from *Metal Cutting Principles*, M.C. Schaw, 1984, Oxford University Press. Reprinted with permission. Ref. 9.

Solution:

The setup time for a sensitive drill press with a vice, from the data in Table 9–5, is 15 minutes for a two spindle drill press for the two different drill sizes.

The length of cut is the thickness of the workpiece, since the holes go entirely through the piece, the pretravel would be 1/8 inch for drilling, the overtravel would be also 1/8 inch, and the lead, for a standard drill with an included angle of 118 degrees, is found by the following equation:

$$l = (D/2) \times \operatorname{Tan} 31$$

which becomes

$$l = D/2 \times 0.60 = 0.30\,D \tag{9-5}$$

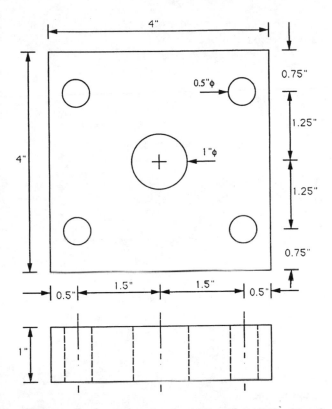

Figure 9–4 Illustration for drilling Example Problem 9–4.

where

 l = Lead in inches (millimeters)
 D = Drill diameter in inches (millimeters)

The total length the drill moves is; for each of the 1/2 inch diameter holes:

 L = depth of hole + lead + pretravel + overtravel
   = 1.00 + 0.3 × 0.5 + 1/8 + 1/8
   = 1.40 inches

for the 1 inch diameter hole:

 L = depth of hole + lead + pretravel + overtravel
   = 1.00 + 0.3 × 1 + 1/8 + 1/8
   = 1.55 inches

The revolutions per minute can be determined from the expression in Table 9-1 for drilling, which is, for the U.S. units:

$$N = 12 \, V \, / \, \pi \, D_c$$

for each of the 1/2 inch diameter holes:

$$N = \frac{12 \times 350}{3.1416 \times 1/2}$$
$$= 2674 \text{ rpm}$$

for the one inch diameter hole:

$$N = \frac{12 \times 350}{3.1416 \times 1}$$
$$= 1337 \text{ rpm}$$

The feed per revolution for each of the holes can be found from the data in Table 9-8 which states:

$$f_r = 0.02 \times D$$

This gives a feed of 0.010 inch/revolution for each of the 1/2 inch holes and a feed of 0.020 inch/revolution for the 1 inch hole.

The feed rate is the product of the feed/revolution and the rpm, that is:

$$F = f_r \times N$$

which results in, for each of the 1/2 inch holes:

$$F = 0.010 \times 2674 = 26.74 \text{ inches/minute}$$

for the 1 inch diameter hole:

$$F = 0.020 \times 1337 = 26.74 \text{ inches/minute}$$

The drilling time for the holes is obtained from:

$$T = L \, / \, F$$

for each of the 1/2 inch holes:

T = 1.40 inches / 26.74 inches/minute

= 0.0523 minutes/hole

or 0.209 minutes for all 4 holes

for the 1 inch hole:

T = 1.55 inches / 26.74 inches/minute

= 0.0580 minutes

Thus the total time for drilling all five holes would be the sum of the times, that is

T = 0.209 + 0.0580 = 0.267 min/piece

The handling time, which also includes the indexing time, from Table 9-3 is 0.30 minutes. The total time, if the allowances of 9 percent to machining and 15 percent to handling time are applied, would be:

T = 1.09 × 0.267 + 1.15 × 0.30

= 0.291 + 0.345

= 0.636 minutes

The fact that the handling time is greater than the drilling time is a result of the high speeds used in drilling aluminum. If the material was mild steel, the drilling time would have been larger than the handling time.

The setup time for the two spindle drill press was 15 minutes, and if the 150 percent adjustment is applied, the total setup time would be 22.5 minutes. The total time to produce the lot of 50 parts would be:

Total Time = Setup Time + 50 × Time/Piece

= 22.5 + 50 × 0.636

= 22.5 + 31.8

= 54.3 minutes or 0.905 hours

If one wishes to determine the metal removal rate, the value can be calculated from the formulas in Table 9-1. For drilling, the relation is:

$Q = \pi D_c^2 F / 4$

$= 3.1416 \times (1/2)^2 \times 26.74 / 4$

= 5.25 cubic inches/minute for the 1/2 inch drill

It is left for the student to show that the metal removal rate for the 1 inch drill is 21.0 cubic inches/minute.

ESTIMATIONS BASED UPON CUTTING PATH LENGTH AND VELOCITY

Another method for determining the cutting time is by using the cutting path length and the cutting velocity. The optimal cutting velocity can be determined by methods as illustrated in Appendix A, and thus this method permits a more direct optimization of the process. If the velocity used is the same as that used to determine the rpm for the feed based method, the results will be identical to those obtained by the feed based methods. The basic formula for the cutting path length and cutting velocity method is:

$$(T = Z / V = \text{cutting path length / cutting velocity}) \tag{9–6}$$

This method is similar to the traditional method as the specific cutting parameters of feed, speed, and depth of cut (or drill diameter) must be specified.

Example Problem 9–5

Calculate the time to drill the four 1/2 inch holes and the 1 inch hole as illustrated in Figure 9–4 by the cutting path length and velocity method. Compare the results obtained with those of Example Problem 9–4.
Solution:

The expressions for the cutting path length for the various processes are in Table 9–1, and for drilling in U.S. units the equation is:

$$Z = \pi \, D_c \, L / 12 \, f_r$$

For the 1/2 inch diameter holes, the total length for each hole is 1.4 inches and for the 1 inch diameter the length is 1.5 inches. The feed is 0.010 inch/revolution for the 1/2 inch diameter holes and 0.020 inch/revolution for the 1 inch diameter hole. The cutting velocity is 350 ft/min for both hole diameters. The values of the cutting path length, Z, and the cutting time, T, for the two hole diameters can now be calculated.

For the 1 inch diameter drill the value of Z is:

$$Z = 3.1416 \times 1.0 \times 1.55 / (12 \times 0.020)$$
$$= 20.29 \text{ ft}$$

The cutting time is:

$$T = Z / V = 20.29 \text{ ft} / 350 \text{ ft/min} = 0.0580 \text{ min}$$

For the 1/2 inch diameter drill the value of Z is:

$$Z = 3.1416 \times 1/2 \times 1.40 / (12 \times 0.010)$$
$$= 18.33 \text{ ft}$$

The cutting time for the four holes is:

$$T = 4 \times Z / V = 4 \text{ holes} \times 18.33 \text{ ft/hole} / 350 \text{ ft/min}$$
$$= 0.209 \text{ min}$$

These results are the same as the values calculated previously for the 1 inch diameter hole and the 4 holes of 1/2 inch diameter. Equation 9-6 is used in optimization models to determine the optimal cutting speed. The time that the tool is actually cutting metal, t_c is given by:

$$t_c = Y \times T \tag{9-7}$$

where

  Y = Fraction of tool path that tool is cutting metal
  T = Total time tool is on cutting path
  t_c = Time tool is actually cutting material

The significance of the two time values is that T is used for the time values needed for cost estimating, whereas t_c is the time value needed for tool life considerations; it is the actual cutting time for the operation. For turning these time values are close, but for drilling the value of t_c is about 70–90 percent of T, and for the interrupted cutting of milling and shaping the t_c values are much lower. The ratio has a maximum value of 50 percent for milling and a maximum value of 70 percent for shaping. The primary concern for cost estimating is the value of T, but engineers must be aware of the other value (t_c) and understand the difference. The tool life value is used to determine the tool costs and the tool changing costs. Details of the metal cutting economics model, which follows the cutting path length and cutting velocity calculations, are presented in Appendix A.

FEATURE BASED ESTIMATING

The feature based cost estimation method, or The Approximate Method (10), classifies machined parts into seven different categories. The machining time can then be estimated based upon the part classification and the weight of the part before machining. The formulas have been derived from more complex expressions and have made assumptions about the volume/surface area ratio, the material, batch size, and etc. The feature based expressions have been published for only one category of parts, the primary rotational parts.

The feature code, feature description, and process operations used to obtain the feature are presented in Table 9–9. The basic expressions are given by Radovanovic (10) in his thesis, but the final reduced expressions are not presented in the thesis. The expression for rotational parts is presented by Boothroyd (2,11), but the other feature based expressions for the other shape categories are not presented. The expressions for the primary rotational parts are:

$$T = t_{mc} + t_{mp} + t_{np} \tag{9–8}$$

$$t_{mc} = 2.74 \times W^{(0.86)} + 6.68 \times W^{(0.57)} \tag{9–9}$$

$$t_{mp} = 49.9 \times W^{(0.47)} \tag{9–10}$$

$$t_{np} = 90.5 + 1.1 \times W \tag{9–11}$$

Table 9–9 Feature Code, Feature Description, and Operations Utilized for Obtaining Feature

Feature code	Feature description	Machining operations for obtaining feature*
1	Primary Rotational	Turning and Grinding
2	Primary Rotational with Secondary Operations	Turning, Drilling, Threading, and Grinding
3	Primary Planar	Milling and Grinding
4	Primary Planar with Secondary Operations	Milling, Drilling, Threading, and Grinding
5	Primary Rotational and Primary Planar	Turning, Milling, and Grinding
6	Primary Rotational, Primary Planar, and Secondary	Drilling, Turning, Milling, Threading, and Grinding
7	Secondary	Drilling, Threading, and Milling

*Operations are listed in decreasing order of process percentage of work content. Adapted from Ref. 10.

where

  T = Total Time per unit (machining and setup)
  t_{mc} = Machining Time for finishing operations (seconds/piece)
  t_{mp} = Machining Time for roughing operations (seconds/piece)
  t_{np} = Setup and other nonproductive time (seconds/piece)
  W = Weight of workpiece (lbs)

It must be emphasized that these expressions are approximate and have numerous assumptions embedded in them. In particular, these expressions are for carbon steel; approximately 60 percent of the material is removed by machining; adjustments for pretravel are included; a fixed relationship exists between volume and surface area; and etc. They are important, however, in that they present a new approach to estimating for machining and for a rapid evaluation of new designs.

Example Problem 9-6

Use the feature based time expressions for rotational parts and calculate the time to produce 100 units of the part illustrated in Figure 9-3. Compare the results with those obtained for Example Problem 9-1 and discuss the differences.
Solution:
  From Figure 9-1, the volume of the original part can be determined as:

$$V = (\pi / 4) \times 3^2 \times 6$$
$$= 42.4 \text{ in}^3$$

The density of steel, from Table 7-4, is 0.285 lb/cubic inch, so the weight of the part is:

$$W = 42.4 \text{ in}^3 \times 0.285 \text{ lb/}(\text{in}^3)$$
$$= 12.1 \text{ lbs}$$

The machining and nonproductive times can be calculated from Equations 9-9, 9-10, and 9-11 which give:

$$t_{mc} = 2.74 \times (12.1)^{0.86} + 6.68 \times (12.1)^{0.57}$$
$$= 23.4 + 27.7$$
$$= 51.1 \text{ seconds}$$
$$t_{mp} = 49.9 \times (12.1)^{0.47}$$
$$= 161.1 \text{ seconds}$$

The total machining time is the sum of these two times; that is:

$$t_m = t_{mc} + t_{mp}$$
$$= 51.1 + 161.1$$
$$= 212.2 \text{ seconds } (3.54 \text{ minutes})$$

This time of 3.54 minutes is comparable with the 2.90 minutes after the adjustment for allowances of 9 percent, or the value of 3.16 minutes. The difference between these two methods is less than 15 percent for this example.

The nonproductive time includes the setup time plus the part handling times. The estimate of the nonproductive time from Example Problem 9-1 would be the difference between the total time per piece of 4.045 minutes less the 3.16 minutes for machining, or 0.885 minutes. The nonproductive time as calculated would be:

$$t_{np} = 90.5 + 1.1 \times 12.1$$
$$= 103.8 \text{ seconds } (1.73 \text{ minutes})$$

The nonproductive time for the feature based method is nearly twice that of the feed based method, but that is because the feature based time is based upon a more complex setup with five tools instead of one tool, more handling for a more complex part, and etc.

The results from the feature based time estimating appear to be encouraging and the cutting time values were reasonable for the sample problem. The setup and handling times are developed separately in the thesis (10) and these expressions may be reformulated. The technique of feature based time estimating has great potential for concurrent engineering environments. The conceptual cost-size estimating expressions of Table 8-8 are also feature based relationships using part volume rather than part weight.

SUMMARY AND CONCLUSIONS

The machining relationships for turning, milling, drilling, and shaping have been presented and illustrated with example problems. The models presented have assumed that the cutting speeds have been determined for the high efficiency cutting range and that tool life considerations have been included in the determination of the cutting speed. The unit tool changing times are considered to be part of the allowances and have not been added separately. If the tool changing time and the tool life values are available, the unit tool changing time can be calculated, but this calculation is beyond the scope of this chapter. Further details concerning tool life optimization are included in Appendix A.

The relationships for the other cutting processes can be presented in a similar manner and the calculations follow the same general procedure. The distinguishing features that are needed for other processes are the feeds and speeds, which were different for the four processes presented. The setup times, handling times, and allowances tend to be valid for most processes, but the feeds and speeds tend to be different.

The feature based time estimating is rather new and has been presented in detail for only primary rotational parts. The relationships need to be developed for the other feature shape categories. Feature based time estimating has potential for reasonably accurate estimates early in the design process when the manufacturing process details are not known.

The costs for the machining operations can be determined from the times calculated by applying the appropriate labor and overhead rates. The total costs would not only include the operation costs, but also the material costs and the scrap costs. Machining is the most costly of the manufacturing processes, and the determination of the time estimates is essential not only for costing, but also for scheduling and production control.

EVALUATIVE QUESTIONS

1. What are the three primary variables in metal cutting? Give a definition of each.
2. There are five elements that are included in the unit piece time. What are these five elements? Describe which are productive and which are nonproductive?
3. On the average, what percentage of the material is removed by machining to produce a light part (less than 60 pounds)?
4. The shape illustrated in Figure 9–5 is to be machined from a 6 inch long bar which initially is two inches in diameter. The cuts are rough

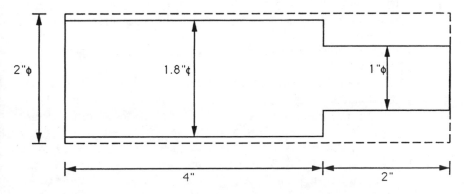

Figure 9–5   Part shape to be generated by turning for Question 4.

cuts, the material is mild steel, and HSS tools are used. The pretravel and overtravel amounts are 1/8 and 1/4 inches respectively, a universal chuck is used, and the typical allowances are applied. A batch of 100 pieces are to be produced.

- What cutting speed and feed range should be used? (for the problem solution, use the highest feed value)
- Determine the number of passes to be made and the average diameter for each pass.
- Estimate the total setup time.
- Estimate the total cutting time per piece, then determine the part handling time, and finally apply the appropriate allowances to determine the allowed time for cutting and the allowed time to produce a part.
- What is the total time allowed to produce the batch of 100 pieces?

5. A soft cast iron block, 1.2 inches thick, 4 inches wide and 4 inches long is to be reduced to 1.0 inch thick by removing material from each side, two holes, one 1 inch in diameter and the second 1/2 inch in diameter, are to be drilled as indicated in Figure 9–6. High speed steel tools are used for both operations. Assume the total pretravel and overtravel distance for shaping is 1 inch and for drilling is 3/16 inch. A mechanical shaper is used with R = 1.6 and a sensitive drill press is used to drill the holes. A vice is used to hold the parts in both operations.

- What feed, cutting speed, and depth of cut should be used for each of the shaping cuts?
- What feed and cutting speed should be used for each of the holes to be drilled?
- Estimate the cutting time for the shaping operation, then estimate the total allowed time/piece for the shaping operation.
- Estimate the cutting time for the drilling for both holes, then estimate the total allowed time/piece for the drilling operation.
- Estimate the allowed setup time for the shaping and for the drilling operations.
- If a lot of 60 parts are made, what is the allowed time to produce the lot of parts?
- What are the metal removal rates for the shaping operation (rough cuts) and the two drilling operations, in cubic inches per minute?

6. Use the feature based method to estimate the time to machine the surface of the part in Figure 9–5 and compare the results with those obtained in Question 4. If the 1 inch diameter section is increased in length from 2 inches to 3 inches and the other section reduced by the same length, what is the change in the results of the feature based method?

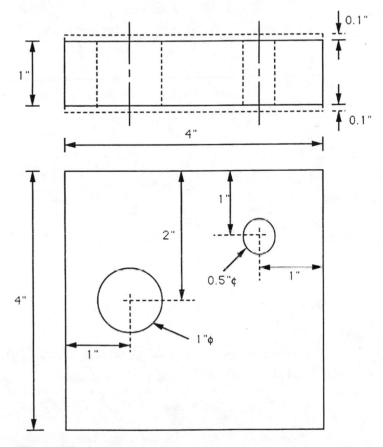

Figure 9–6 Part to be made by shaping top and bottom surfaces and by drilling two holes as described in question 5.

7. A slot is to be milled in an aluminum block as indicated in Figure 9–7. The HSS milling cutter is 50 mm in diameter and has 12 teeth. The pretravel is 5 mm and the overtravel is also 5 mm. A vice is used to hold the part and the feed used is 0.100 mm/tooth. A order of 400 parts has been obtained.
   - What is the cutting speed, cutter rpm, and feed rate in mm/min?
   - Estimate the cutting time and the allowed time/piece for the milling operation.
   - What is the allowed time to produce the order of 400 parts?
   - What is the maximum metal removal rate when cutting?

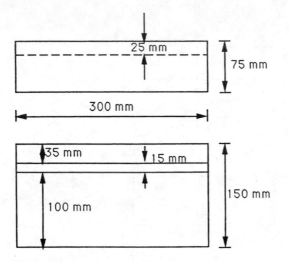

Figure 9–7   Illustration for milling of slot for question 9-7.

BIBLIOGRAPHY

1. Adithan, M. and Pabla, B. S., *Production Engineering, Estimating and Costing*, Konark Publishers, Delhi, 1989, pp. 146–177.
2. Boothroyd, G., and Knight, W. A., *Fundamentals of Machining and Machine Tools*, Marcel Dekker, 2nd edition, 1989, pp. 175–204, 399–465.
3. Ostwald, P. F., *American Machinist Manufacturing Cost Estimating Guide*, 1982 Edition, McGraw Hill, p. 382.
4. Creese, R. C., "Unit Cost and Unit Production Standards for the Minimum Cost Metal Cutting Model", *AFS Transactions*, Vol.92, 1984, pp. 515–518.
5. Creese, R.C., "Standards for the Minimum Cost and Maximum Production Metal Cutting Models: Turning, Shaping, Drilling, and Milling", *AFS Transactions*, Vol. 93, l985, pp. 183–186.
6. Drozda, T. J. and Wicks, C., Editors, *Tool and Manufacturing Engineers Handbook, Volume 1—Machining*, 1983, Society of Manufacturing Engineers, Dearborn, Michigan, pp. 8-2.
7. Bolz, R. W., *Production Processes*, Conquest Publications, Novelty, Ohio, 1974, p. 135.
8. Schey, J. A., *Introduction to Manufacturing Processes*, Second Edition, 1987, McGraw Hill, p. 505.

9. Shaw, M. C., *Metal Cutting Principles*, Oxford University Press, 1984, Oxford, England, p. 474.

10. Radovanovic, P., *Approximate Cost Estimating for Machined Components*, University of Rhode Island, MS Thesis, Department of Industrial Engineering and Manufacturing Engineering, 1989, p. 140.

11. Boothroyd, G. and Reynolds, C., *Approximate Machining Cost Estimates*, Report No. 17, Department of Industrial and Manufacturing Engineering, University of Rhode Island, pp. 5–11.

10
Basic Costing for Welding Processes

INTRODUCTION

The joining processes consist of fasteners, welding, and adhesive bonding. Fasteners include both those for permanent assembly and those for nonpermanent assembly such as nuts and bolts. Adhesive bonding includes processes which rely on adhesion rather than cohesion, and includes processes such as brazing, soldering, gluing, and bonding by epoxies. The main joining process is welding, which includes the various arc welding processes, resistance welding, mechanical fusion welding techniques (friction welding, explosion welding, diffusion bonding), and optical beam welding methods, including laser and electron beam welding. These joining processes are quite different and the cost methods are therefore varied, so this chapter will deal with the main joining process, namely arc welding, and the methodology of obtaining arc welding costs.

ARC WELDING VARIABLES

The process variables and cost terms used in arc welding are presented in Table 10-1 with the symbols used in the formulas developed and the corresponding units. A brief description of the variables and terms is presented to indicate the importance of the variable and how it is determined. The equations and variables will be expressed in U.S. units and in the corresponding metric units. The descriptions of the variables are:

Travel Speed (S)—This is one of the primary welding variables and refers to the speed of the electrode during welding. The speeds can range from

Table 10–1 Process Variables and Cost Terms for Arc Welding

Process variables	Symbol	U.S. units	Metric units
Travel Speed	S	inches/minute	millimeters/sec
Welding current	I	amperes	amperes
Welding Voltage	V	volts	volts
Operator Factor	OF	decimal	decimal
Electrode Metal yield	EMY	decimal	decimal
Machine (power supply) efficiency	M	decimal	decimal
Gas Flow Rate	GFR	cubic ft/hr	cubic meters/hr
Wire Feed Rate	WFR	inches/minute	meters/minute
Electrode Weight per unit Length	EWL	lbs/inch (lbs/foot)	kilograms/meter
Deposition Rate	DR	lbs/hour	kilograms/hour
Duty Cycle	DC	percent	percent
Flux Consumption Rate	FCR	lb flux/lb metal	kg flux/kg metal
Energy consumed per unit length	H	joules/inch	joules/mm
Weight of Weld Metal Deposited	WMD	lb/in	kilograms/meter
Length of weld	L	foot	meter
Welding Time	WT	minute	minute
Cost Terms:			
Labor Rate	LR	$/hour	$/hour
Overhead Rate	OR	$/hour	$/hour
Electrode Cost	EC	$/lb	$/kilogram
Gas Cost	GC	$/cubic foot	$/cubic meter
Flux Cost	FC	$/lb flux	$/kg flux
Power Cost	PC	$/kwhr	$/kwhr
Tooling Cost	TC	$	$

Common Conversion Terms:

1 inch/min	=	0.423 mm/sec		1 mm/sec	=	2.36	inch/min
1 inch/min	=	0.254 m/min		1 m/min	=	39.37	inch/min
1 lb/inch	=	17.9 kg/m		1 kg/m	=	0.0559	lb/inch
1 lb/hr	=	0.454 kg/hr		1 kg/hr	=	2.20	lb/hr
1 lb	=	0.454 kg		1 kg	=	2.20	lb
1 ft^3/hr	=	0.0283 m^3/hr		1 m^3/hr	=	35.3	ft^3/hr
1 in^2	=	645 mm^2		1 mm^2	=	0.00155	in^2
1 in	=	25.4 mm		1 mm	=	0.03937	in

5 inches/minute (2 millimeters/second) for a manual process to over 1000 inches/minute (400 millimeters/second) in automatic pipe welding processes. It is not only important for cost determination, but it also indicates how fast the welder should be moving the electrode.

Welding current (I)—This is the primary variable which has an important effect upon the weld penetration as well as the deposition rate. For the same energy input, current has a greater effect upon penetration than voltage or travel speed.

Welding Voltage (V)—This is a primary variable and has an effect upon weld bead width, that is, the greater the voltage, the greater the width of the weld bead.

Operator Factor (OF)—This is a major term in the determination of the welding economics. It is the ratio of the arc time to the total welding cycle time. The total welding cycle time includes the arc time, the positioning and tacking of the pieces, cleaning and brushing, removal of slag, and any other element in the weld cycle. The weld cycle does not include setup time for the job.

Electrode Metal Yield (EMY)— The electrode metal yield is the fraction of the weight of the electrode which becomes weld metal. This varies considerably with the welding process. The electrode metal yield is also called the deposition efficiency ratio.

Machine (power supply) efficiency (M)—The welding power supply has some losses and these must be included in the power costs. Most arc welding power supplies are approximately 90 percent efficient, or 0.90 on a decimal basis.

Gas Flow Rate (GFR)—The shielding gas used to protect the weld metal in gas welding is measured in cubic feet/hr. In metric units the gas flow rate is in cubic meters/hour.

Wire Feed Rate (WFR)—In automatic welding processes, this represents the rate at which the welding filler wire is fed into the weld arc and gets melted. The welding filler wire also acts as the electrode. The U.S. units are usually inches/minute whereas the metric units are meters/minute.

Electrode Weight per unit Length (EWL)—This is the weight per unit length of the welding filler wire in automatic and semiautomatic processes and is dependent upon the wire diameter and material. It can be obtained by weighing a piece of wire and dividing the weight by the length. The U.S. units are usually pounds/inch or sometimes pounds/foot, whereas the metric units are kilograms/meter.

Deposition Rate (DR)—The deposition rate is the amount of weld metal that can be deposited in one hour. It is dependent primarily upon the welding process, welding current, filler metal yield, and electrode size. The U.S. units for deposition rate are pounds/hour and the metric units are kilograms/hour.

Duty Cycle (DC)—This is the percent of a ten minute period that the power supply can be run at the rated current and voltage without overheating. Automatic welding processes require power supplies with high duty cycles, around 100 percent, whereas the duty cycle for manual welding power supplies can be as low as 20 percent. The duty cycle implies that the power supply can dissipate a limited amount of heat, and this can be expressed by:

$$I^2 \times DC = constant \qquad\qquad (10\text{--}1)$$

where

I = Welding current in amperes
DC = Duty Cycle in %

Flux Consumption Rate (FCR)—In the submerged arc welding process, a granular flux is used to shield the weld metal from the atmosphere. Some flux becomes crystallized and cannot be reused and the amount of crystallized flux is related to the weld metal deposited. The flux consumption rate is the amount of flux crystallized or otherwise consumed per unit of weld metal deposited. This is a ratio quantity, such as pounds flux/pounds weld metal or kilograms flux/kilograms weld metal, which is the same numerical value in both unit systems.

Energy consumed per unit of weld length (H)—This is a term that can be used to compare different welding processes and is a function of the three primary variables. The first expression is for the U.S. units and the second, which has the letter a in the equation number, is for the metric units.

$$H = 60 \times VI/S \qquad\qquad (10\text{--}2)$$

or

$$H = VI/S \qquad\qquad (10\text{--}2a)$$

where

H = Joules/unit length of weld length (unit length is inches for the U.S. and millimeters for the metric expression)
V = Welding Voltage in volts
I = Welding current in amperes
S = Travel Speed in inches per minute or millimeters per second

Weight of Weld Metal Deposited (WMD)—This term describes the amount of weld metal deposited per unit length of weld. This is equivalent to the product of the weld metal cross-sectional area times the weld metal density, that is:

$$WMD(lb/in) = Weld\,Area(in^2) \times Metal\,Density(lb/in^3) \qquad (10\text{--}3)$$

or

$$WMD(kg/m) = Weld\,Area(mm^2) \times Metal\,Density(kg/m^3) \times 10^{-6}$$

$$(10\text{--}3)$$

Length of weld (L)—This is the length that is welded and is a major variable in determining welding time and welding costs. The U.S. unit for length of weld is the foot, and the corresponding metric unit is the meter.

Welding Time (WT)—This is the time allowed for the total welding cycle and includes both the arc time and the non-arc time per piece. The usual unit for time in welding is the minute, but sometimes seconds are used in metric calculations. The time unit for both systems will be the minute in the following formulas. This is obtained from the total length of weld, travel speed, and operator factor in the following manner:

$$WT(min) = [L(ft) \times 12\,in/ft] / [S(in/min) \times OF] \qquad (10\text{--}4)$$

or

$$WT(min) = [L(m) \times 1\,000mm/m] / [S(mm/sec) \times 60\,sec/min \times OF]$$

$$(10\text{--}4a)$$

where

     WT = Welding Time
      L = Length of weld
      S = Travel Speed
    OF = Operator Factor

These variables will be utilized in determining the cost components in both the U.S. and metric systems of units.

WELDING COST COMPONENTS

The welding costs can be viewed in terms of the fixed and variable cost components. These two components will be analyzed in more detail, starting with the fixed costs.

Fixed Costs

1. Tooling Costs—For production lots, it is generally economical to have special jigs and fixtures to hold the work or welding electrode, to perform the welding more rapidly. These are frequently special purpose and must be costed to the particular job.
2. Setup Costs—These costs depend upon the welding process and the type of work performed. Some time estimates for setup for different welding processes reported by Ostwald (1) are in Table 10–2. Automatic welding processes tend to have more complex welding setups than the manual or semiautomatic processes.

Variable Costs

The variable costs in welding are generally classified as labor, overhead, material (electrode), shielding (gas or flux), and power costs. The costs can be considered either (i) on the basis of dollars per foot ($/ft) or dollars per meter ($/m) of weld length, or (ii) on the basis of dollars per pound ($/lb) or dollars per kilogram ($/kg) of weld metal deposited. The units normally selected for consideration are the $/ft ($/m), as the weld length can frequently be obtained from the component diagram. The units of $/lb ($/kg) can be obtained from the $/ft ($/m) units by dividing by the metal density and the weld cross-sectional area, that is:

$$\$/lb = \frac{\$/ft \div 12 \text{ in/ft}}{[\text{ metal density} (lb/in^3) \times \text{weld cross-section area} (in^2)]} \qquad (10-5)$$

Table 10–2 Setup Times for Selected Welding Processes

Welding Process	Automation* Level	Setup time (min)	
		Mean	Range
Shielded Metal Arc Welding	Manual	18	—
Flux-Cored Arc Welding	Semiautomatic	24	—
Flux-Cored Arc Welding	Automatic	180	120–240
Submerged Arc Welding	Semiautomatic	30	—
Submerged Arc Welding	Automatic	180	120–240
Gas Metal Arc Welding	Semiautomatic	24	—
Gas Tungsten Arc Welding	Manual	24	—

*Automation Level Manual—manual wire feed and manual travel speed. Semiautomatic—automatic wire feed and manual travel speed. Automatic—automatic wire feed and automatic travel speed. Adapted from Ref. 1. Reprinted with permission of *American Machinist*.

or

$$\$/kg = \frac{\$/m \times 1m^2/10^6 \, mm^2}{[\text{metal density } (lb/m^3) \times \text{weld cross-section area } (mm^2)]} \quad (10\text{--}5a)$$

The expressions will be developed for both the U.S. units and the corresponding metric units. This will permit the solving of problems in either set of units. The first expression will be the U.S. units and the following equation, with the suffix a, is for the corresponding metric units. The five major components of the variable welding cost will be developed for both the U.S. units and metric units in terms of dollars per unit length.

1. Labor Cost—The labor cost in $/ft ($/m) is obtained from the labor rate, travel speed, and operator factor in the following equation:

$$LC(\$/ft) = \frac{LR(\$/hr) \times 12 \, in/ft}{[60 \, min/hr \times S(in/min) \times OF]} \quad (10\text{--}6)$$

or

$$LC(\$/m) = \frac{LR(\$/hr)}{[3600sec/hr \times 1 \, m \, / \, 1000 \, mm \times S(mm/sec) \times OF]}$$
$$(10\text{--}6a)$$

where

    LC = Labor Cost
    LR = Labor Rate
     S = Travel Speed
    OF = Operator Factor

The question now becomes; what are the expected values for the operator factor and the travel speeds? Table 10–3 gives some of the typical values used for operator factors. The travel speeds depend upon weld thickness, material, and process. Some typical values are presented in Table 10–4. Another expression for labor cost involves deposition rate, and is:

$$LC(\$/ft) = \frac{[LR(\$/hr) \times WMD(lb/in) \times 12 \, in/ft]}{[DR(lb/hr) \times OF]} \quad (10\text{--}7)$$

or

$$LC(\$/m) = \frac{[LR(\$/hr) \times WMD(kg/m)]}{[DR(kg/hr) \times OF]} \quad (10\text{--}7a)$$

Table 10–3 Operator Factor for General and Specific Welding Processes

Welding Process Description	Operator Factor	
	Range	Typical Value
In General		
Manual Welding Processes	0.05–0.40	0.30
Semiautomatic Welding Processes	0.10–0.60	0.40
Automatic Welding Processes	0.40–1.00	0.60
Specific Welding Processes		
Shielded Metal Arc Welding		0.30
Gas Metal Arc Welding	0.41–0.66	0.50
Flux Cored Arc Welding		0.50
Submerged Arc Welding	0.34–0.63	0.50

Adapted from Refs. 2, 3, and 4.

Table 10–4 Travel Speeds For Arc Welding Processes

A   Travel Speeds for Different Arc Welding Process for 3/8 inch (9.5mm) Butt Weld
(From Lincoln (5))

Welding Process	Travel Speed	
	in/min	mm/sec
Shielded Metal Arc Welding	4.25	1.8
Flux Cored Arc Welding	10.0	4.2
Submerged Arc Welding—Semiautomatic	15.0	6.3
Submerged Arc Welding—Automatic	18.0	7.6

B   Typical Travel Speed Ranges Used For Arc Welding Processes on Steel (Adapted
From Lincoln (5))

Welding Processes	Travel Speed Range	
	in/min	mm/sec
Shielded Metal Arc Welding <0.14inches*	15–25	6–11
>0.14inches*	5–15	2–6
Submerged Arc Welding <0.25 inches*	30–100	13–42
>0.25 inches*	8–30	3–13
FluxCoreArcWelding <0.14inches*		
Fully Automatic	100–200	42–85
Semiautomatic	10–25	4–11
Gas Metal Arc Welding	10–25	4–11
Gas Tungsten Arc Welding	10–18	4–8

*Weld Thickness Limits

where

$$LC = \text{Labor Cost}$$
$$LR = \text{Labor Rate}$$
$$WMD = \text{Weld Metal Deposited}$$
$$DR = \text{Deposition Rate}$$
$$OF = \text{Operator Factor}$$

Note that the ratio of DR / WMD is equivalent to the the travel speed in inches/hr or in m/hr. If travel speeds are not available, they can be estimated from the formulas:

$$S(\text{in/min}) = DR(\text{lb/hr}) / [WMD(\text{lb/in}) \times 60\,\text{min/hr}] \tag{10–8}$$

or

$$S(\text{mm/sec}) = DR(\text{kg/hr}) / [WMD(\text{kg/m}) \times 1\text{m} / 1000\text{mm} \times 3600\text{sec/hr}] \tag{10–8a}$$

If Equation 10–7 is to be used for the labor costs, expressions for the deposition rate need to be developed. From an examination of the deposition rate curves (4,5), expressions were developed for nonmanual and manual welding processes. The expressions developed for nonmanual processes were:

$$DR(\text{lb/hr}) = 0.033 \times I(\text{amps}) \tag{10–9}$$

or

$$DR(\text{kg/hr}) = 0.015 \times I(\text{amps}) \tag{10–9a}$$

and for manual processes were:

$$DR(\text{lb/hr}) = 0.033 \times I(\text{amps}) - 1.7 \tag{10–10}$$

or

$$DR(\text{kg/hr}) = 0.015 \times I(\text{amps}) - 0.77 \tag{10–10a}$$

where

$$DR = \text{Deposition Rate}$$
$$I = \text{Current}$$

For example, if manual welding is used and the current is 100 amps, the deposition rate would be 1.60 lbs/hour or 0.73 kg/hr.

2. Overhead Costs—The overhead cost is calculated in a manner similar to that for labor costs. The only difference is that the overhead rate is used instead of the labor rate in equations 10–6 and 10–7. The overhead costs (OC) thus become:

$$OC(\$/ft) = \frac{[OR(\$/hr) \times 12 \text{ in/ft}]}{[60 \text{min/hr} \times S(\text{in/min}) \times OF]} \qquad (10-11)$$

or

$$OC(\$/m) = \frac{[OR(\$/hr)]}{[3600 \text{ sec/hr} \times 1m / 1000\text{mm} \times S(\text{mm/sec}) \times OF]}$$

$$(10-11a)$$

where

OC = Overhead Cost
OR = Overhead Rate
 S = Travel Speed
OF = Operator Factor

Another set of expressions for the determination of the overhead cost is:

$$OC(\$/ft) = \frac{[OR(\$/hr) \times WMD(\text{lb/in}) \times 12 \text{ in/ft}]}{[DR(\text{lb/hr}) \times OF]} \qquad (10-12)$$

or

$$OC(\$/m) = \frac{[OR(\$/hr) \times WMD(\text{kg/m})]}{[DR(\text{kg/hr}) \times OF]} \qquad (10-12a)$$

where

OC = Overhead Cost
OR = Overhead Rate
WMD = Weld Metal Deposited
DR = Deposition Rate
OF = Operator Factor

The labor and overhead costs are generally the greatest portion of the total variable welding costs, that is from 60 to 90 percent of the the total variable welding cost.

3. Material (Electrode) Costs—The material cost for welding represents the electrode costs, not the material costs of the parts being assembled. The methods for calculation are different for the manual processes and the automatic and semiautomatic processes, where the filler wire is automatically fed into the weld pool. The calculation method generally used for automatic and semiautomatic welding is:

$$VEC(\$/ft) = \frac{[WFR(in/min) \times EWL(lb/in) \times EC(\$/lb) \times 12\,in/ft]}{[S(in/min) \times EMY]}$$

(10–13)

or

$$VEC(\$/m) = \frac{[WFR(m/min) \times EWL(kg/m) \times EC(\$/kg)]}{[S(mm/sec) \times 60sec/min \times 1m\,/\,1000mm \times EMY]}$$

(10–13a)

where

VEC = Variable Electrode Cost
WFR = Wire Feed Rate
EC = Electrode Cost
S = Travel Speed
EMY = Electrode Metal Yield
EWL = Electrode Weight per unit Length

The equation primarily used for manual welding, but sometimes used for semiautomatic and automatic welding, is:

$$VEC(\$/ft) = WMD(lb/in) \times EC(\$/lb) \times 12\,in/ft\,/\,EMY \quad (10-14)$$

or

$$VEC(\$/m) = WMD(kg/m) \times EC(\$/kg)\,/\,EMY \quad (10-14a)$$

where

VEC = Variable Electrode Cost
WMD = Weld Metal Deposited
EC = Electrode Cost
EMY = Electrode Metal Yield

The electrode metal yield is dependent upon the welding process, and some of the typical values are given in Table 10–5. The ranges of electrode metal yield were presented by Cary (5) and the typical values

Table 10-5 Electrode Metal Yield Factors for Various Welding Processes

	Electrode Metal Yield*	
Welding process description	Normal** range	Typical value
Shielded Metal Arc Welding—average		0.60
—14" Electrode	0.55–0.65	
—18" Electrode	0.60–0.70	
—28" Electrode	0.65–0.75	
Submerged Arc Welding	0.95–1.00	1.00
Gas Metal Arc Welding—Carbon Dioxide	0.90–0.95	0.92
—Other Gases	0.95–1.00	1.00
Flux Core Arc Welding (with carbon dioxide)	0.80–0.85	0.85

*The electrode metal yield is sometimes called deposition efficiency ratio.
**From Howard B. Cary, *Modern Welding Technology*, 2nd Ed., © 1989 p. 616. Adapted by permission of Prentice Hall, Englewood Cliffs, New Jersey.

were selected based upon the range and values used previously by the authors.

4. Shielding Gas/Flux Costs—The shielding costs are the costs for the shielding gases or fluxes that are used to protect the weld metal from the atmosphere. These are included in the cost of the electrode materials for shielded metal arc welding and in the flux costs in flux core arc welding. However, the shielding gas costs for gas metal arc welding, gas tungsten arc welding, and, if used, in flux core arc welding must be determined. Also, the cost of the flux used in submerged arc welding must be included as it is used to shield the weld from the atmosphere. The cost for the shielding gas can be determined by:

$$VGC(\$/ft) = \frac{[GFR(ft^3/hr) \times GC(\$/ft^3) \times 12\,in/ft]}{[S(in/min) \times 60\,min/hr]} \qquad (10\text{-}15)$$

or

$$VGC(\$/m) = \frac{[GFR(m^3/hr) \times GC(\$/m^3)]}{[S(mm/sec) \times 3600\,sec/hr \times 1\,m/1000\,mm]}$$

$$(10\text{-}15a)$$

where

VGC = Variable Gas Cost
GFR = Gas Flow Rate
GC = Gas Cost
S = Travel Speed

The AWS recommended gas flow rates (2) are approximately 10 ft^3/hr (0.28m^3/hr) per 100 amperes of the weld current used, with a minimum value of 10 ft^3/hr (0.28m^3/hr).

The flux cost for the submerged arc welding process is determined by:

$$VFC(\$/ft) = WMD(lb\,metal/in) \times FCR(lb\,flux/lb\,metal)$$
$$\times FC(\$/lb\,flux) \times 12\,in/ft \qquad (10\text{-}16)$$

or

$$VFC(\$/m) = WMD(kg\,metal/m) \times FCR(kg\,flux/kg\,metal)$$
$$\times FC(\$/kg\,flux) \qquad (10\text{-}16a)$$

where

VFC = Variable Flux Cost
WMD = Weld Metal Deposited
FCR = Flux Consumption Rate
FC = Flux Cost

The flux consumption rate ranges from 1.0 to 1.5 and, according to Cary (4), a value of 1.0 is frequently used.

5. Power Costs—The variable power cost depends primarily upon the utility rates, which vary considerably throughout the world. The expression for the variable power cost is:

$$VPC(\$/ft) = \frac{[I(amps) \times V(volts) \times PC(\$/kwhr)/1000] \times 12in/ft}{[S(in/min) \times 60min/hr \times M]}$$
$$(10\text{-}17)$$

or

$$VPC(\$/m) = \frac{[I(amps) \times V(volts) \times PC(\$/kwhr)/1000]}{[S(mm/sec) \times 3600sec/hr \times 1\,m/1000\,mm \times M]}$$
$$(10\text{-}17a)$$

where

VPC = Variable Power Cost
I = Welding current
V = Welding Voltage
PC = Power Cost
S = Travel Speed
M = Machine efficiency

Variable power cost can also be calculated from the weight of weld metal deposited and deposition rate by:

$$VPC(\$/ft) = \frac{[I(amps) \times V(volts) \times PC(\$/kwhr) / 1000] \times WMD(lb/in) \times 12\,in/ft}{[DR(lb/hr) \times M]}$$

(10–18)

or

$$VPC(\$/m) = \frac{[I(amps) \times V(volts) \times PC(\$/kwhr)/1000] \times WMD(kg/m)}{[DR(kg/hr) \times M]}$$

(10–18a)

where

$\qquad$ VPC = Variable Power Cost
$\qquad$ I = Welding current
$\qquad$ V = Welding Voltage
$\qquad$ PC = Power Cost
$\qquad$ WMD = Weight of weld Metal Deposited
$\qquad$ DR = Deposition Rate
$\qquad$ M = Machine efficiency

These five components of the variable cost, when summed, represent the total variable cost for the welding calculations. Example problems are presented in a later section to illustrate the application of the formulas presented.

MULTIPLE PASS WELDING

In many cases it will take more than one pass to complete the weld, and each pass may be at a different travel speed. Rather than determine the costs for each pass, an overall travel speed (5) can be used which is computed as:

$$S = \frac{1}{1/S1 + 1/S2 + \cdots + 1/Sn}$$

(10–19)

where

$\qquad$ S = Overall travel Speed
$\qquad$ S1 = Travel Speed of first pass
$\qquad$ S2 = Travel Speed of second pass
$\qquad$ .. = Travel Speed of .... pass
$\qquad$ Sn = Travel Speed of last pass

For example, if two passes are made, one at 10 inches per minute and the second at 20 inches per minute, the overall travel speed is:

$$S = \frac{1}{1/10 + 1/20}$$
$$= 20/3$$
$$= 6.67 \text{ inches/minute}$$

Equation 10–19 is also valid for metric units. For example if two passes are made, one at 0.4 mm/sec and the second at 0.8 mm/sec, the overall travel speed is:

$$S = \frac{1}{1/0.4 + 1/0.8}$$
$$= 0.267 \text{ mm/sec}$$

Note: The overall travel speed is lower than the lowest of the individual travel speeds.

ILLUSTRATIVE WELDING PROBLEMS

Example Problem 10–1

Two pieces are welded together as illustrated in Figure 10–1. The pieces are a low carbon steel, 12 inches long, welded on a power supply with a 20 percent duty cycle and a current rating of 200 amps. If the welding procedure calls for 160 amps, 20 volts, travel speed of 10 inches per minute; and if the operator factor is 0.40, determine:

The allowed time to weld the two pieces together excluding setup time.
The energy generated per unit length during welding.
Whether the power supply will overheat.

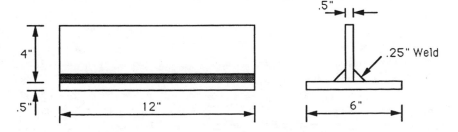

Figure 10–1 Illustration of fillet weld for Example Problem 10–1.

Solution:

Using Equation 10–4,

$$WT(min) = L(ft) \times 12\ in/ft\ /[S(in/min) \times OF]$$

where

L = 2 × 12inches / 12 in/ft = 2 feet
S = 10 in/min
OF = 0.40
WT = 2ft × 12in/ft / 10 in/min × 0.4
   = 6.0 minutes

(The arc time is equal to WT × OF, which is 2.4 minutes for this problem.)
b. The energy generated per unit length is found from Equation 10–2

$$H = 60\ sec/min \times V \times I\,/\,S(in/min)$$

where

V = 20 Volts
I = 160 Amperes
S = 10 in/min
H = 60 × 20 × 160 / 10
   = 19,200 joules/inch

c. The amount of energy that can be dissipated by the power supply is represented by a constant C1:

$$C1 = I^2 \times DC = 200^2 \times 20 = 800,000\ (maximum\ energy\ permissible)$$

In a ten minute period, the power supply would be operating 10 × OF minutes, that is 10 × 0.4 = 4 minutes or the duty cycle would be 40 percent; thus the energy to be dissipated would be represented by a constant C2. The value of C2 is:

$$C2 = 160^2 \times 40 = 1,024,000$$

which is greater than 800,000; so the power supply would overheat. (If the operator factor was 0.3, the power supply would not overheat, as C2 would be 768,000, which is less than 800,000.) If C2 is less than C1 the power supply will not overheat, whereas if C2 is greater than C1 the power supply will overheat.

Example Problem 10–2

A metal box is to be welded as indicated in Figure 10–2. It has a base of 6 inches by 10 inches with a wall height of 4 inches. The inside corners are to be 1/4 inch fillet welds, the material is a low carbon steel sheet which is 0.20 inches thick. Using the welding and cost parameters in Table 10–6, determine the time and cost to produce a lot of 40 boxes (excluding material cost). Some of the process data used is from the Lincoln Procedure Book (5) or estimated from the data listed.

Solution:

The weight of the weld metal deposited per unit length is the product of the weld cross-sectional area and the weld metal density. Since the material is steel, it has a density of 0.28 lb/cubic inch. The fillet weld has a triangular cross-sectional and its area is:

$$\begin{aligned} \text{Area} &= 1/2 \, b \times h \\ &- 1/2 \times 1/4 \times 1/4 \\ &= 1/32 \text{ square inches} \end{aligned}$$

Therefore, from Equation 10–3,

$$\begin{aligned} \text{WMD} &= 1/32 \times 0.28 \\ &= 0.00875 \text{ lb/in} \end{aligned}$$

Although the deposition rate is not required, it can be obtained by rearranging Equation 10–8 and solving for DR by:

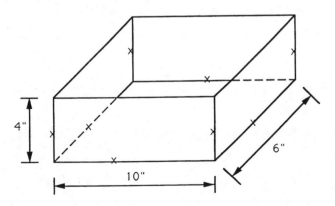

Figure 10–2   Metal box dimensions for Example Problem 10–2.

Table 10–6 Welding Process Parameters and Cost Parameters for Example
Problem 10-2

Welding Process Parameters	
Process	Shielded Metal Arc Welding (SMAW)
Travel Speed	9 inches/min (3.8 mm/sec)
Welding Current	200 Amps
Welding Voltage	20 Volts
Machine Efficiency	0.90
Duty Cycle	60 percent
Operator Factor	0.30 (Table 10–3)
Electrode Metal Yield	0.65 (Table 10–5 for 18 inch electrode)
Gas Flow Rate	Not Applicable for SMAW
Wire Feed Rate	Not Applicable for SMAW
Electrode Wt. per length	Not Applicable for SMAW
Flux Consumption Rate	Not Applicable for SMAW
Deposition Rate	Calculate from travel speed
Weight of Weld Metal Deposited	Calculate from weld size
Weld Cost Parameters	
Labor Rate	12.00 $/hr
Overhead Rate	18.00 $/hr
Gas Cost	Not Applicable for SMAW
Flux Cost	Not Applicable for SMAW
Material (electrode) Cost	0.25 $/lb (0.55 $/kg)
Power Cost	0.10 $/kwhr

$$
\begin{aligned}
DR &= S(in/min) \times 60\ min/hr \times WMD(lb/in) \\
&= 9 \times 60 \times 0.00875 \\
&= 4.7\ lb/hr
\end{aligned}
\tag{10--20}
$$

The length of the weld, L, is found from the information in Figure 10–2, and
is:

$$
\begin{aligned}
L &= [2 \times 10 + 2 \times 6 + 4 \times 4]inches\ /\ 12\ in/ft \\
&= 4\ ft
\end{aligned}
$$

The labor cost per ft from Equation 10–6 is:

$$
\begin{aligned}
LC &= 12.00\ \$/hr \times 12\ in/ft\ /\ [60\ min/hr \times 9\ in/min \times 0.30] \\
&= 0.889\ \$/ft
\end{aligned}
$$

Similarly, the overhead cost per foot from Equation 10–11 is:

$$OC = 18.00 \text{ \$/hr} \times 12 \text{ in/ft} / [9 \text{ in/min} \times 60\text{min/hr} \times 0.30]$$
$$= 1.333 \text{ \$/ft}$$

There is no separate shielding gas or flux cost in the SMAW process. The variable material (electrode) cost is found from Equation 10–14 by:

$$VEC = 0.00875 \text{ lb/in} \times 0.25 \text{ \$/lb} \times 12 \text{ in/ft} / 0.65$$
$$= 0.040 \text{ \$/ft}$$

The power cost is found from Equation 10–17 by:

$$VPC = \frac{[200 \times 20 \times 0.10 / 1000]\text{\$/hr} \times 12 \text{ in/ft}}{[9 \text{ in/min} \times 60 \text{ min/hr} \times 0.90]}$$
$$= 0.0098 \text{ \$/ft}$$
$$= 0.010 \text{ \$/ft}$$

The total variable cost is the sum of:

$$TVC = LC + OC + VEC + VPC$$
$$= 0.889 \text{ \$/ft} + 1.333 \text{ \$/ft} + 0.040 \text{ \$/ft} + 0.010 \text{ \$/ft}$$
$$= 2.272 \text{ \$/ft}$$

Note that most of the cost is the labor and overhead costs. Therefore these two components are frequently used and the other two components, electrode material cost and power cost, are often neglected in manual welding cost calculations.

The total weld length per part is 4 ft, so the variable cost per part is:

$$VC = 2.272 \text{ \$/ft} \times 4 \text{ ft} = \$9.088 \text{ per unit}$$

From Table 10–2, the setup time would be approximately 18 minutes, and the setup cost would be the setup time times the sum of the labor plus overhead rates, that is:

$$Setup \ Cost = 18 \text{ minutes} \times [12.00 \text{ \$/hr} + 18.00 \text{ \$/hr}] / 60 \text{ min/hr}$$
$$= \$9.00$$

The cost of 40 pieces would be $40 \times \$9.088 = \$363.52$. The total cost, including setup cost, is $\$372.52$

The time to produce a unit is:

WT = L / [S × OF]
= 4 ft × 12 in/ft / [9 in/min × 0.3]
= 17.77 min

The total time to produce 40 units is:

WT(40) = (40 × 17.77) + 18 (setup)
= 728.8 min or 12.15 hr

Example Problem 10–3

This is the same problem as Example 2 except that the welding is to be done by the Gas Metal Arc Welding (GMAW) and thus the processes can be compared. The overhead rate has been increased to reflect the higher equipment costs. The data is in Table 10–7 and reflects the differences in the processes. Solution:
The variable labor cost, from Equation 10–6, is:

$$LC(\$/ft) = \frac{[12.00 \$/hr \times 12 in/ft]}{[60 min/hr \times 16 in/min \times 0.50]}$$
$$= 0.300 \$/ft$$

The variable overhead cost, from Equation 10–11 is:

$$OC(\$/ft) = \frac{[24.00 \$/hr \times 12 in/ft]}{[60 min/hr \times 16 in/min \times 0.50]}$$
$$= 0.600 \$/ft$$

The variable material (electrode) cost, from Equation 10–13, is:

$$VEC(\$/ft) = \frac{[87 in/min \times 0.0019 3 lb/in \times 0.25 \$/lb \times 12 in/ft]}{[16 in/min \times 0.95]}$$
$$= 0.033 \$/ft$$

The variable gas cost, from Equation 10–15, is:

$$VGC(\$/ft) = \frac{[40 ft^3/hr \times 0.30 \$/ft^3 \times 12 in/ft]}{[16 in/min \times 60 min/hr]}$$
$$= 0.150 \$/ft$$

Table 10-7 Welding Process Parameters and Cost Parameters for Example Problem 10-3

Welding Process Parameters	
Process	Gas Metal Arc Welding (GMAW)
Travel Speed	16 inches/min (6.8 mm/sec)
Welding Current	400 Amps
Welding Voltage	27 Volts
Machine Efficiency	0.90
Duty Cycle	60 %
Operator Factor	0.50 (Table 10-3)
Electrode Metal Yield	0.95 (Table 10-5)
Gas Flow Rate	40 cubic ft/hr (1.13 cubic m/hr)
Wire Feed Rate	87 inches/min (2.21 m/min)
Electrode Wt. per Length	0.00193 lb/in (0.0345 kg/m)
Flux Consumption Rate	Not Applicable for GMAW
Deposition Rate	Calculated from travel speed
Weight of Weld Metal Deposited	0.00875 lb/in (0.157 kg/m) (from Example Problem 10-2)
Welding Cost Parameters	
Labor Rate	12.00 $/hr (same)
Overhead Rate	24.00 $/hr (increased from 18 $/hr)
Gas Cost	0.30 $/cubic foot (10.59 $/m³)
Flux Cost	Not Applicable for GMAW
Material (electrode) Cost	0.25 $/lb (0.55 $/kg)
Power Cost	0.10 $/kwhr
Setup Time	24 min (Table 10-2)

The variable power cost, from Equation 10-17, is:

$$\text{VPC}(\$/\text{ft}) = \frac{[400\,\text{amps} \times 27\,\text{volts} \times 0.10\,\$/\text{kwhr} / 1000] \times 12\,\text{in}/\text{ft}}{[16\,\text{in}/\text{min} \times 60\,\text{min}/\text{hr} \times 0.9]}$$

$$= 0.015\ \$/\text{ft}$$

The total variable cost (TVC) is the sum of these components:

$$\text{TVC} = 0.300 + 0.600 + 0.033 + 0.150 + 0.015$$
$$= 1.098\ \$/\text{ft}$$

Since a unit contains 4 feet of weld length, the welding cost per unit is:

VC = 4 × 1.098 = $ 4.392/unit

For 40 units, the cost is

Total Cost = 40 × 4.392 + Setup Cost for 40 units
           = $ 175.68 + 24min × [(12 $/hr + 24 $/hr) / 60 min/hr]
           = $ 175.68 + $ 14.4
           = $ 190.08

The SMAW cost was $ 372.52.
The welding time per unit is:

WT = L / [S × OF]
   = 4 ft × 12 in/ft / [16 in/min × 0.50]
   = 6 minutes

Thus for 40 units

WT(40) = (40 units × 6 min/unit) + 24 min (setup)
       = 264 min or 4.4 hr

The SMAW process took 728.8 minutes or 12.15 hr.

In general the improved operator factors and faster welding speeds offset the higher overhead costs and thus automatic and semiautomatic welding tends to be more economical as well as faster than manual welding. One should note that power, gas, and electrode variable costs are a greater portion of the total variable cost for the GMAW process than for the SMAW process.

Example Problem 10-4

An open end cylindrical tank, 1.5 meters in height and 1 meter in diameter is to be welded from 2 pieces, as indicated in Figure 10-3. The plate, 4 mm thick, is to be formed into a cylinder and welded along the 1.5 m length with a square butt weld with a gap of 2 mm. The base is to be placed inside the cylinder 8 mm, and a 4 mm fillet weld is used to join the base to the walls. The gas metal arc welding (GMAW) process is to be used, and the data is in Table 10-8. Calculate the total variable welding cost and unit welding time for one tank.
Solution:

The weld area for the butt weld and fillet welds are:

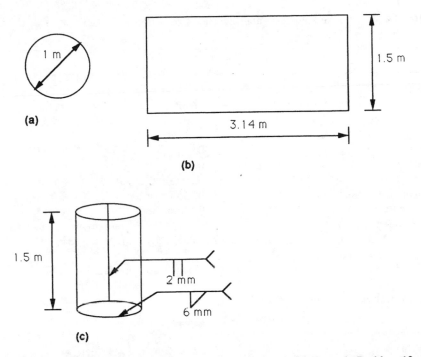

Figure 10-3 Part dimensions for cylindrical tank for Example Problem 10-4. (a) Tank bottom piece, (b) tank wall piece, (c) assembled tank and well description.

$$A(\text{butt}) = 2 \text{ mm} \times 4 \text{ mm}$$
$$= 8 \text{ mm}^2$$

and

$$A(\text{fillet}) = 1/2 \times 4 \text{ mm} \times 4 \text{ mm}$$
$$= 8 \text{ mm}^2$$

After adjustment of about 15 to 25 percent for convex surfaces and etc. the weld areas are still approximately identical, so the same welding parameters can be used. If they were significantly different, these would be evaluated separately, as two different welds. The total weld area for these welds will be considered as 10 square millimeters. The metal is steel, and the density is 7905 kg/m³, so the weld metal deposited, from Equation 10-3a, is:

Table 10–8 Welding Process Parameters and Cost Parameters for Example Problem 10–4

Welding Process Parameters	
Process	Gas Metal Arc Welding (GMAW)
Travel Speed	5.2 mm/sec (12.3 in/min)
Welding Current	150 Amps
Welding Voltage	20 Volts
Machine Efficiency	0.90
Duty Cycle	60 %
Operator Factor	0.50 (Table 10–3)
Electrode Metal Yield	0.95 (Table 10–5)
Gas Flow Rate	0.8 cubic m/hr (28.2 cubic ft/hr)
Wire Feed Rate	6.6 m/min (260 in/min)
Electrode Wt. per Length	0.00503 kg/m (0.000281 lb/in)
Flux Consumption Rate	Not Applicable for GMAW
Deposition Rate	Calculated from travel speed
Weight of Weld Metal Deposited (calculated from weld area)	0.079 kg/m (0.00442 lb/in)

Welding Cost Parameters	
Labor Rate	12.00 \$/hr
Overhead Rate	24.00 \$/hr
Gas Cost	10.00 \$/cubic meter (0.283 \$/cubic ft)
Flux Cost	Not Applicable for GMAW
Material (electrode) Cost	1.00 \$/kg (0.454 \$/lb)
Power Cost	0.10 \$/kwhr
Setup Time	24 min (Table 10–2)

$$\begin{aligned} WMD &= 10 \text{ mm}^2 \times 7905 \text{ kg/m}^3 \times 10^{-6} \text{ m}^2/\text{mm}^2 \\ &= 0.079 \text{ kg/m} \end{aligned}$$

The length of the weld is the total of the two welds, as they are being performed with the same welding parameters; otherwise, each weld would need to be calculated separately. Thus, using the data in Figure 10–3, the weld length is:

$$\begin{aligned} L &= \text{Length of Butt Weld} + \text{Length of Fillet Weld} \\ &= 1.5 \text{ m} + 3.14 \text{ m} \\ &= 4.64 \text{ m} \end{aligned}$$

The variable labor cost is found from Equation 10–6a, and is:

$$LC(\$/m) = \frac{[12.00\,\$/hr]}{[3600\,sec/hr \times 1\,m/1000mm \times 5.2\,mm/sec \times 0.50]}$$
$$= 1.282\,\$/m$$

The variable overhead cost is found via Equation 10–11a, and is:

$$OC(\$/m) = \frac{[24.00\,\$/hr]}{[3600\,sec/hr \times 1\,m/1000\,mm \times 5.2\,mm/sec \times 0.50]}$$
$$= 2.564\,\$/m$$

The variable material (electrode) cost is found via Equation 10–13a, and is:

$$VEC(\$/m) = \frac{(6.6\,m/min \times 0.00503\,kg/m \times 1.00\,\$/kg)}{(5.2\,mm/sec \times 60\,sec/min \times 1\,m/1000mm \times 0.95)}$$
$$= 0.112\,\$/m$$

The variable gas cost is obtained from Equation 10–15a, and is:

$$VGC(\$/m) = \frac{(0.8\,m^3/hr \times 10.00\,\$/m^3)}{(5.2\,mm/sec \times 3600\,sec/hr \times 1m/1000\,mm)}$$
$$= 0.427\,\$/m$$

The variable power cost is obtained from Equation 10–17a, and is:

$$VPC(\$/m) = \frac{(150\,amps \times 20\,volts \times 0.10\,\$/kwhr/1000)}{(5.2\,mm/sec \times 3600\,sec/hr \times 1m/1000mm \times 0.9)}$$
$$= 0.018\,\$/m$$

The total variable cost (TVC) is the sum of these five components

$$TVC = 1.282 + 2.564 + 0.112 + 0.427 + 0.018$$
$$= 4.403\,\$/m$$

Since the total weld length of the unit is 4.64 meters, the variable welding cost per unit would be:

$$VC = 4.64\,m/unit \times 4.403\,\$/m$$
$$= 20.426\,\$/unit$$

The total welding time per unit, from Equation 10–4a is:

$$WT = \frac{(4.64m \times 1000 \text{ mm/m})}{(5.2 \text{ mm/sec} \times 60 \text{ sec/min} \times 0.5)}$$
$$= 29.74 \text{ minutes/unit}$$

This is the time to weld one unit and does not include the setup time. Similarly, the welding cost is the variable welding cost per unit and does not include the setup costs.

DISCUSSION AND CONCLUSIONS

The primary process variables governing the welding economics are the travel speed (or deposition rate) and the operator factor. The newer welding processes permit higher travel speeds and increase the operator factor, but have higher overhead rates and longer setup times. The formulas presented permit an evaluation of different welding processes for a variety of welding jobs. The setup times in Table 10–2 are higher for automatic welding because they are usually applied to more complex work, and would be somewhat lower for simpler tasks. Nevertheless, the setup time for automatic and semiautomatic welding is usually more than that for manual welding.

Although deposition rate can give the equivalent values for the economic evaluations, the use of travel speed permits an easier analysis of the time values and gives the operator a better understanding of his rate of working.

In general, the labor and overhead costs are over 70 percent of the total variable costs for most of the welding processes, and even over 90 percent for most manual arc welding processes. The formulae presented and methodology illustrated enables one to determine the welding costs for most of the arc welding processes.

EVALUATIVE QUESTIONS

1. Define the following welding terms: operator factor, travel speed, overall travel speed, electrode metal yield, and duty cycle.
2. A multiple pass weld has three passes and travel speeds of 10 in/min, 15 in/min, and 20 in/min. What is the overall travel speed in in/min?
3. Calculate the welding time for Example Problem 10–1 if the travel speed was 14 inches/min instead of 10 inches/min. Also calculate the heat generated per unit length with the higher travel speed.
4. Change the travel speed in Example Problem 10–2 from 9 inches per minute to 12 inches per minute, and determine the cost and time to make the tanks.
5. Change the operator factor from 0.50 to 0.40 in Example Problem 10–3 and determine the costs and time to make the tanks.

Table 10–9 Welding Process Parameters and Cost Parameters for Question 6
Using Submerged Arc Welding Process

Welding Process Parameters	
Process	Submerged Arc Welding (SAW)
Travel Speed	39 inches/min (16.5 mm/sec)
Welding Current	625 Amps
Welding Voltage	32 Volts
Machine Efficiency	0.90
Duty Cycle	100 %
Operator Factor	0.50 (Table 10–3)
Electrode Metal Yield	1.00 (Table 10–5)
Gas Flow Rate	Not Applicable for SAW
Wire Feed Rate	Not given
Electrode Weight per Length	0.00537 lb/inch (.0961 kg/m)
Flux Consumption Rate	0.70
Deposition Rate	Calculate from travel speed
Weight of Weld Metal Deposited	0.00875 lb/inch (0.157 kg/m) (previously calculated)
Welding Cost Parameters	
Labor Rate	12 $/hr
Overhead Rate	36 $/hr
Gas Cost	not applicable
Flux Cost	0.15 $/lb (0.33 $/kg)
Material (electrode) Cost	0.20 $/lb (0.44 $/kg)
Power Cost	0.10 $/kwhr
Setup Time	3 hours

6. Redo Example Problem 10–2 for the submerged arc welding process. The data provided in Table 10–9 is to be used.
7. Redo Example Problem 10–3 in the metric units in Table 10–7 and use a total length of 1220 mm instead of 4 ft.
8. Redo Example Problem 10–4 in the U.S. units in Table 10–8. The total length would be 15.22 ft instead of 4.64 m.

BIBLIOGRAPHY

1. Ostwald, P. F., *American Machinist Manufacturing Cost Estimating Guide*, 1982 Edition, McGraw Hill, pp. 275–288.
2. Wadhwa, A. B., "Simplified Standard Data for Welding", *Industrial Engineering*, Dec. 1974, pp. 24–29.

3. Connor, L. P., Editor, *Welding Handbook—Welding Technology*, 8th Ed., Vol.1, American Welding Society, 1989, pp. 265—286.
4. Cary, H. B., *Modern Welding Technology*, Prentice Hall, 1989, p. 616.
5. *The Procedure Handbook of Arc Welding*, The Lincoln Electric Company, Cleveland, Ohio, 12th Edition, 1973, pp. 6.1.1–6.7.2
6. Lindberg, R. A., and Braton, N. R., *Welding and Other Joining Processes*, Allyn and Bacon, Inc., 1976, pp. 470–507.

11

Basic Costing for Casting Processes

INTRODUCTION

Metal casting is the manufacturing process which converts raw materials to final shape in the most direct route. It is the pouring of liquid metal into a mold cavity to produce the desired shape of the product. Casting has an inherent cost advantage over machining and forging for producing product details, by eliminating the need for intermediate shapes (1). The major disadvantages are that the mechanical properties of forgings are often better than castings and the surface finish of machined parts are generally better than other methods. Often products are cast and the necessary surfaces are machined to meet the design requirements.

The costing information on casting in the literature is limited when compared to that of machining or welding. Some basic details are presented by Adithan and Pabla (2), and a detailed investigation was done by Ajmal (3). Other sources (4,5,6) have taken a cost accounting approach, and Westover (6) gives a detailed example for collecting data and formula development. Usually the data is not available for a detailed cost analysis and this is especially true when attempting to compare the cost of casting with the other processes.

The formulas developed in this section are presented on the unit basis of the pound. The formulas are applicable to any weight basis, such as the kilogram or ton, if both the weight and weight rate units ($/weight) are consistent. The pound unit has been used for illustrative purposes, and is used throughout the chapter for consistency. The kilogram and $/kilogram units can be used wherever pound and $/pound units are used.

CASTING PROCESSES

There are a variety of casting processes and only a few can be considered for comparison purposes. The major processes are sand casting, permanent mold casting, investment casting, and die casting. The casting processes can be classified according to mold use (single or multiple use) and pattern use (single or multiple use). Table 11–1 classifies the major processes according to mold and pattern use. In general, the variable unit production costs, such as labor and overhead, are high for single use molds, but the mold/die costs are very high for the multiple use molds.

The capabilities of the casting processes are varied. Table 11–2 illustrates some of the differences between the four processes under consideration. The rankings have only three categories, and at least one process was classified into each category.

Table 11–1 Classification Scheme for Casting Processes

Casting process	Mold use	Pattern use
Sand Casting	S	M
Permanent Mold Casting	M	*
Investment Casting	S	S
Die Casting	M	*

M = multiple use
S = single use
*Processes with multiple use molds do not use patterns for each casting as the mold is the pattern.

Table 11–2 Process Attributes of Four Important Casting Processes

Process attribute	Sand casting	Permanent mold casting	Investment casting	Die casting
Casting Alloy Range	1	2	1	3
Surface Finish	3	2	1	1
Tolerance Capability	3	2	1	1
Thin Section Capability	3	2	1	1
Size and Shape Restrictions	1	3	2	3
Production Quantity Limits	1	2	2	3
Process Cost	1	2	3	2

1 = few or no limitations, best
2 = some limitations, average
3 = highly restricted, worst

The general production flow in a foundry is illustrated in Figure 11–1. The major cost areas of a foundry are generally considered to be patternmaking, core making, molding, melting and pouring, and cleaning and finishing (3). As the environmental costs have become a greater concern, the disposal costs of sand, slag, sludge, air and water are large enough to become a cost center. However, little data exists on the cost of disposal of foundry waste products at this time.

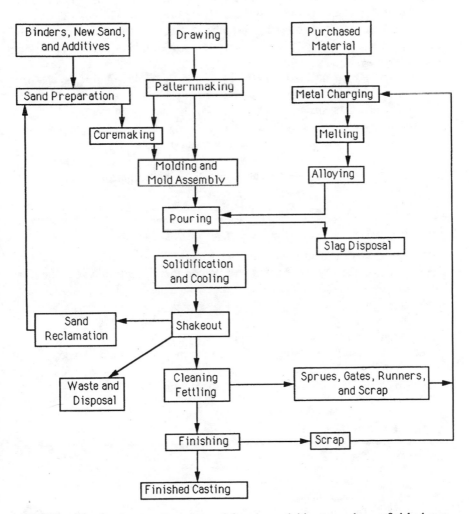

Figure 11–1 Process flow chart of foundry activities to produce a finished casting by sand casting.

COST ELEMENTS FOR SAND CASTING

The major elements in the estimation of foundry costs are material costs, labor costs, direct foundry expenses, overhead expenses, and environmental costs. The environmental costs involve disposal costs (slag, sludge, and sand disposal), water treatment, and air cleaning. There is little data on these costs, but these costs are becoming major cost items and need to be considered in foundry cost evaluations. The environmental costs are generally related to the other major cost elements and will be considered as part of those costs. Each of the four major cost elements will be discussed in more detail. The costs discussion will be related to the sand casting process, but some of the equations can be directly applied to the other processes, while others will need some modification.

The casting costs generally can be related to the mold volume and the portions for metal, cores, and molding sand. Other items such as sleeves for risers (feeders) and filters are additional costs for the casting process. Table 11–3 lists the major cost items in the mold and the mold volume components, and Figure 11–2 illustrates some of the cost items of Table 11–3.

The major cost items will now be defined in detail and expressions presented for their calculation. The emphasis is upon the material and labor costs.

Material Costs

The material costs primarily are the metal costs, the core costs and the molding sand costs. Each of these items will be considered separately, but the total volume of these is equal to the flask volume as indicated in Figure 11–2.

Metal Costs

To compute the metal costs, the total metal poured, the return metal (gates, runners, and risers), the casting scrap, and the melt loss should be known. The total metal poured minus the return metal, casting scrap, and melt loss is the casting weight. The relationship between these items is:

Table 11–3 Major Cost Items for Casting

Cost item
Metal Volume (Casting, Gating, Riser, etc.)
Core Volume (Size and Number)
Flask Volume (Total Volume)
Molding Sand Volume
Other (Sleeves, Filters, etc.)

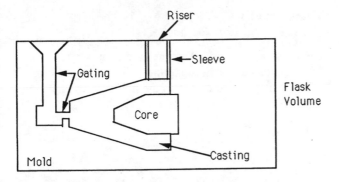

Figure 11-2 Illustration of sand casting mold to indicate some of the cost items in Table 11-3.

$$TWP = CW \times [1/(1 - SR)] \times [1/Y] \times [1/(1 - ML] \times [1/(1 - FSR)]$$

$$(11-1)$$

where

TWP = Total Weight of metal Poured (lb)
  CW = Casting Weight (lb)
  SR = Casting Scrap Rate (decimal)
    Y = Yield (decimal)
  ML = Melt Loss (decimal)
  FSR = Finishing and cleaning scrap rate (decimal)

The yield is related to the casting weight and poured weight by:

$$Y = CW/PW \qquad (11-2)$$

where

CW = Casting weight
PW = Poured weight (casting plus process returns)

The poured weight is the casting weight plus the gating (sprue, runner, and gates) and risers. The yield values are readily available at the foundry for various classes of castings.

The casting scrap per casting can be determined from the casting scrap rate, finishing and cleaning scrap rate, and the casting weight, that is:

$$CS = CW \times SR/[1 - SR] \times [1/(1 - FSR)] \qquad (11-3)$$

where

CS = Casting Scrap weight per casting (lb)
CW = Casting Weight (lb)

SR = Casting Scrap Rate (decimal)
FSR = Finishing and cleaning Scrap Rate (decimal)

The finishing and cleaning scrap rate is the percentage of completed castings which are scrapped in the cleaning or finishing operations. The amount of finishing and cleaning scrap can be determined from the finishing and cleaning scrap rate and the casting weight, that is:

$$CSFC = CW \times FSR / [1 - FSR] \tag{11-4}$$

where

CSFC = Casting Scrap weight from Finishing and Cleaning (lb)
CW = Casting Weight (lb)
FSR = Finishing and cleaning Scrap Rate (decimal)

The returns consist of the gates and risers from all castings, both the scrapped castings as well as the good castings. The return weight per casting is:

$$RW = CW \times [(1 - Y) / Y] \times [1 / (1 - SR)] \times [1 / (1 - FSR)] \tag{11-5}$$

where

RW = Return Weight (lb)
CW = Casting Weight (lb)
Y = Yield (decimal)
SR = Scrap Rate (decimal)
FSR = Finishing and cleaning Scrap Rate (decimal)

The melt loss (oxidation, dust, slag, etc.) is generally a small quantity and can be expressed as:

$$MLW = CW \times [ML / (1 - ML)] \times [1 / Y] \times [1 / (1 - SR)]$$
$$\times [1 / (1 - FSR)] \tag{11-6}$$

where

MLW = Melt Loss Weight (lb)
CW = Casting Weight (lb)
ML = Melt Loss (decimal)
Y = Yield (decimal)
SR = Casting Scrap Rate (decimal)
FSR = Finishing and cleaning Scrap Rate (decimal)

The total weight poured is equal to the casting weight, melt loss weight, casting scrap weight, cleaning and finishing scrap weight, and return weight. That is:

$$TWP = CW + CS + MLW + CSFC + RW \tag{11-7}$$

Example Problem 11-1

Determine the total pouring weight, melting loss weight, casting scrap weight, finishing and cleaning scrap weight, and return weight for a 20 pound casting with a yield of 60 percent, casting scrap rate of 10 percent, melt loss of 2 percent, and a finishing and cleaning scrap rate of 3 percent.
Solution:
From Equation 11-1, the total weight poured is:

$$
\begin{aligned}
TWP &= 20 \times [1 / (1 - 0.10)] \times [1 / 0.60] \times [1 / (1 - 0.02)] \\
&\quad \times [1 / (1 - 0.03)] \\
&= 38.96 \text{ lb}
\end{aligned}
$$

From Equation 11-6, the melt loss weight is:

$$
\begin{aligned}
MLW &= 20 \times [0.02 / (1 - 0.02)] \times [1 / 0.60] \times [1 / (1 - 0.10)] \\
&\quad \times [1 / (1 - 0.03)] \\
&= 0.78 \text{ lb}
\end{aligned}
$$

From Equation 11-3, the casting scrap weight is:

$$
\begin{aligned}
CS &= 20 \times [0.10 / (1 - 0.10)] \times [1 / (1 - 0.03)] \\
&= 2.29 \text{ lb}
\end{aligned}
$$

From Equation 11-4, the finishing and cleaning scrap weight is:

$$
\begin{aligned}
CSFC &= 20 \times [0.03 / (1 - 0.03)] \\
&= 0.62 \text{ lb}
\end{aligned}
$$

From Equation 11-5, the return weight is:

$$
\begin{aligned}
RW &= 20 \times [(1 - 0.60) / 0.60] \times [1 / (1 - 0.1)] \times [1 / (1 - 0.03)] \\
&= 15.27 \text{ lb}
\end{aligned}
$$

Note that 38.96 lb − 0.78 lb − 2.29 lb − 15.27 lb − 0.62 lb = 20.00 lb, which is the casting weight.

If the hot metal costs are $ 1.00 per pound, scrap and returns have a credit of $ 0.50/lb and melt loss has an environmental cost of $ 3.00/lb, the total cost for the casting would be:

Cost of metal poured	= 38.96 lb × $ 1.00/lb =	$ 38.96
Environmental cost	= 0.78 lb × $ 3.00/lb =	2.34
Casting scrap credit	= 2.29 lb × $ 0.50/lb =	− 1.145
Returns credit	= 15.27 lb × $ 0.50/lb =	− 7.635
Finishing scrap	= 0.62 lb × $ 0.50/lb =	− 0.31
Total Metal Cost		$ 32.21

Although the casting only weighs 20 pounds and hot metal costs $ 1.00/lb, the metal cost is $ 32.21 or $ 1.61/lb and not $ 20.00 or $ 1.00/lb. Note that it takes 38.96 pounds of hot metal to make the 20 pound casting, and the hot metal and environmental costs must be recovered.

Core Costs

The core costs include the costs of the cores used in the casting, the costs of cores broken in the core room and in molding, the cost of the cores in scrapped castings, and the core disposal costs. These costs can be expressed in terms of the total core weight needed for a specific casting, given the core room and molding losses and the casting scrap losses. The total core weight needed is:

$$TCW = CCW \times [1 / (1 - CSR)] \times [1 / (1 - SR)] \times [1 / (1 - FSR)]$$

$$(11\text{-}8)$$

where

TCW = Total Core Weight (lb)
CCW = Casting Core Weight (lb)
CSR = Core and molding Scrap Rate (decimal)
SR = Casting Scrap Rate (decimal)
FSR = Finishing and cleaning Scrap Rate (decimal)

Example Problem 11-2

If a casting has a casting core weight of 10 pounds, the core and molding room core scrap rate is 15 percent, the casting scrap rate is 10 percent, and the finishing and cleaning scrap rate is 3 percent, what core weight should be charged to each casting?
Solution:
From Equation 11-8, the value would be:

$$TCW = 10 \times [1 / (1 - 0.15)] \times [1 / (1 - 0.10)] \times [1 / (1 - 0.03)]$$
$$= 13.5 \text{ lb}$$

This is the same amount of core sand that would need to be disposed. Thus if the core sand costs \$ 0.10/lb and the disposal costs are \$ 0.05/lb (\$ 100.00/ton), then the core sand costs for the casting would be:

$$\text{Cost for Core Sand} = 13.51 \times [\$ \, 0.10/lb + \$ \, 0.05 \, lb]$$
$$= \$ \, 2.03$$

Molding Sand Costs

The molding sand is less expensive than the core sand, but the quantity of sand used is so large that the molding sand cost is often the most expensive material cost for the casting. Most molding sands are reclaimed, but losses occur due to dust, fines, burn- on, etc., so a certain percentage of new sand must be added to the system, as well as for replacing some of the binder materials. The discarded sand tends to be expensive as the disposal costs can be high. For example, the disposal costs for sand from a brass/bronze foundry can be \$ 150.00 per ton because of the lead contained in the sand. The total molding sand per casting is:

$$\text{TSW} = \text{SMW} \times [1/(1-\text{SML}] \times [1/(1-\text{SR})] \times [1/(1-\text{FSR})] \qquad (11\text{--}9)$$

where

TSW = Total molding Sand Weight per casting (lb)
SMW = Sand Mold Weight per casting (lb)
SML = Sand Mold Losses (decimal)
SR = Casting Scrap Rate (decimal)
FSR = Finishing and cleaning Scrap Rate (decimal)

The sand mold losses are generally smaller than the core and molding scrap rate, as cores can be broken in the core room, in transportation to the molding line, and when inserted into the mold. The sand mold losses generally occur only in the molding line.

The new system sand is usually a percentage of the total molding sand weight and can be expressed as:

$$\text{NSS} = \text{A} \times \text{TSW} \qquad (11\text{--}10)$$

where

NSS = New System Sand (lb)
A = Decimal fraction of new system sand to total molding sand
TSW = Total molding Sand Weight (lb)

Similarly, the waste sand for disposal can be expressed as a percentage of the total molding sand weight and can be expressed as:

$$WSD = B \times TSW \tag{11-11}$$

where

WSD = Waste Sand for Disposal (lb)
  B = Decimal fraction of waste sand to total molding sand
TSW = Total molding Sand Weight (lb)

The molding sand cost for the casting would be the cost for the molding sand, the new system sand, and the disposal costs for the waste sand.

Example Problem 11-3

Determine the molding sand costs if the sand mold weight for the casting is 150 lb, the sand mold losses are 5 percent, the casting scrap rate is 10 percent, the finishing and cleaning scrap rate is 3 percent, the new system sand is 8 percent, the waste sand fraction is 6 percent, the molding sand costs $ 0.02/lb, the new sand costs $ 0.04/lb, and the disposal costs are $ 0.06/lb.
Solution:
From Equation 11-9, the total molding sand weight is:

$$
\begin{aligned}
TSW &= 150 \text{ lb.} \times [1 / (1 - 0.05)] \times [1 / (1 - 0.10)] \times [1 / (1 - 0.03] \\
&= 180.9 \text{ lb}
\end{aligned}
$$

From Equation 11-10, the new system sand is:

$$
\begin{aligned}
NSS &= 0.08 \times 180.9 \text{ lb} \\
&= 14.5 \text{ lb}
\end{aligned}
$$

From Equation 11-11, the waste sand for disposal is:

$$
\begin{aligned}
WSD &= 0.06 \times 180.9 \text{ lb} \\
&= 10.9 \text{ lb}
\end{aligned}
$$

The total molding sand costs would be the sum of the molding sand cost, the new system sand cost, and the waste sand disposal costs which would be:

$$
\begin{aligned}
\text{Total Cost of Molding Sand} &= [(180.9 - 14.5)\text{lb} \times \$ 0.02/\text{lb}] \\
&\quad + (14.5 \text{ lb} \times \$ 0.04/\text{lb}) \\
&\quad + (10.9 \text{ lb} \times \$ 0.06/\text{lb}) \\
&= \$ 4.56
\end{aligned}
$$

From the examples, the total material cost would be the sum of the metal cost, molding sand cost, and core sand cost:

$$\text{Total Material Cost} = \$ 32.21 + \$ 2.03 + \$ 4.56$$
$$= \$ 38.80$$

Labor Costs

The labor costs can be identified with the basic cost centers of patternmaking, core making, molding, melting and pouring, and cleaning and finishing. These costs are determined by different methods, but most foundries use the same general approach. The general approaches (3,4) followed for the foundry cost centers are:

Patternmaking

The patternmaking costs are generally treated as a fixed cost, similar to the setup cost (6) in machining. The labor cost in the patternmaking is part of the total patternmaking cost and is not treated as a variable cost. Thus the pattern-making labor costs will not be considered in further detail.

Core making

The core making cost is generally treated as a variable cost and the labor cost, like the material cost, is determined for each casting. The labor costs should be adjusted for the losses in the core making and molding as well as for the scrap castings.

Molding

The molding labor cost is determined in a manner similar to that of the core making labor cost, and is determined for each mold. The labor costs should be adjusted for the losses in molding and the scrap castings.

Melting and Pouring

The labor costs for melting and pouring are usually included in the metal costs. Thus separate labor costs for melting and pouring generally do not occur, and these will not be considered in further detail.

Cleaning and Finishing

The labor costs for cleaning and finishing are, like the core making and molding, assigned for each casting. The amount of cleaning and finishing varies considerably with the casting design, and thus needs to be evaluated for each casting product. Since many of the scrapped castings are removed before finishing, the adjustments for casting scrap rate and core and molding scrap rate are lower.

The expressions for the determination of labor costs for the core making, molding, and cleaning and finishing will now be developed. The unit times for these operations for the particular casting, the labor rates, and overhead rates must be known. The coremaking labor cost would be determined by:

$$CMUC = CMUT \times CMUL \times [1 / (1 - CSR)] \times [1 / (1 - SR)]$$
$$\times [1 / (1 - FSR)] \qquad (11\text{-}12)$$

where

    CMUC = Core making Unit Labor Cost ($/casting)
    CMUT = Core making Unit Time (min/casting)
    CMUL = Core making Labor Rate ($/min)
      CSR = Core and Molding Scrap Rate (decimal)
       SR = Casting Scrap Rate (decimal)
      FSR = Finishing and cleaning Scrap Rate (decimal)

If the core making time is 2 minutes for each core and a casting has two cores, the labor rate is 0.15 $/min(9.00 $/hr), the core and molding scrap rate is 5 percent, the casting scrap rate is 10 percent, and the finishing and cleaning scrap rate is 3 percent, the coremaking unit labor cost per casting would be:

$$CMUC = [2 \text{ cores} \times 2\text{min} / \text{core}] \times 0.15 \text{ \$/min} \times [1 / (1 - 0.05)]$$
$$\times [1 / (1 - 0.10)] \times [1 / (1 - 0.03)]$$
$$= \$ 0.73/\text{casting}$$

Similarly, the molding unit labor cost can be expressed as:

$$MULC = MULT \times MLR \times [1 / (1 - SML)] \times [1 / (1 - SR)]$$
$$\times [1 / (1 - FSR)] \qquad (11\text{-}13)$$

where

    MULC = Molding Unit Labor Cost ($/casting)
    MULT = Molding Unit Time (min/casting)
     MLR = Molding Labor Rate ($/min)
     SML = Sand Mold Losses (decimal)
      SR = Casting Scrap Rate (decimal)
     FSR = Finishing and Cleaning Scrap Rate (decimal)

If the unit molding time is 25 minutes, the molding labor rate is 0.30 $/min (18 $/hr), the sand mold losses are 7 percent, the casting scrap rate is 10 percent, and the finishing and cleaning scrap rate is 3 percent, the molding unit labor cost per casting would be:

$$\text{MULC} = 25 \text{ min} \times 0.30 \text{ \$/min} \times [1 / (1 - 0.07)] \times [1 / (1 - 0.10)]$$
$$\times [1 / (1 - 0.03)]$$
$$= \$ 9.24/\text{casting}$$

The cleaning and finishing labor costs per casting can be evaluated from:

$$\text{CULC} = \text{CULT} \times \text{CLR} \times [1 / (1 - \text{FSR})] \qquad (11\text{--}14)$$

where

CULC = Cleaning and finishing Unit Labor Cost (\$/casting)
CULT = Cleaning and finishing Unit Time (min/casting)
CLR = Cleaning and finishing unit Labor Rate (\$/min)
FSR = Cleaning and finishing Scrap Rate (decimal)

The cleaning and finishing scrap rate is the scrap generated in the cleaning room and during the following finishing operations. This is lower than the casting scrap rate, as many of the scrap castings with obvious surface defects will be removed prior to grinding or any other finishing operations. If the cleaning and finishing unit time is 5 minutes per casting, the cleaning and finishing unit labor rate is \$ 0.25/min (15.00 \$/hr), and the cleaning and finishing scrap rate is 3 percent, then the cleaning and finishing unit labor cost per casting would be:

$$\text{CULC} = 5 \text{ min/casting} \times \$ 0.25/\text{min} \times [1 / (1 - 0.03)]$$
$$= \$ 1.29/\text{casting}$$

The unit labor times are needed for core making, molding, and finishing, and these are a function of the casting volume and surface area. From some available data (6) the following expressions have been developed based upon casting weight and core weight. These expressions are only approximations, but fit the data reported for three casting bays with an error of 10 percent. These expressions are presented in Table 11–4.

The expressions in Table 11–4 were developed from data for ferrous castings in the 30 to 300 pound weight range and for cores in the 8 to 150 pound range. The foundry from which the data was obtained was in England. However, separate expressions can be developed for the type of casting produced at a particular foundry.

Other Direct Expenses

Some of the other direct expenses are the expenditures for patterns and core boxes. These are usually treated as fixed costs similar to setup costs as they

Table 11–4 Expressions for Estimating Times for Molding, Core making, and Finishing Operations

Operation	US units	Metric units
Molding Time	MULT = 3.1 × CW + 14	MULT = 6.8 × CW + 14
Core making Time	CMUT = 2.36 × Y −0.40	CMUT = 5.2 × Y − 0.40
Finishing Time	CULT = 0.80 × CW	CULT = 1.76 × CW

Units For Variables
CW = Casting Weight (lb or kg); range: 30–300 lb, (14–136Kg)
Y = Core weight (lb or kg); range: 8–150lb, (3–68Kg)
MULT = Molding Unit Labor Time (min)
CMUT = Core Making Unit labor Time (min)
CULT = Cleaning and finishing Unit Labor Time (min)
Adapted from Ref. 3.

are not directly related to the production quantity. The pattern costs must be recovered whether 10 castings or 10,000 castings are made. In some cases, such as the investment casting process, a pattern is made for each casting and this cost can then be directly related to the production quantity and would be included in the material costs. On the other hand in the high pressure die casting process, the cost of the dies and tooling can approach $ 500,000.

If the production quantity is large, the pattern costs can be spread over the expected pattern life. However, with the rapid changes in design, patterns can become obsolete in a rather short time.

Overhead Expenses

The overhead expenses for equipment usage, supervisory staff, inspection staff, administration, etc. can be assigned by one or more of the method presented in Chapter 4. The overhead rates are often 150–200 percent of the direct labor rates for the core making, molding and cleaning areas (4).

COSTING FOR OTHER CASTING PROCESSES

The cost elements for the other casting processes, such as permanent mold casting, die casting, and investment casting would follow the same general procedure as those for sand casting. The magnitude of the costs would be vastly different for the cost elements. For example, the pattern costs of sand casting would be considerably smaller than the die costs for use in die casting a similar part. On the other hand, the molding costs in die casting are nonexistent, while they are rather high in investment mold casting. Thus the cost drivers for the different casting processes are different, and generalizations about costs in casting are difficult to make.

The high cost of patternmaking in the sand casting process and of tooling in the die casting process have led to the use of CAD, simulation, NC machining, and other computer aids to reduce the costs in these areas and also to improve the casting quality. The use of computers can reduce product and pattern or mold, design problems gating and risering design and location problems, and even cleaning and finishing problems, in the design stage, before the tooling or castings are produced. The greatest cost reductions are obtained in the design stage, not on the production floor.

Specific formulas were presented by Zenger (7) for sand casting, permanent mold casting, die casting and investment casting. These process cost expressions represented the production and tooling costs; they do not include the scrap, materials (product or mold), or etc. The equations were expressed in terms of casting volume (cubic inches) and the number of parts produced. The unit process costs are:

$$C(SC) = 8.2 \times V^{0.72} + 1030 \times V^{0.51} / N \tag{11-15}$$

$$C(PM) = 0.3 + 2 \times V^{0.7} + (517 + 101 \times V) / N \tag{11-16}$$

$$C(DC) = 0.56 + 0.3 \times V + 3660 \times V^{0.27} / N \tag{11-17}$$

and

$$C(IC) = 15.3 \times V^{0.57} + 1700 \times V^{0.3} / N \tag{11-18}$$

where

$C(SC)$ = Unit process cost for Sand Casting, \$/unit
$C(PM)$ = Unit process cost for Permanent Mold casting, \$/unit
$C(DC)$ = Unit process cost for Die Casting, \$/unit
$C(IC)$ = Unit process cost for Investment Casting, \$/unit
V = Casting Volume, cubic inches
N = Number of parts for tooling life

If the volume is in cubic centimeters, the formulas become:

$$C(SC) = 1.09 \times V^{0.72} + 247 \times V^{0.51} / N \tag{11-19}$$

$$C(PM) = 0.3 + 0.28 \times V^{0.7} + (517 + 6.16 \times V) / N \tag{11-20}$$

$$C(DC) = 0.56 + 0.018 \times V + 1720 \times V^{0.27} / N \tag{11-21}$$

and

$$C(IC) = 3.11 \times V^{0.57} + 735 \times V^{0.3} / N \qquad (11-22)$$

where

C(SC), C(PM), C(DC), C(IC), and N are the same as previously defined
and
V = casting volume, cubic centimeters

For total unit costs, other costs such as the material costs, finishing costs, and core costs would be required. These formulas represent a starting point for the determination of the casting unit costs for these processes, and more research is needed. This does present a new approach to the determination of the casting unit costs and this is important.

SUMMARY AND CONCLUSIONS

The major cost items for the casting process are the material costs, labor costs, other direct expenses, and overhead expenses. The primary emphasis is on the determination of the material and labor costs, as the overhead expenses are usually a function of these items. The other direct expenses category is often treated as a fixed cost or as a machine hour type cost. In general, little data exists in the literature for the determination of time standards for molding, core making, and finishing, and data must be developed for the particular plant. The new environmental regulations are having a major impact upon the material costs in the foundry and must be considered in the cost estimates.

The expressions presented can be used without modification for the evaluation of metric problems; the only caution is that the variable units must be changed throughout. This implies that both the weight and rate units of $/weight must be changed to the same weight basis. The expressions developed indicate the major effect of scrap upon unit product costs, and permit the determination of the cost of scrap in material and labor costs.

EVALUATIVE QUESTIONS

1. A 15 lb casting has a yield of 60 percent, scrap rate of 10 percent, and a melt loss of 3 percent. Determine the total poured weight, the scrap weight, the return weight, and the melt loss weight for each casting.
2. If, for Question 1, the hot metal cost is $ 1.50/lb, the scrap and return credit is $ 0.40/lb, and the environmental cost is $ 3.00/lb, what is the total metal cost for the 15 lb casting?

3. The core used for Question 1 weighs 3 lb and the core and molding scrap rate is 8 percent. Determine the total amount of core material weight to be charged per casting.
4. If the core sand costs $ 0.10/lb and the core sand disposal costs $ 0.05/lb, what is the total material cost for the core?
5. If the sand/metal ratio is 8 (that is, 8 lb sand per lb metal) for the mold, and the sand mold losses are 7 percent, determine the total molding sand weight per casting for the casting in Question 1.
6. If the sand cost is $ 0.03/lb, new sand costs are $ 0.06/lb, and the sand disposal costs are $ 0.05/lb, determine the total material cost for the mold if the new system sand fraction is 11 percent and the waste sand fraction is 8 percent.
7. Determine the total material costs for the casting from the data in Questions 1 through 6.
8. If the data in Table 11–4 is applicable, determine the molding time, the core making time, and the finishing time for the casting in Question 1.
9. If the labor rate for molding is $ 30/hr, for coremaking $ 24/hr, and for cleaning and finishing is $ 18/hr, determine the total labor costs if the cleaning and finishing scrap rate is 6 percent and the data of Question 8 is applicable.
10. What are the total material and labor costs for the casting?
11. If a riser sleeve is used which costs $ 0.40/sleeve, what amount should be added per casting? Assume that it is not recovered from broken molds or scrapped castings.
12. Rework Example Problem 11–1, but change the casting weight from 20 lbs to 20 kg and the costs from $ 1.00/lb to $ 1.00/kg, $ 0.50/lb to $ 0.50/kg, and $ 3.00/lb to $ 3.00/kg.
13. Estimate the tooling and process costs for a die casting which is to be produced in a lot of 10,000 units. The casting volume is 25 cubic centimeters.

BIBLIOGRAPHY

1. Michaels, J. V. and Wood, W. P., *Design to Cost*, Wiley Interscience, 1989, New York, pp. 145–179.
2. Adithan, M. and Pabla, B. S., *Production Engineering, Estimating and Costing*, 1989, Konark Publishers, Delhi, pp. 190–196.
3. Ajmal, A., *The Development of a Microcomputer-Aided Interactive Process Planning and Estimating System for Use in A Jobbing Foundry*, Ph.D. Thesis, University of Manchester, March 1986, p. 400.

4. Working Group E5, "The Construction of the Cost Estimate", *The British Foundryman*, Nov. 1984, pp. 490–495.

5. *Cost Accounting Methods for Iron Foundries*, Iron Castings Society, 1981, p. 186.

6. Westover, J. A., *Cost Accounting*, American Foundrymen's Society, 2nd Ed., Des Plaines, IL, 1985, p. 83.

7. Zenger, D.C., *An Early Material/Process Cost Estimating System for Product Designers*, Ph.D. Thesis, University of Rhode Island, 1989.

12

Basic Costing for Forging Processes

INTRODUCTION

Metal forming is one of the two primary shaping processes (the other being casting) for obtaining a near net shape or final product shape. Metal forming is a plastic deformation process in which a basic shape is transformed into the desired product shape. This process has much higher yields and better mechanical properties than machined products. The advantages of forming over casting are that, in general, formed products have better mechanical properties, better structural integrity, and a better surface finish, but usually have higher costs.

Certain shapes, such as thin flat pieces (for example coins) or long sections, such as structural beams, rail, and pipe are extremely well suited to some forming processes. The high tooling cost often limits the forming processes to high volume products when competing with casting and/or machining. The tooling costs, therefore, are one of the major cost components in the forming operations.

There are two major categories of the metal forming processes, bulk deformation processes and sheet metal deformation processes. The bulk deformation processes generally have drastic dimensional changes in all three directions and high compression forces are involved. Examples of the bulk deformation processes are forging, extrusion, and rolling. The sheet metal deformation processes generally have little change in the thickness direction and tensile stresses are dominant. Examples of sheet metal deformation processes are shearing, bending, drawing, and press forming. A comprehensive reference on deformation processes has recently been written by Mielnik (1).

The emphasis of costing in this chapter is upon the forging process as it is one of the major forming processes and more cost information was available on that process than on any other process. The cost drivers of the forging process are typical of those of the bulk deformation processes, and the methodologies presented can be extended to the other processes. The major problem for the authors is that little cost information on other processes was available in the literature.

COSTING METHODOLOGIES FOR FORGING PROCESSES

There has been very little published information concerning the costing of formed products, and thus it has been difficult to make a cost comparison of formed products with the other processes. However, most information has been published about forging, and that is the forming process that is considered here. There are two basic approaches; the basic standard time approach (2,3) and the relative cost approach (4). The major cost elements of both approaches, are the material costs, labor and overhead costs, and the direct expense costs, which is primarily the tooling costs.

The basic standard time approach determines the cost for the part directly, whereas the relative cost approach determines a relative cost. The relative cost is the ratio of the cost of the desired part to that of a reference part. This also includes a ratio between three of the major cost components for the reference part. The advantage of the relative cost method is that it permits an evaluation of different designs rapidly on a relative basis and can be computerized, but it relies on developing a variety of relative factors to the reference part. The basic standard time approach will be illustrated first and then the relative cost approach will be discussed.

BASIC STANDARD TIME COSTING APPROACH

The major cost items in the forging process are the material costs, the labor costs, direct expenses (such as tooling), and overhead expenses. The material costs are generally somewhat higher than for casting as the initial material required for processing is of higher quality. The labor costs tend to be lower than casting as the processing times are lower. The direct expenses are higher, as the tooling requires higher mechanical properties and frequently is under more adverse temperature conditions than in most casting processes.

Material Costs

There are several types of material losses that occur in forging, the most common ones being shear loss, tonghold loss, scale loss, flash loss, and sprue loss.

These losses can be a significant amount of the total material, up to 60 percent of the net weight of the product. The losses are described as follows (2):

Shear Loss—If the blank is cut from billets or bars, the material removed by sawing as well as the small pieces left at the end are lost. These losses are generally taken as five percent of the net weight.

Tonghold Loss—Drop forging operations are performed by holding the stock at one end with tongs. A small length, about 1 inch or equal to the diameter of the stock, whichever is greater, is added to the stock for holding. The loss would be the cross-sectional area times the length of tonghold.

Scale Loss—The forging process is generally performed in an air atmosphere; therefore the oxygen in the air will oxidize the surface of iron products and form scale. The scale falls off the surface at each stroke of the hammer. Scale loss for iron is about six percent of the net weight. The scale loss will vary with material, as some materials oxidize more rapidly than others.

Flash Loss—When dies are used for forging, some metal comes out at the parting line of the top and bottom halves of the die. This prevents damage to the dies, and some flash is required, generally about 0.1 inch thick and 3/4 inch wide at the parting line. The flash volume is dependent upon the product surface area at the parting line. This is usually the largest loss item.

Sprue Loss—When the part is forged by holding the stock with tongs, the tonghold and metal in the die are connected by a portion of metal called the sprue or runner. This is removed when the part is complete, and is approximately seven percent of the net weight.

Since the losses are generally expressed as a percentage of the net weight, and the gross weight is the sum of the net weight plus the losses, the following expression can be used to determine the material required:

Gross Amount = Net Amount × (1 + losses)

or

$$GA = NA \times (1 + SL + TL + SCL + FL + SRL) \qquad (12\text{-}1)$$

where

GA = Gross Amount (lb or kg)
NA = Net Amount (lb or kg)
SL = Shear/sawing Loss (decimal)

TL = Tonghold Loss (decimal)
SCL = Scale Loss (decimal)
FL = Flash Loss (decimal)
SRL = Sprue/Runner Loss (decimal)

The decimal flash loss can be obtained by the ratio of the volume of flash material to the volume of the net product.

Example Problem 12-1

If a low carbon steel part with a density of 0.25 lb/cubic inch has a volume of 8 cubic inches, flash volume of 1 cubic inch, sawing loss of 5 percent, tonghold loss of 6 percent, scale loss of 4 percent, and sprue/runner loss of 7 percent, what is the total gross weight in pounds?
Solution:
If the net volume is 8 cubic inches, the net weight is:

$$NA = \text{Volume} \times \text{Density}$$
$$NA = 8 \text{ cubic inches} \times 0.25 \text{ lb/cubic inch}$$
$$= 2 \text{ pounds}$$

The flash fraction is:

$$FL = \text{flash volume / net volume}$$
$$= 1 / 8$$
$$= 0.125$$

Therefore, the gross amount is:

$$GA = 2 \text{ lb} \times (1.00 + 0.05 + 0.06 + 0.04 + 0.125 + 0.07)$$
$$= 2 \text{ lb} \times 1.345$$
$$2.69 \text{ lb}$$

Now if in the process, 3 percent of the materials are scrapped (SR = Scrap Rate [decimal]) because of defects, the total gross amount is:

$$TGA = GA / (1 - SR) \tag{12-3}$$

That is, for the example,

$$TGA = 2.69 / (1 - 0.03)$$
$$= 2.773 \text{ lb}$$

The corresponding material cost is the product of the gross amount times the material rate. The scrap and returns do not have much value as they must be reprocessed, and thus the scrap value is only 5 to 30 percent of the raw material cost. Thus if, for the sample problem, the raw material cost is $ 3.00 per lb and the scrap is $ 0.30 per lb, and the recovered scrap does not include the scale or shear loss, the material cost would be:

$$\text{Return Scrap} = \text{Net Amount} \times [(TL + FL + SRL) / (1 - SR) + SR / (1 - SR)]$$
$$= 2.00 \text{ lb} \times [(0.06 + 0.125 + 0.07) / 0.97 + 0.03 / 0.97]$$
$$= 2.00 \times [0.255 + 0.03] / 0.97$$
$$= 0.588 \text{ lb}$$

$$\text{Waste Material} = \text{Net Amount} \times (SL + SCL) / (1 - SR)$$
$$= 2.00 \text{ lb} \times (0.05 + 0.04) / 0.97$$
$$= 0.186 \text{ lb}$$

$$\text{Gross Material} = \text{Net amount} + \text{Return Scrap} + \text{Waste Material}$$
$$= 2.00 \text{ lb} + 0.588 \text{ lb} + 0.186 \text{ lb}$$
$$= 2.774 \text{ lb}$$

$$\text{Total Material Cost} = 2.774 \text{ lb} \times 3.00 \text{ \$/lb} - 0.588 \text{ lb} \times 0.30 \text{ \$/lb}$$
$$= 8.15 \text{ \$/unit}$$

Labor Costs

Labor costs for hot forging are difficult to determine as little has been published with respect to time standards. Ostwald (4) presented some basic data and the time values in Table 12–1 were derived from that source.

Example Problem 12–2

A 1500 lb forging press is used to make two pieces with a gross weight of 1.42 lb per forging from a bar that is 1 inch in diameter, 12.125 inches long, and weighs 3.6 pounds. A crew of 2 is used. What is the time to produce a lot of 200 units, that is, the time to process 100 bars (2)?
Solution:

$$T = 2.67 + (0.070 \times 1 \times 12.125)$$
$$= 3.52 \text{ min/bar}$$

This is the total crew time, that is 1.76 min for each member.

Table 12–1 Setup Times and Total Crew Time Values For Forge Presses as a Function of Press Rating

A U.S. Units

Forge press rating (pounds)	(crew size)	Setup time (crew min.)	Crew minutes/piece (minutes/piece processed)
1500	2	60	$2.67 + 0.070 \times D \times L$
3000	2	90	$2.91 + 0.100 \times D \times L$
5000	3	120	$4.95 + 0.0586 \times D \times L + 0.0205 \times GA$
12000	4	180	$5.19 + 0.1066 \times D \times L + 0.0355 \times GA$

D = Diameter of raw billet, in
L = Length of raw billet, in
GA = Weight (gross amount) of raw billet, lb

B Metric Units

Forge press rating (kN)	(crew size)	Setup time (crew min)	Crew minutes/piece (minutes/piece processed)
6.4	2	60	$2.67 + 109 \times D \times L$
13.3	2	90	$2.91 + 155 \times D \times L$
22.2	3	120	$4.95 + 90.8 \times D \times L + 0.0451 \times GA$
53.4	4	180	$5.19 + 165 \times D \times L + 0.0781 \times GA$

D = Diameter of raw billet, meters
L = Length of raw billet, meters
GA = Weight (gross amount) of raw billet, kg
Adapted from Ref. 3. Reprinted with permission of *American Machinist*.

The total labor time for 100 bars is the labor time plus the setup time, which is:

$$
\begin{aligned}
TL &= 100 \times 3.52 + 60 \\
&= 352 + 60 \\
&= 412 \text{ minutes}
\end{aligned}
$$

where

TL = total labor time including setup time

In this problem, 200 pieces will be produced. In addition, the total operating time is:

TM = 100 bars × 3.52 Crew minutes / bar / 2 crew members

    = 176 minutes (operating)

and the machine will be tied up for a total time of:

TTM = TM + setup

    = 176 + (60 / 2)

    = 206 minutes

where

    TM = Total operating time
    TTM = Total operating time plus setup time

Thus if the labor rate was 20 $/hr and the machine rate was 30 $/hr, the labor costs and machine costs for the lot would be:

Labor Cost = 412 minutes × 20 $/hr / 60 min/hr

    = $ 137.33

Machine Cost = 206 minutes × 30 $/hr /60 min/hr

    = $ 103.00

If there is a 3 percent scrap loss, then the labor cost and machine cost would be for 200 × (1.00 − 0.03) or 194 good units. Thus the unit labor and machine cost per unit would be:

Unit (labor and machine) Cost = ($ 137.33 + $ 103.00) / 194

    = $1.24/unit

Other Direct Expenses

One of the largest expenses in forging operations is the cost of the die to produce the forgings. This frequently is the largest cost item, even more than the material or operating cost of the presses. This is particularly true in complex shaped components, where it is expensive to make the die and also the die life is reduced. In addition, alloys which require high temperatures for working generally have low die life and thus correspondingly high die costs.

The cost of dies for forging can range from $ 500 to over $ 250,000 depending upon die material, part area and volume, part material and complexity, and part precision required. An expression derived from limited data (5) for the die cost for a simple part for U.S. units is:

$$DC(\$) = 350 - 2.38 \times X + 6.08 \times X^2 \qquad (12\text{--}4)$$

where

DC = Die Cost in $
  X = Part length in inches

and for metric units is

$$DC(\$) = 350 - 0.937 \times X + 0.942 \times X^2 \qquad (12\text{--}4a)$$

where

DC = Die Cost in $
  X = Part length in centimeters

Thus if the part was 10 inches long, simple shape, and of an easily formed material, the die cost would be approximately:

$$\begin{aligned} DC &= 350 - 23.8 + 608 \\ &= \$\,934.20 \end{aligned}$$

Overhead Expenses

The overhead expenses for the equipment usage, supervisory staff, administration, etc. can be assigned by one or more of the methods presented in Chapter 4. The overhead rates are frequently applied to the direct labor hours or to machine hours, and range from 150 to 300 percent of the direct labor or machine hour rate.

RELATIVE COSTING APPROACH

The relative costing approach for forging is primarily used for comparing costs of different forging designs. The costs are relative to a reference forging with a reference cost ratio for material costs, operating costs, and tooling costs to the total cost. The reference cost ratio used(4,6) is 50 percent for material costs, 30 percent for operating costs, and 20 percent for tooling costs. This is determined by plant practices, materials, and methods. Thus for a particular part, the ratio is:

$$CF/CFR = 0.5 \times Cmr + 0.30 \times Cor + 0.20\,Ctr \qquad (12\text{--}5)$$

where

CF = Cost of Forging the part under consideration
CFR = Cost of Reference Forging

Cmr = Relative material Cost
Cor = Relative operating Cost
Ctr = Relative tooling Cost

The problem is how to evaluate Cmr, Cor, and Ctr. In the expressions that follow, the metric units are those used by Poli and Knight and the units in parentheses are the typical U.S. units. Poli and Knight (4) have two files, a material data file and a shape data file for the calculations. The shape data file uses a three digit code to identify the particular forging shape. The equations for the relative cost factors are:

$$Cmr = Dr \times Cr \times Kf \times V / [196,000] \qquad (12\text{--}6)$$

where

Cmr = Relative material cost
Dr = Ratio of material density to reference material density
Cr = Ratio of material price/lb to reference material price/lb
Kf = Ratio gross-to-net weight for part and reference material
V = Part Volume in cubic millimeters (196,000 = volume of reference material in cubic millimeters; if part volume is in cubic inches, the volume of the reference material is 11.96)

The values of Dr and Cr are in the material data file and Kf is in the shape data file. The value of V is the volume of the part under consideration.

$$Cor = Co \times N \qquad (12\text{--}7)$$

where

Cor = Relative operating Cost
Co = Relative operation cost per operation
N = Number of operations

The number of operations is from the shape data file and the relative operation cost is determined as a function of the equipment energy capacity. The equipment energy capacity is determined from:

$$E = Ap \times Mlf \times Slf \qquad (12\text{--}8)$$

where

E = Energy capacity for equipment in kg-m (or ft-lb)
Ap = Plane area of part with flash in square millimeters (or square inches)
Mlf = Material load factor in kg-m/square millimeter (or ft-lb/square inch)
Slf = Shape load factor

The material load factor (Mlf) is from the material data file, the shape load factor (Slf) is from the shape data file, and the plane area of the part (Ap) with flash is from the part drawing. Figure 12–1 illustrates how the operation cost in $/operation relates to the energy capacity.

The equation for the relative die cost is a complex expression:

$$Ctr = Ap \times Cdc \times N \times [Dmf \times R + Sdmf \times (1 - R)] / [Mdlf \times Sdlf \times K]$$

where   (12–9)

Ctr = Relative die Cost
Ap = Plane Area of part in square millimeters (or square inches)
Cdc = Relative die Cost per unit area
N = Number of operations
Dmf = Die material cost factor
R = Die material cost proportion

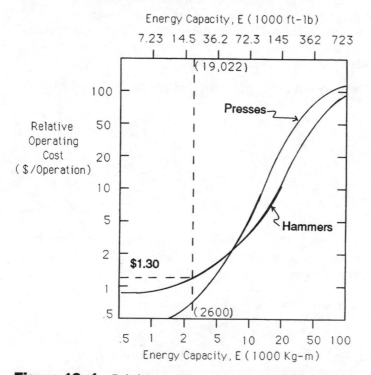

Figure 12–1   Relative operation cost as a function of energy capacity for press and hammer forges. (Adapted from Knight and Poli (4). Used with permission of *Machine Design*.)

Sdmf = Shape die machining factor
Mdlf = Material die life factor
  Sdlf = Shape die life factor
    K = Reference die surface area = 17,671 sq millimeters (If Ap is in
        square inches, the value of the reference die surface area is 27.39
        square inches)

The values of the relative die cost per unit area (Cdc) and die material cost
proportion (R) are found in Figure 12–2 as a function of the plane area of the
part. The number of operations (N), shape die life factor (Sdlf),and shape die
machining factor (Sdmf) are found from the shape data file. The die material
cost factor (Dmf) and material die life factor (Mdlf) are found in the material
data file. The plane area of the part (Ap) is from the part drawing.

The type of information available in the material and shape data files is
illustrated in Table 12–2. This indicates the magnitudes of the variables, but
does not fully illustrate the wide variety of shapes considered.

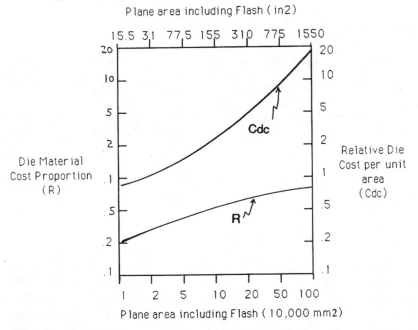

Figure 12–2   Die material cost proportion (R) and relative die cost (Cdc) per unit
area as a function of the plane area of the forged part. (Adapted from Knight and Poli
(4). Used with permission of *Machine Design*.)

Table 12–2 Material and Shape Data Files for Relative Costing

A   Material Data File

Mat'l class	Materials	Material load factor (Mlf)**	Material die life factor (MDlf)	Die Material cost factor (Dmf)	Relative material density (Dr)	Relative material cost (Cr)
0	Aluminum Alloy					
	Group A	0.054	1.0	1.0	0.35	4.70
	Group B	0.087	1.0	1.0	0.35	4.94
2	Carbon and Alloy Steels					
	Group A*	0.065	1.0	1.0	1.00	1.00
	Group B	0.076	0.8	1.0	1.00	1.29
4	High Alloys Steels					
	Stainless-A	0.130	0.3	1.2	1.01	7.37
	Nickel Alloy	0.130	0.3	1.2	1.02	16.16

*Reference Material
**Units for Mlf are kg-m/mm^2. The conversion to US units is 1 kg-m/mm^2 = 4662 ft-lb/in^2

B   Shape Data File

Shape code 1–2 shape config-uration	Digits 3 shape complex-ity	Ratio of gross-to -net weight (Kf)	Shape Load factor (Slf)	Shape die life factor (Sdlf)	Shape die machining factor (Sdmf)	Number of operatons (N)
*1–0	0	1.00	1.00	1.00	1.00	1
1–1	5	1.06	1.15	0.80	1.10	3
1–1	6	1.09	1.35	0.60	1.10	4
1–2	6	1.10	1.40	0.55	1.15	4

*Reference Shape Configuration and Complexity Adapted from Ref. 4. Reprinted with permission of *Machine Design*.

Example Problem 12–3

Determine the relative cost of an austenitic stainless steel part with a shape configuration code of 1–1 and complexity code of 6. The stainless steel part has a plane area of 15,000 square millimeters (23.25 square inches), a volume of 200,000 cubic millimeters (12.20 cubic inches), and is formed using a hammer forge.

Solution:

Using Equation 12–6 and taking the values from Table 12–2, the relative material cost is:

$$Cmr = 1.01 \times 7.37 \times 1.09 \times 200{,}000 / 196{,}000$$
$$= 8.28$$

or

$$Cmr = 1.01 \times 7.37 \times 1.09 \times 12.20 / 11.96$$
$$= 8.28$$

The energy capacity for equipment is determined from Equation 12–8:

$$E = 15{,}000 \text{ square millimeters} \times 0.130 \text{ kg-m/sq mm} \times 1.35$$
$$= 2{,}633 \text{ kg-m}$$

or

$$E = 23.25 \text{ sq in} \times 0.130 \text{ kg-m/sq mm}$$
$$(\text{mu } 4662 \text{ ft-lb/sq in} / (1 \text{ kg- m/sq mm}) \times 1.35$$
$$= 19{,}022 \text{ ft-lb}$$

Using Figure 12–1, the operation cost for a hammer forge is approximately $ 1.30 for an energy capacity of 2,600 kg-m (or 19,022 ft-lb) and the number of operations from Table 12–2 is 4, so the relative operation cost, using Equation 12–7 is:

$$Cor = \$ 1.30 \times 4$$
$$= \$ 5.20$$

Using Fig. 12–2, the die material cost proportion for a plane area of 15,000 sq mm (or 23.25 sq in) is 0.30 and the relative die cost per unit area is $ 1.00. Now using Equation 12–9, the relative die cost is:

$$Ctr = \frac{15{,}000 \times 1.00 \times 4 \times [1.2 \times 0.30 + 1.1 \times (1.0 - 0.3)}{[0.3 \times 0.60 \times 17{,}671]}$$
$$= 21.32$$

or

$$Ctr = \frac{23.25 \times 1.00 \times 4 \times [1.2 \times 0.30 + 1.1 \times (1.0 - 0.3)}{[0.3 \times 0.60 \times 27.39]}$$
$$= 21.32$$

Now, using Equation 12–5, the cost ratio is:

$$CF / CFR = (0.5 \times 8.28) + (0.3 \times 5.20) + (0.2 \times 21.32)$$
$$= 9.96$$

It costs 9.96 times the reference part cost to make the austenitic stainless steel part. All costs—material cost, operation cost, and tooling cost—are greater than the reference plain carbon steel part. The data based information is fairly standard, but the cost information in Figures 12–1 and 12–2 is difficult to obtain and would be continually changing.

SUMMARY AND CONCLUSIONS

There is only a sparse amount of cost data on metal forming processes available in the literature, and the emphasis of this chapter has been upon forging operations. Two different costing approaches, the standard costing approach and the relative costing approach, were investigated. The standard cost approach has poor data for estimating operation times and tooling costs. The relative costing approach is designed primarily for comparing different forging designs, not for comparing forging to other processes. The weak links in the relative costing approach are in the determination of the relative operating cost, die material cost proportion, and relative die cost per unit area.

Although both approaches lack extensive published cost data, they are procedurally correct and would give valid results if sufficient cost data were available. One advantage of the standard costing approach is that it requires the calculation of the standard production time and thus indicates the production rate. The relative costing approach does not require the production level and would tend to be more useful at the conceptual design stage.

EVALUATIVE QUESTIONS

1. What are the main components in the standard costing approach for forging?

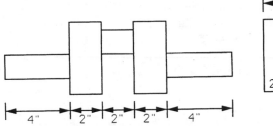
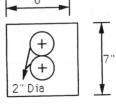

Figure 12–3   Crankshaft for Question 3.

2.   What is the primary objective in the relative costing approach and how does that differ from the standard costing approach?

3.   The crankshaft illustrated in Figure 12–3 is made from low carbon steel that costs $ 0.75/lb with a recovered scrap value of $ 0.10/lb. The scrap defects are 2 percent, the flash is 6 percent, the shear loss is 3 percent, the scale loss is 5 percent, and the tonghold plus sprue/runner loss totals 8 percent. The density of the steel is 0.25 lb/cubic inch.
   •   Determine the part volume (cubic inches).
   •   Determine the total gross amount of material needed per part (lb).
   •   Determine the amount of return scrap (lb).
   •   Determine the net total material cost ($) per unit.

4.   Find the relative cost ratio for an aluminum alloy, Group A, for a part of shape configuration code 1–1 and shape complexity code 6. Assume the part volume is 12 cubic inches with a plane area of 25 square inches. (note 1 inch = 25.4 mm.)

5.   The crank shafts of Question 12–3 are made on a 12,000 lb press from a 7 inch diameter round, 6.45 inches in length. Estimate the total labor time and total machine time to produce a lot of 1000 crank shafts and assume the density to be 0.25 lb/cubic inch. What is the weight of the starting round? Estimate the total labor cost and machine cost if the labor rate is $ 20.00/hr and the machine cost is $ 30.00/hr.

6.   If the crank shaft had a complexity factor of 2, estimate the die cost. Complexity factor is the ratio of the volume of the rectangular or cylindrical envelope for a part to the volume of the part itself.

BIBLIOGRAPHY

1.   Mielnik, E. M., *Metalworking Science and Engineering*, 1991, McGraw Hill.

2. Adithan, M. and Pabla, B. S., *Production Engineering Estimating and Costing*, 1989, Konark Publishers, Dehli, pp. 198–203.
3. Ostwald, P.F., *American Machinist Manufacturing Cost Estimating Guide*, 1982, McGraw Hill, pp. 40, 111–118.
4. Knight, W. A. and Poli, C., "A Systematic Approach to Forging Design", *Machine Design*, Jan. 24, 1985, pp. 94–99.
5. Lyman, T. Editor, *Metals Handbook—Forging and Casting*, Vol. 5, 8th Edition, 1970, pp. 19–40.
6. Ludema, K. C., Caddell, R. M., and Atkins, A. G., *Manufacturing Engineering*, Prentice Hall, 1987, pp. 361–366.

13

Cost Indexes, Cost Capacity Factors, and Improvement Curves (Learning Curves)

INTRODUCTION

Cost estimates need to be adjusted for timing, size, and learning, and this can be done with the use of cost indexes, cost capacity factors and improvement curves. The study for an equipment investment analysis can be updated using cost indexes rather than reworking the study if the equipment has not changed substantially since the last analysis. The effect of equipment size can be analyzed through cost capacity factors rather than obtaining a new data base to study a larger piece of equipment. The costs of start-up operations can be estimated through improvement curves or learning curves, and thus the steady state operation costs can be predicted from the initial operating costs. These tools will be illustrated in the following sections.

COST INDEXES

Cost indexes are used to update cost values from one period in time to another. The advantage of cost indexes over an inflation rate adjustment is that inflation varies, not only over time but from one area to another. The cost indexes are for an area, but location factors can permit adjustments for different locations. The general formula for adjusting data for different time periods by cost indexes is:

$$C(t) = C(r) \times I(t) / I(r) \tag{13-1}$$

where

$C(t)$ = Cost at time of interest
$C(r)$ = Cost at time of reference
$I(t)$ = Cost Index at time of interest for location of interest
$I(r)$ = Cost Index at time of reference for location of interest

There are several cost indexes, such as those proposed by Engineering News Record (ENR), Marshall and Swift, Chemical Engineering, and Nelson Refinery Construction (1,2). The Engineering News Record data for Construction Cost (3) and the Marshall and Swift (4) data for manufacturing and metal-working equipment are presented in Table 13-1.

If, for example, a 3,000 pound forging hammer was purchased in 1970 for $ 8,000, what would be the expected cost of this equipment if purchased in 1980? Since this is manufacturing equipment, the Marshall and Swift Index would be used, and from Equation 13-1:

$$C(1980) = \$ 8,000 \times 730.9 / 330.4$$
$$= \$ 17,700$$

The equipment cost has increased by 2.2 times over that particular 10 year period. If the machine was purchased in 1980 for $ 17,700, what would be the expected purchase price in 1990?

Table 13-1 Cost Index Data for Selected Years for Construction Costs and Metalworking Equipment

Year	Construction cost index* base 1913 = 100	Manufacturing metalworking equipment cost index** base 1926 = 100
1960	824	242.4
1965	971	263.2
1970	1381	330.4
1975	2212	497.7
1980	3237	730.9
1985	4195	906.0
1986	4295	912.1
1987	4406	923.6
1988	4519	963.8
1989	4615	1011.2
1990	4732	1038.9

*From Ref. 3. Reprinted with permission of *Engineering News-Record*.
**From Ref. 4. Reprinted with permission of Marshall & Swift.

C(1990) = $ 17,700 × 1038.9 / 730.9

= $ 25,200

Note that the equipment cost has increased by 1.4 times during the second ten year period. This indicates that a significant amount of inflation occurred during the 1970s in comparison to the 1980s. If one goes from 1970 to 1990 directly, the following is obtained;

C(1990) = $ 8,000 × 1038.9 / 330.4

= $ 25,200

This indicates the consistency of the index approach for adjusting costs over different time intervals.

If a new building or plant site is to be built, then the construction cost index would be used. Although there are a wide variety of cost indexes for the chemical and construction industries, there are few for the manufacturing industries. One problem with cost indexes is that they are historical, and usually one wants to predict future costs. This forces an estimation of the cost index for that future period.

COST CAPACITY FACTORS

The cost capacity factors permit calculations for facilities at different capacities. This is done as indicated by Equation 13-2 which is:

$$C(Sd) = C(Sr) \times [Q(Sd) / Q(Sr)]^X \qquad (13-2)$$

where

C(Sd) = Cost at desired size
C(Sr) = Cost at reference size
Q(Sd) = Capacity at desired size
Q(Sr) = Capacity at reference size
    X = Cost capacity factor for equipment or facility

In general, the value of X is approximately 0.6, but it usually varies between 0.5 to 0.8 and the maximum range is from 0.3 to 1.30 In general it is less than 1.0, because if it is greater than 1.0 there is no economy of scale and it is more economical to have multiple units rather than a single large unit. Table 13-2 shows some cost capacity factors for various types of equipment, but most of these pertain to chemical industry equipment, as little information is available for the various types of manufacturing equipment.

Table 13–2 Approximate Cost Capacity Factor for Various Types of Equipment

Equipment description	Equipment size range	Capacity units	Cost capacity value	Exponent range
Belt Conveyor	30" to 72" wide 10 to 100 ft long	in-ft	1.00	
Buildings	single story	floor area, rooms	.85	.75–.90
	multiple story	floor area, rooms	.75	.70–.85
Vertical Molding Machine	360–1000 sq in	average mold volume	.74	
Shredder		tons/hr	.62	
Magnetic Separator		tons/hr	.27	
Aluminum Separator		tons/hr	.68	
General Manufacturing Equipment			.60	.50–.95

Values estimated from various sources including Refs. 1, 2, 5, and 6.

To illustrate the application of the cost capacity equation, let one consider that a 3000 lb forging press cost $ 4,000 and it was desired to estimate the cost of a 5000 lb press. It is assumed that the 0.60 cost capacity factor applies, then, using Equation 13–2 the following is obtained:

$$C(5000 \text{ lb}) = \$ 4,000 \times [5000 / 3000]^{0.6}$$
$$= \$ 5,435$$

Thus the cost does not increase at the same rate as the capacity, but this is typical of most equipment.

Equations 13–1 and 13–2 can be combined together so that timing and capacity are accounted for in the same expression and that is:

$$C(t,Sd) = C(r,Sr) \times [I(t)/I(r)] \times [Q(Sd)/Q(Sr)]^X \qquad (13-3)$$

where

$C(t,Sd)$ = Cost at time of interest for desired capacity
$C(r, Sr)$ = Cost at time and capacity of reference
$I(t)$ = Cost Index at time of interest
$I(r)$ = Cost Index at time of reference
$Q(Sd)$ = Capacity at desired level
$Q(Sr)$ = Capacity at reference level
X = Cost capacity factor

The following example will illustrate the application of Equation 13–3. If a foundry purchased a 15 ton induction melting furnace in 1970 and planned to install a 25 ton induction melting furnace in 1990, what would be the estimated cost for 1990 if the 1970 cost was $ 25,000? From Equation 13–3:

$$C(90,25 \text{ ton}) = \$ 25,000 \times [1038.9/330.4] \times [25/15]^{0.6}$$
$$= \$ 107,000$$

COMBINED INDEXES

Consider the building of a new manufacturing plant in 1990 and estimate its cost from the building of a previous plant in 1970. The plant is a one story facility and the total cost was 4 million dollars, 1 million for the building and 3 million for the equipment. The original building has an area of 50,000 square feet and the new building needs 70,000 square feet. The capacity of the original plant was 7,000 tons per year and the capacity of the new plant is 10,000 tons per year. The best approach is to separate the individual estimates and then determine the total estimate. Thus the cost of the new building would be based on the construction cost index and the capacity factor for a single story building, which results in:

$$C(90;70,000) - \$1,000,000 \times [4732/1381] \times [70,000/50,000]^{0.85}$$
$$= \$ 4,561,000$$

The cost of the new equipment would be based on the manufacturing equipment index and the capacity factor for general manufacturing equipment, which results in:

$$C(90;10,000) = \$ 3,000,000 \times [1038.9/330.4] \times [10,000/7,000]^{0.6}$$
$$= \$ 11,684,000$$

The total cost estimate would be the sum of the building and equipment estimates, which is $ 16,215,000. This estimate can be improved if more details about the equipment and the cost capacity relationships for that type of equipment are known.

LEARNING CURVE ADJUSTMENTS

When new products are made that are quite different from the standard products, it takes more time, as workers are not familiar with that type of work. As they become more experienced or learn how to do the task better, it takes less time. Since time standards are based on the time for an experienced and skilled worker, the time to perform the task will be longer than what the standard time would be. Another instance when learning occurs is in the installation of new equipment, as it takes time (learning) to come up to standard. This is often referred to as training or launching costs. If one can plan for these effects, then the associated costs can be controlled and management has a better idea of whether the learning is on schedule. A detailed explanation of the formulas developed is presented in the thesis by Madhu Sudhan (7).

Learning curves are better understood as improvement curves, as they lead to improved productivity. A 90 percent learning curve really implies a 10 percent improvement in productivity and not a 90 percent improvement. There are two different bases for improvement curves, the average unit time basis and the unit time basis. If the work is complex assembly work, such as the assembly of airplanes, the average unit time basis works best. If the production is individual units or small assemblies, then the unit time basis is more suitable. The discussion will be limited to the unit time system, and the relationship is expressed in the following equation.

$$Y(N) = A \times N^B \qquad\qquad (13\text{--}4)$$

where

    $Y(N)$ = Time (min) for Nth unit of production
    A = Time (min) for 1st unit of production
    B = Exponent of improvement curve (learning curve)

The improvement or learning rate is determined from the amount of learning or improvement that occurs as the production level doubles. If the learning rate is 90 percent, the unit time will be reduced 10 percent as the production is doubled. If the first unit takes 100 minutes, the second unit will take 90 minutes if the learning rate is 90 percent. The fourth unit will then take 90 percent of 90 minutes or 81 minutes, and etc. The value of B can be found from:

$$B = \text{Log}[\,(100 - I)\,/\,100]\,/\,\text{Log}(2) \qquad\qquad (13\text{--}5)$$

where

    I = Improvement rate as percent

If the improvement rate is 10 percent and the first unit time is 20 minutes, then B is:

$$\begin{aligned} B &= \text{Log}[(100 - 10)\,/\,100]\,/\,\text{Log}(2) \\ &= -0.152 \end{aligned}$$

and the time for the eighth unit is:

$$Y(8) = 20 \times (8)^{-0.152}$$
$$= 14.58 \text{ min}$$

Another parameter of importance is the cumulative time to produce a specific number of units. This is obtained by the integration of Equation 13–4 and the following result is obtained:

$$TC(N) = [A / (B + 1)] \times [(N + 0.5)^{(B+1)} - (0.5)^{(B+1)}] \qquad (13-6)$$

where

    $TC(N)$ = Total Cumulative time to produce N units
        N = Number of units
        A = Time taken for 1st unit of production
        B = Exponent of improvement curve (learning curve)

The integration requires the approximation of a discrete function by a continuous function, so there is some small error, which is less than five percent for typical data.

For the previous example, the cumulative time to produce the eight units is approximately:

$$TC(8) = [20 / (-0.152 + 1)] \times [8.5^{(-0.152+1)} - 0.5^{(-0.152+1)}]$$
$$= [23.58] \times [6.140 - 0.555]$$
$$= 131.68 \text{ min}$$

The average time per unit is the cumulative time divided by the number of units and that is:

$$T(ave) = TC(N) / N \qquad (13-7)$$

where

    $T(ave)$ = Average unit Time
    $TC(N)$ = Total Cumulative time to produce N units
        N = Number of units

For the previous problem, the average unit time would be:

$$T(ave) = 131.68 / 8$$
$$= 16.46 \text{ minutes}$$

Thus the time saved over the production of the first 8 units is the difference between the cumulative time for the 8 units and 8 times the first unit time. The time saved would be:

$$
\begin{aligned}
TS &= N \times A - TC(N) \\
&= 8 \times 20 - 131.68 \\
&= 28.32 \text{ minutes}
\end{aligned}
\qquad ((13\text{-}8))
$$

This could also have been obtained from the average unit time:

$$
\begin{aligned}
TS &= N \times [\, A - T(ave)\,] \\
&= 8 \times [\, 20 - 16.46\,] \\
&= 28.32 \text{ minutes}
\end{aligned}
\qquad ((3\text{-}9))
$$

MULTIPLE IMPROVEMENT RATES

It has been stated that the improvement rate (or learning rate) changes during the start-up phases and there may be more than one learning rate. Usually the first improvement rate is the largest and the second is smaller, but the theory developed applies to any case. Only two rates will be considered, but it can be extended to additional rates. The two different rates can be represented as:

$$
Y(N) = A1 \times N^{B1} \text{ for } N = 1, 2, \ldots, N1
\qquad (13\text{-}10)
$$

and

$$
Y(N) = A2 \times N^{B2} \text{ for } N = N1 + 1, N1 + 2, \ldots, N2
$$

where

A1 = Intercept of unit improvement curve from 1 to N1
A2 = Intercept of unit improvement curve from N1 + 1 to N2
B1 = Exponent for first improvement curve (I1)
B2 = Exponent for second improvement curve (I2)

Therefore

$$
B1 = Log[\,(100 - I1)\, / \,100\,]\, / \,Log2
\qquad (13\text{-}11)
$$

and

$$
B2 = Log[\,(100 - I2)\, / \,100\,]\, / \,Log2
$$

where

I1 = first improvement rate expressed as percent
I2 = second improvement rate expressed as percent
The total cumulative time to produce N units is:

$$TC(N) = [A1 / (B1 + 1)] \times [(N1 + 0.5)^{(B1+1)} - (0.5)^{(B1+1)}]$$
$$+ [A2 / (B2 + 1)] \times [(N2 + 0.5)^{(B2+1)} - (N1 + 0.5)^{(B2+1)}] \quad (13\text{-}12)$$

Also, at the point where the improvement rates are the same, the values for the two curves must be equal, that is:

$$A1 \times N1^{B1} = A2 \times N1^{B2} \quad (13\text{-}13)$$

This relationship is used to find the value of A1 or A2 when either A1 or A2 is known and both B1 and B2 are known. The parameters for the case of two improvements is illustrated in Figure 13-1, which is plot of the unit and cumulative times versus the number of units of production on a log-log scale. Note that the slope of the unit curve for the first interval is B1 and the slope of the cumulative curve for the same interval is (1 + B1), where B1 is a negative

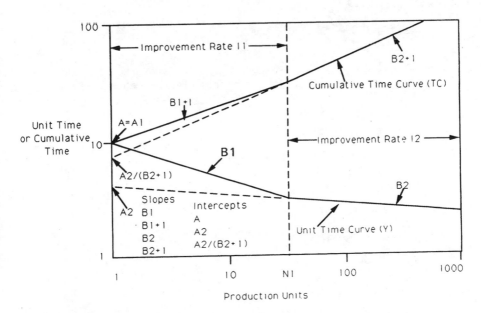

Figure 13–1 Cumulative and unit time curves for two improvement rates.

value. For the second interval, the slopes are B2 and (1 + B2) for the unit and cumulative curves, respectively. The intercept for the unit curve in the second interval is A2, and the intercept for the cumulative curve for the second interval is A2 / (B2 + 1). For the first interval, the intercept value for the unit curve is A1 (which is equivalent to A) and the intercept of the cumulative curve is A1 / (B1 + 1).

Example Problem 13-1

Consider the instance when the first unit takes 30 minutes, and the improvement for the process is 10 percent to unit 12 and 5 percent to unit 50, which is when the improvement rate due to learning is considered to become zero. What should be the standard unit time at unit 50 when the learning is considered to end?
Solution:
    Determine the improvement curve exponents for the 5 and 10 percent learning rates using Equation 13-11

$$B1 = Log[(100 - 10) / 100] / Log\ 2$$
$$= -0.152$$

and

$$B2 = Log[(100 - 5) / 100] / Log\ 2$$
$$= -0.074$$

The value of A2 is needed and it can be found from Equation 13-13:

$$A2 = A1 \times N1^{B1} / N1^{B2}$$
$$= A1 \times N1^{(B1 - B2)}$$
$$= 30 \times 12(-0.152 - [-0.074])$$
$$= 24.71\ minutes$$

Now Y(50) can be found using Equation 13-10:

$$Y(50) = 24.71 \times 50^{-0.074}$$
$$= 18.50\ min$$

Example Problem 13-2

In many instances, the data available is standard data and one needs to know how long it should take to produce the first unit. If, for example, the standard

time is based upon the 50th unit and it takes 18.5 minutes, what should be the time for the first unit if the learning rates are 10 percent for the first 12 units and 5 percent for units after the first twelve.
Solution:

Note that there are two break points, one at 12 units, where the improvement rate changes from 10 to 5 percent, and one at 50 units, where the improvement rate changes from 5 to 0 percent.

Determine the improvement rate curve exponents for the 0 percent, 5 percent, and 10 percent improvement rates using Equation 13-5:

$$B1 = Log[(100 - 10) / 100] / Log\ 2$$
$$= -0.152$$

$$B2 = Log[(100 - 5) / 100] / Log\ 2$$
$$= -0.074$$

$$B3 = Log[(100 - 0) / 100] / Log\ 2$$
$$= 0.0$$

Using equation 13-13 for the value between curves 2 and 3:

$$A2 \times N2^{B2} = A3 \times N2^{B3}$$
$$A2 = A3 \times N2^{(B3-B2)}$$
$$= 18.5 \times 50^{(0-[-0.074])}$$
$$= 24.71\ minutes$$

Then using Equation 13-13 again to solve for the value between curves 2 and 1, and determine A1:

$$A1 \times N1^{B1} = A2 \times N1^{B2}$$
$$A1 = A2 \times N1^{(B2-B1)}$$
$$= 24.71 \times 12^{(-0.074-[-0.152])}$$
$$= 30.00\ minutes$$

Thus the time allowed for the first unit would be 30 minutes for the improvement rates and break points given. In the aircraft industry, the usual break points are 10 and 250 units (8) with improvement rates of 25 and 20 percent. These lead to a considerable decrease in time standards, and since the time standards are in thousands of hours per unit, the cost implications are substantial.

Example Problem 13–3

Another issue of concern is to determine the time above the standard time until the standard is reached. The total time until the standard is reached is the launch time and the time above the standard time is the time lost due to learning. For the example considered, the standard time is 18.5 minutes but this was obtained only on the 50th unit. What was the total time for the 50 units and the time lost in the learning process? Use the values of $B1 = -0.152$, $B2 = -0.074$, $A1 = 30$ minutes, and $A2 = 24.71$ minutes

Solution:

From Equation 13–12, the total time for the 50 units is:

$$
\begin{aligned}
TC(50) &= [30 / (-0.152 + 1)] \times [(12.5)^{(-0.152+1)} - (0.5)^{(-0.152+1)}] \\
&\quad + [24.71 / (-0.074 + 1)] \times [(50.5)^{(-0.074+1)} - (12.5)^{(-0.074+1)}] \\
&= [35.38] \times [8.514 - 0.555] + [26.68] \times [37.779 - 10.369] \\
&= 281.59 + 731.30 \\
&= 1{,}012.89 \text{ minutes}
\end{aligned}
$$

The total standard time for 50 units when each unit time is 18.50 minutes is 925 minutes, therefore the lost time for the first 50 units is:

$$
\begin{aligned}
\text{Lost Time} &= TC(50) - 50 \times 18.50 \\
&= 1{,}012.89 \times 925 \\
&= 87.89 \text{ or } 88 \text{ minutes}
\end{aligned}
$$

The lost time, or time spent in learning or gaining experience, can be rather large if one is doing complex assemblies, such as making airplane engines, diesel locomotives, or ships, where many details are modified during the production and methods are changed. In simple parts, the lost time is smaller as little new learning occurs and few, if any, changes are made from the original design and production plan.

SUMMARY AND CONCLUSIONS

Cost indexes and cost capacity factors are important adjustment factors to update previous cost estimates to current design criteria. The cost indexes are primarily for different time periods, but newer indexes include adjustments for various locations, which is important for the global production market in which we are involved. Capacity factors are common for the chemical and construction industries, but little data is available for the manufacturing industries. More data needs to be developed so that manufacturing industries can be more competitive.

Improvement curves, better known as learning curves or experience curves, can be used to predict the lost time in the start-up of new processes or in the production of new, complex products. The use of multiple improvement rates reflects the differences in prototype production, trial production, and standard production. Improvement curves can be used to predict the standard time from the prototype times, to predict the prototype times from the standard time, and to predict the effect of different improvement rates. The effects of improvement (learning) must be included in the estimates when complex products are produced as the unit time values will change considerably during the learning phase.

EVALUATIVE QUESTIONS

1. Explain what cost indexes are and how they are used. Explain cost capacity factors and how they are used.

2. A foundry purchased a molding machine capable of producing 60 molds per hour in 1970 for $ 350,000. Estimate the cost for purchasing this machine in 1990. If a machine capable of producing 90 molds per hour is desired for 1990, what is your estimate of the cost?

3. A machining center purchased in 1965 cost $ 100,000 and was capable of a material removal rate of 10 cubic inches per minute. A new machining center is to be purchased with the same capabilities in 1990. What is an estimate of its cost? If the material removal rate is 20 cubic inches per minute, what would be the cost estimate?

4. A welding fabrication shop was built in 1960 at a total cost of $ 1,500,000 with one third of the cost for the building and the remainder for the equipment. The plant had an area of 50,000 square feet and a welding deposition capacity 1 ton/day. If the new plant has an area of 80,000 square feet and a welding deposition capacity of 2 tons/day, what would be the expected cost of the new facility?

5. A new crew is being assigned to a job involving the use of a forging hammer. The improvement rate is estimated to be 15 percent over the first 250 pieces until they are experienced. The standard time per piece is estimated at 5 minutes/piece. What is the time estimate for the first piece? What is the time estimate for the tenth piece? What is the estimate for the first 250 pieces? What is the estimate of the lost time by using an inexperienced crew versus the experienced crew? If the crew has four members, what is the estimate of the lost man-hours?

6. A new complex casting is being molded in the foundry. The first unit takes 4 hours and the expected improvement rate is 10 percent for the first 12 units and 5 percent to unit 50 when the improvement rate due to learning is negligible. What should be the expected time for the 5th

unit? What should be the expected time for the 15th unit? What should be the expected time for the 50th unit?

BIBLIOGRAPHY

1. Couper, J. R. and Rader, W. H., *Applied Finance and Economic Analysis for Scientists and Engineers*, 1986, Van Nostrand, pp. 24–106.
2. Park, W. R. and Jackson, D. E., *Cost Engineering Analysis*, 1984, John Wiley and Son, pp. 127–145.
3. *Engineering News-Record*, McGraw Hill, March 29,1990, p. 71 and July 3, 1991, p. 120.
4. *Marshall Validation Service*, Marshall and Swift, Los Angeles, July 1991, Section 98, p. 9.
5. Canada, J. R. and Sullivan, W. G., *Economic and Multiattribute Evaluation of Advanced Manufacturing Systems*, Prentice Hall, 1989, pp. 116–118.
6. Frazier, A.M., *Process Design and Economic Evaluation of Preparing a MSW/Coal Fuel for Existing Combustion Facilities*, M.S. Thesis, Civil Engineering Department, West Virginia University, 1991, pp. 47–73.
7. Madhu Sudhan, B.P., *Manufacturing Time Estimation Using Multiple Improvement Curves in the Concurrent Engineering Environment*, M.S. Thesis, Industrial Engineering, West Virginia University, 1990, p. 110.
8. Noton, B. R., "Cost Drivers in Design and Manufacture of Composite Structures", *Engineered Materials Handbook*, Vol. 1, ASM Publications, Metals Park, Ohio, 1988, pp. 419–427.

14

Facility Capital Cost Estimation and the Estimation of Operating Costs

INTRODUCTION

There has been little, if any, published data for the estimation of capital costs and operating costs in the manufacturing sector. Most of the work has been done in the construction industry and for the chemical process industry. This lack of data and methodologies has prevented comparisons of the different manufacturing processes. The purpose of this chapter is to present some of the methods that have been used in the chemical and construction industries to illustrate the methodologies, and determine what information is needed to apply these methods in the manufacturing sectors.

The chapter will emphasize the two different cost estimates, that is the estimation of the capital required and the estimation of the operating costs. The relations illustrated will use the data available, but more accurate data bases must be developed for the manufacturing sector.

CAPITAL COST ESTIMATION

There are various methods of estimating the capital costs of a project, but only five will be considered, as they are typical of the methods used. The five methods are: detailed design estimating, the turnover ratio method, the single factor method, the knowledge and experience (K and E) method, and the AACE total capital requirements procedure. Detailed design estimating is the most accurate and is required for detailed estimates; the AACE procedure is for budgetary estimates for plants, and processes; the K and E method is for individual equipment items or process lines, and the turnover ratio and single factor methods are for the conceptual or magnitude estimates.

Detailed Design Estimating

The detailed design estimate, or the definitive estimate, as defined by AACE (1, 2) is: an estimate prepared from very defined engineering data. The engineering data includes as a minimum, nearly complete plot plans and elevations, piping and instrument diagrams, one line electrical diagrams, equipment data sheets and quotations, structural sketches, soil data and sketches of major foundations, building sketches and a complete set of specifications. This category of estimate covers all types, from the minimum described above to the maximum definitive type which would be made from "approved for construction" drawings and specifications. It is normally expected than an estimate of this type would be accurate to plus 15 percent and minus 5 percent.

Although this definition is more applicable to facility construction, it does give an indication of the depth of detail needed for the estimate. This same type of detail is needed in making detailed estimates for the manufacturing industry for new facility construction or major renovations and process changes. Changes such as a new machining cell, new melt shop, or new pipe mill would require such detail for final approval.

Turnover Ratio

The turnover ratio is a management accounting term used to evaluate the performance of a company. However, it can be used to estimate the capital investment required for a business venture. The use of the turnover ratio for investment determination appears in only a few references (3,4) as other estimation methods would be more reliable. The turnover ratio determines the maximum investment from the expected sales and revenues and not from the equipment or facilities used to produce the product. The turnover ratio is:

$$\text{Turnover Ratio} = \frac{\text{Annual Sales}}{\text{Total Investment}} \qquad (14\text{-}1)$$

If the expression is rearranged, the investment can be evaluated by:

$$\text{Total Investment} = \frac{\text{Annual Sales}}{\text{Turnover Ratio}} \qquad (14\text{-}2)$$

where

Total Investment = Total plant investment ($)

Annual Sales = Total annual sales ($)
Turnover Ratio = Ratio (dimensionless)

The turnover ratio is frequently evaluated on an industry wide basis; for example, in the chemical industry the value is 0.9 whereas in the steel industry the value is 1.1. The value of 0.7 can be extended to the metalworking industry with caution.

Example 14-1

A new foundry is being planned and is expected to produce 500,000 kilograms of salable castings per year. The castings have an average selling price of $ 5.50/kg. What is the expected investment for the facility?
Solution:
The annual sales would be

Annual Sales = 500,000 kg × $ 5.50/kg
= $ 2,750,000

The total investment can be found using Equation 14-1 and is:

Total Investment = $ 2,750,000 / 0.7
= $ 3.9 million

The disadvantage of the investment ratio method is that it does not adjust for the capacity of the plant. If the plant is doubled in size, the investment would also double and that occurs only when the cost capacity index is unity. For more accurate estimates, the turnover ratio should be designated for a specific capacity level and then the investment costs can be adjusted for the capacity variance.

Single Factor Method

The single factor method uses one factor to predict the overall investment cost of the facility. The factor most frequently used is the delivered equipment cost. This has been used with success in the chemical industry for nearly 50 years. The chemical industry has three sets of factors: one for the solid processing plant, one for the solid fluid processing plant, and one for the fluid processing plant. The plant design closest to the manufacturing sector is the solid processing plant, and these factors will be considered. These factors, often called the Lang Factors, have been presented by Peters and Timmerhaus (6) so the total plant cost, fixed capital investment, and total capital investment can be calculated and analyzed with considerably more detail than the original Lang Factors. The accuracy of an estimate by the single factor method is an order of magnitude estimate; that is within plus 50 percent to minus 30 percent.

The factors are given for a major process plant addition and some adjustment can be made for smaller equipment purchases where less construction would be required for installation. However, delivered equipment costs represent 18–35 percent of the total plant costs (4). The factors for the solid processing plant (5,6) are presented in Table 14–1 and the adjusted factors are for small additions. The adjusted factors represent the author's view of the reduced cost for installing equipment in an existing facility. The factor values considerable expenses for site preparation and fees that are associated with new sites.

The direct plant costs include the purchased equipment, the installation of the purchased equipment, the purchase and installation of the controls, the piping, electrical, buildings, yard improvements, installed service facilities, and land. If the plant is at a completely undeveloped site, the total fixed capital investment may increase by 100 percent.

The indirect costs are primarily engineering, supervision, and construction expenses. The fees and contingency represent the expected profit and omissions or unforeseen costs from incomplete engineering. The contingency fee would decrease as the level of detail increases.

Example 14–2

A small die-casting shop is being built and three main pieces are required: a melting unit, the die-casting machine, and the trimming unit. The estimated costs for the equipment are:

Table 14–1 Ratio Factors for Capital Investment Based upon Delivered Equipment Costs

Item	Factor(5)	Adjusted factor
1. Total Direct Plant Cost	2.64	2.05
2. Indirect Costs	0.72	0.36
Total Plant Cost	3.36	2.41
3. Fees and Contingency	0.51	0.24
Fixed Capital Investment	3.87	2.65
4. Working Capital	0.68	0.47
Total Capital Investment	4.55	3.12

Adapted from Ref. 6.

Item	Cost
Melting Unit	$ 220,000
Die-Casting Machine	400,000
Trim Unit	80,000
Total	$ 700,000

What is the expected total plant cost and the total fixed capital investment?

Solution:

The plant is a new plant so the factor values will be used rather than the adjusted factor values. The values can be obtained using the factors from Table 14-1:

$$\text{Total Plant Cost (PCT)} = 3.36 \times \$\,700{,}000$$
$$= \$\,2.35 \text{ million}$$

$$\text{Fixed Capital Investment (FCI)} = 3.87 \times \$\,700{,}000$$
$$= \$\,2.71 \text{ million}$$

$$\text{Total Capital Investment (TCI)} = 4.55 \times \$\,700{,}000$$
$$= \$\,3.19 \text{ million}$$

The total plant cost (PCT) rather than the total capital investment is usually the value desired. If this was the addition to an existing die casting shop, the values would decrease to:

$$\text{Total Plant Cost (PCT)} = 2.41 \times \$\,700{,}000$$
$$= \$\,1.69 \text{ million}$$

$$\text{Fixed Capital Investment (FCI)} = 2.65 \times \$\,700{,}000$$
$$= \$\,1.86 \text{ million}$$

$$\text{Total Capital Investment (TCI)} = 3.12 \times \$\,700{,}000$$
$$= \$\,2.18 \text{ million}$$

The total capital investment, which includes the working capital, is not used as much as the total plant cost. The total plant cost is frequently used for depreciation calculations. The total capital investment includes the land cost, which is highly dependent upon the site, and the working capital, which is usually a function of the annual operating costs.

Knowledge and Experience (K and E) Method for Estimating

A new approach for estimating the cost of equipment has been proposed and developed by Greg Stamp (7) at Proctor and Gamble. This technique was for the pricing of developmental equipment and was entitled DE × CID, which is an acronym for Developmental Equipment × Costing Improvement Database. The key of this procedure is the determination of the developmental equipment factor. This developmental equipment factor is determined from a knowledge and experience level. The steps in this process will be explained in more detail.

The knowledge and experience method (7) is a five step procedure used to determine the total delivered cost of a piece of equipment or a process line. The steps are:

1. Determine the knowledge and experience level.
2. Determine the developmental equipment factor.
3. Determine the number of units to be developed.
4. Determine the replacement value for the equipment after development.
5. Calculate the total delivered equipment cost.

The determination of the knowledge and experience level can be estimated from the knowledge and experience factors in Table 14–2. This information was obtained in a different format (8) and has been modified for more general usage. The factors considered in determining the knowledge and experience level are: type of concept, existing equipment similarity, design base, equipment base, vendor experience, company product similarity, and company experience. Intermediate levels for the amount of knowledge and experience, rather than integers, can be used at the user's discretion.

The developmental equipment factor (DEF) is determined from the knowledge and experience curve illustrated in Figure 14–1. This curve is an approximation of curves illustrated in the paper (7) and at the paper presentation, but it does not represent the actual curve used by Proctor and Gamble, as this information was considered confidential. Each company should develop its own knowledge and experience curve based upon their knowledge and experience levels and developmental equipment costs. Figure 14–1 is for illustrative purposes and considerable variation may exist in different industries or in different companies.

The number of units (NU) to be developed most frequently is one, but in some instances several units may need to be developed simultaneously. This could occur when the company needs to establish a dominant market share quickly.

Table 14-2 Knowledge and Experience Levels as a Function of Seven Factors

Knowledge & Experience Level	Type of Concept (1)	Knowledge and Experience Factors			Vendor Experience (5)	Company Product Similarity (6)	Company Experience (7)
		Existing Equipment Similarity (2)	Design Base (3)	Equipment Base (4)			
1	New	None	Scratch	Scratch	None	None	None
2	New	None	Scratch	Scratch	Slight	None	None
3	New	None	Scratch	Scratch	Slight	Exists	Slight
4	Existing	Equipment Exists	Scratch	Scratch	Slight	Exists	Slight
5	Existing	Equipment Exists	Some Std. Components	Scratch	Moderate	Exists	Slight
6	Existing	Equipment Exists	Many Std. Components	Some Std. Components	Moderate	Exists	Slight
7	Existing	Equipment Exists	Many Std. Components	Many Std. Components	Moderate	Exists	Moderate
8	Vendor	Equipment Exists	Major Re-Design	Major Modification	Modified Vendor Design	Exists	Moderate
9	Vendor	Equipment Exists	Moderate Re-Design	Moderate Modification	Standard Vendor Design	Exists	Moderate
10	Vendor	Equipment Exists	No Re-Design	No Modification	Standard Vendor Design	Exists	Considerable

From Ref. 8.

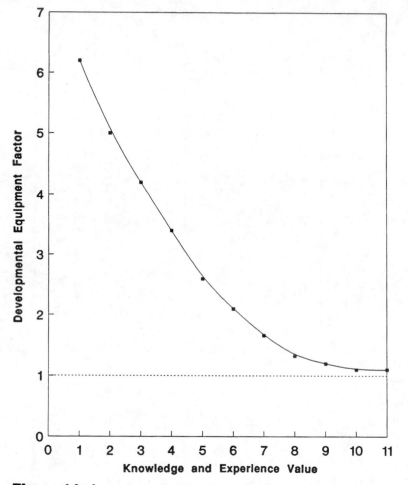

Figure 14–1 Developmental equipment factors as a function of knowledge and experience level. (Adapted from Ref. 7.)

The replacement value (RV), as defined by AACE (2), is "that value of an item determined by repricing the item on a basis of replacing it, in new condition, with another item that gives the same ability to serve, or the same productive capacity, but which applies current economic design, adjusted for the existing property's physical deterioration." The original paper uses the term fair market value instead of replacement value, but the intended meaning was that of replacement value.

The total delivered cost (TDC), can be expressed as the product of the developmental equipment factor, the number of units under development, and the replacement value; that is:

$$TDC = DEF \times NU \times RV \qquad (14\text{--}3)$$

where

TDC = Total Delivered Cost
DEF = Developmental Equipment Factor
 NU = Number of Units being developed
 RV = Replacement Value

Example 14–3

A new double fixturing device is to be developed which permits automatic fixturing during cutting, so all three axes can be cut without manual repositioning. This is a new concept with no existing equipment, designs, product similarity, or company experience. The leading vendor has made some unsuccessful previous attempts to develop this equipment. The replacement value for this equipment is estimated to be $ 300,000, and one unit is to be developed. Estimate the developmental cost.

Solution:

The knowledge and experience level is estimated to be 2 from an analysis of the knowledge and experience factors and Table 14–2. Using this value of 2.0, the developmental equipment factor is estimated to be 5 from Figure 14–1. There is only 1 piece of equipment to be developed, so the developmental equipment cost, using Equation 14–3, is:

$$TDC = 5 \times 1 \times \$\,300{,}000$$
$$= \$\,1{,}500{,}000$$

This indicates that the developmental equipment cost is 5 times the expected replacement cost; that is, future replacements would be only slightly greater than $ 300,000. Note that as the knowledge and experience factor reaches its maximum value of 10, the developmental equipment factor is still approximately 1.25, as there are still installation costs. In order to offset the high developmental costs, there must be significant marketing and profit opportunities from the new equipment.

AACE Total Capital Requirements Procedure*

The AACE Total Capital Requirements Procedure follows AACE Recommended Practice No. 16R-90. The procedure (9) is illustrated in Table 14–3. The AACE procedure was written for the budget type estimate, that is, with an

---

*AACE Recommended Practice No. 16R-90 is reprinted by special permission of AACE and further reproduction is prohibited.

Table 14–3 AACE Components of Total Capital Requirements

I. Total Plant Cost
    A. Process Capital
      1. Direct Cost
        a. Material Costs
          (1) Purchased Equipment Costs
          (2) Installation Material Costs
        Total Direct Material Cost = a(1) + a(2)
        b. Labor Costs
          (1) Labor to Handle and Place Bare Equipment
          (2) Installation Labor
        Total Direct Labor Cost = b(1) + b(2)
      Total Direct Cost = 1a + 1b
                = a(1) + a(2) + b(1) + b(2)

      2. Indirect Costs
        a. Indirect Field Costs (construction equipment,
           construction support, and major tools)
        b. Labor Benefits
        c. Small Tools (<$ 500)
        Total Indirect Field Costs = 2a + 2b + 2c
        Total Process Capital = A1 + A2
               = 1a + 1b + 2a + 2b + 2c
    B. General Facilities
    C. Home Office Overhead and Fee
    D. Contingencies
      1. Project
      2. Process
    Contingency Cost = D1 + D2
    Total Plant Cost = A + B + C + D
II. Prepaid Royalties
III. Start-up Costs (including start-up materials)
IV. Spare Parts
V. Land
VI. Working Capital

Note: Depreciable Capital = I + II + III + IV; Fixed Capital Investment = I + II + III + IV + V; Total Capital Investment = I + II + III + IV + V + VI.
Adapted from Ref. 9. Reprinted with special permission of AACE.

accuracy of plus 30 percent to minus 15 percent. The total plant cost is divided into four components—process capital, general facilities, overhead and fees, and contingencies. The process capital is separated into direct costs (materials and labor) and indirect costs. The cost terms in the AACE method and those of the factor method do not have complete agreement; for example, the total plant cost (PCT) in the factor method does not include the contingency costs, whereas they are included in the AACE method. Each of the components of the AACE Recommended Practice will be discussed in more detail and methods for calculation will be suggested.

Purchased Equipment Costs

The purchased equipment costs are the basis of the calculation procedure. These costs are critical, as many of the other cost values are based upon the purchased equipment costs. The equipment costs can be determined from (9):

1. Firm bids or quotations
2. Previous project equipment costs
3. Published equipment cost data
4. Preliminary vendor quotations
5. Scale-up of data for similar equipment or other capacities
6. Development of cost capacity equations from vendor data

The development of cost capacity equations from vendor data is often necessary, as the vendors may not have the equipment size desired and are reluctant to give a quotation on something they do not have in stock. For example, if one wanted a shotblast unit for 12 tons/day, and the supplier had units of 3, 8, and 20 tons/day, one could develop a cost capacity relationship to predict the cost of a 12 ton/day unit.

Labor Costs to Handle and Place Bare Equipment

The labor costs to handle and place the bare equipment are those associated with unloading, uncrating, and physically placing the equipment at its place of operation. These values can be expressed as a function of purchased equipment cost, and are presented in Table 14–4 for three general classes of equipment. These factors are the decimal fraction of the purchased equipment cost.

Installation Material Costs and Installation Labor Costs

AACE Recommended Practice 16R-90 gives distributive factors for several different chemical processes and bulk material situations. These factors are expressed as a decimal fraction of purchased equipment cost. The set of factors selected had the lowest numerical values, which were for the crushing, grinding, and conveying of bulk materials. The factors, expressed as a decimal

Table 14–4 Factors for Labor to Handle and Place Bare Equipment as a Function of Purchased Equipment Cost

Equipment class and description		Labor factor	
class	equipment class description	Range	Average
1.	Stationary Equipment (no moving parts) (hoppers, chutes, etc.)	0.05–0.15	0.10
2.	Machinery (linear) (conveyors, feeders, etc.)	0.10–0.20	0.15
3.	Rotary Equipment (compressors, pumps, fans, etc.)	0.15–0.35	0.25

Note: For expensive equipment, the relationship is not a constant percentage of the total equipment cost. For example, a compressor may be 25 percent of the first $ 200,000 and then 10 percent for the cost above $ 200,000. Adapted from Ref. 9. Reprinted with special permission of AACE.

Table 14–5 Material and Labor Installation Factors as a Function of the Purchased Equipment Cost

Installation item	Factor	
	material	labor
Foundations	0.04	0.06
Structural Steel	0.04	0.02
Buildings	0.02	0.02
Insulation	0.01	0.015
Instrumentation	0.04	0.016
Electrical	0.08	0.06
Piping	0.05	0.025
Painting	0.005	0.015
Miscellaneous	0.03	0.024
Total	0.315	0.255

Adapted from Refs. 9 and 10. Reprinted with special permission of AACE.

fraction, are presented in Table 14–5 for the installation of the equipment. These are average factors and not for a specific piece of equipment.

The installation material and labor items must be kept separate as the benefits are determined as a function of the labor cost. The installation labor plus the labor to handle and place the bare equipment represents the total direct labor cost (TDLC). Similarly, the purchased equipment cost plus the installation material cost represents the total direct material cost (TDMC).

Indirect Costs

The indirect costs consist of three items: indirect field costs, labor benefits, and the cost of small tools.

The indirect field costs consist of: indirect field labor (supervision, accounting, field engineering, staff engineering, warehousing, etc.); construction support (temporary buildings and roads, field utilities and communications, etc.); construction supplies (welding, safety, office, etc.); cleanup; labor benefits (fringe, travel, subsistence); payroll taxes and insurance; equipment and tools (construction equipment and equipment servicing); and construction camp expenses.

The labor benefits consist of the benefits for both the indirect field labor and the total direct labor costs (TDLC). The small tools cost is handled separately, and consists of tools that are less than $ 500 per tool. The small tool costs are presented as a percentage of the total direct labor cost for different levels of the direct labor cost, as indicated in Table 14–6.

Expressions were developed from curves in the AACE Recommended Practice 16R-90 to determine the indirect field cost and the labor component of the indirect field cost. The curves in the reference had a base labor rate of 20 $/hr and the expressions developed allow for variation from that base rate. The curves are illustrated in Figure 14–2, and these are drawn as straight lines rather than as curves as in AACE document (9). The indirect field cost relation was developed for two ranges of the direct field labor cost. The first was:

$$\text{IFC}(\%) = 51 \times (\text{TDLC} \times 20 \,/\, \text{LR})^{(-0.25)} \qquad ((14\text{–}4))$$

where

IFC(%) = Indirect Field Cost as a percent of the total direct field labor (varies between 75 and 49 percent)
TDLC = Total Direct field Labor in million dollar units (varies between 0.25 and 1.2 units)
LR = Average direct field Labor Rate in $/hr (does not include benefits)

Table 14–6 Small Tool Cost as a Percentage of the Total Direct Labor Cost

Project total direct labor cost range	Small tool cost (%TDLC)
< $ 300,000	5.0 %
$ 300,000–$ 3,000,000	3.5 %
> $ 3,000,000	2.0 %

Adapted from Refs. 9 and 10. Reprinted with special permission of AACE.

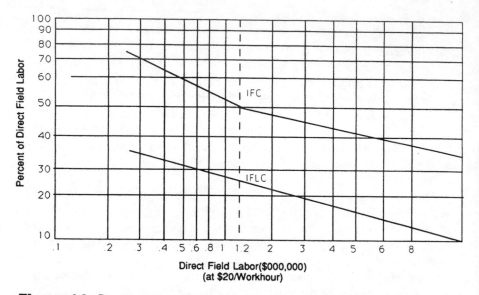

Figure 14–2 The indirect field cost and the indirect field labor cost as a function of the direct field labor cost. (From Ref. 9. Reprinted with special permission of AACE.)

The total indirect field cost expression for the second range was:

$$IFC(\%) = 29 + 21 \times (TDLC \times 20 \, / \, LR)^{(-0.34)} \qquad (14\text{-}5)$$

where

IFC(%) = Indirect Field Cost as a percent of the total direct field labor (varies between 49 and 38 percent)
TDLC = Total Direct field Labor in million dollar units (varies between 1.2 and 15 units)
LR = Average direct field Labor Rate in $/hr (does not include benefits)

The expression for the indirect field labor cost was found to be:

$$IFLC(\%) = 21 \times (TDLC \times 20 \, / \, LR)^{(-0.34)} \qquad (14\text{-}5)$$

where

IFLC(%) = Indirect Field Labor Cost as a percent of the total direct field labor (varies between 8 and 33 percent)
TDLC = Total Direct field Labor in million dollar units (varies between 0.25 and 15 units)
LR = Average direct field Labor Rate in $/hr (does not include benefits)

The labor benefit cost includes the benefits on both the direct labor cost and the indirect field labor cost. The AACE Recommended Practice suggests a value of 35 percent of the total direct and indirect labor cost. The current actual percentage should be used if it is known.

The sum of the indirect field costs, labor benefits, and small tool costs represent the total indirect field costs (TIFC). The sum of the total indirect field costs and the total direct costs is the total process capital (TPC). This can be represented by Equation 14–7 as follows:

$$\text{Total Process Capital} = \text{Total Direct} + \text{Total Indirect Field}$$
$$\text{(TPC)} \qquad \text{Cost (TDC)} \qquad \text{Cost (TIFC)} \qquad (14\text{--}7)$$

General Facilities and Home Office Overhead and Fee

These two items are represented as functions of the total process capital (TPC). The general facilities (GF) cost represents the expenses for roads, laboratories, office buildings, etc., and generally are in the range of 5 to 20 percent (9) of the total process capital. The AACE recommended practice (9) suggests a value of 15 percent unless there is an underlying reason to assume otherwise, but documentation should be provided for the value selected even if it is the suggested value.

The home office overhead and fee (HOOF) represent the profits that must be made by those involved in the work. The home office must have people check the progress of the project and the contractor expects to make a profit. The total costs range from 7 to 15 percent of the process capital (9), and the value suggested by AACE is a total of 15 percent (9).

Contingency Costs

The AACE Recommended Practice suggests two types of contingencies—process and project. The contingency costs—process and project (CCPP)—represent those additional costs that would occur due to the lack of process technology information and the unforeseen costs caused by the incomplete scope of the budget estimate. The process contingency factors are based upon the state of technology. The process contingency factors are expressed as a percentage of the total process capital and are presented in Table 14–7.

The project contingency cost is included to cover the costs that would occur if a detailed costing pattern was followed. For a budget-type process, AACE recommends a range of 15 to 30 percent, with a recommended value of 25 percent of the total plant cost, plus home office overhead and fees, plus any process contingencies.

The total plant cost (PCT) is the sum of the total process capital, general facilities, home office overhead and fee, and the contingency (process and project) costs. The total plant cost can be represented in equation form as:

Table 14–7 Process Contingency Factors for Different Technology Levels as a Function of Total Process Capital

State of technology development			Percentage of total Process capital
New Concept	—	Limited Data	>40 %
Concept	—	Bench Scale Data	30–70%
Pilot Plant	—	Pilot Plant Data	20–35%
Modules	—	Full-Size Modules Operating	5–20%
Commercial	—	Process in Commercial Use	0–10%

Adapted from Refs. 9 and 11.

$$
\begin{array}{llllll}
\text{Total} & = & \text{Total} & + & \text{General} & + & \text{Home Office} & + & \text{Contingency} \\
\text{Plant} & & \text{Process} & & \text{Facilities} & & \text{Overhead and Fee} & & \text{Costs} \\
\text{Cost (PCT)} & & \text{Cost (TPC)} & & \text{(GF)} & & \text{(HOOF)} & & \text{(CCPP)} \\
& & & & & & & & (14\text{–}8)
\end{array}
$$

Prepaid Royalties, Start-up Costs, and Spare Part Costs

The prepaid royalties, start-up costs, and spare part costs (RSS) are the other capital costs which are regarded as depreciable expenses. The royalty charges are usually levied for proprietary processes and AACE recommends a factor of 0.5 to 1.0 percent of the total process capital (9). There may be additional royalties based upon per unit of output for future production, and they would be part of the operating costs.

The start-up costs are those incurred for plant start-up such as operator training, extra maintenance, plant modifications, and etc. The primary recommendations by AACE (9) are:

1. One month of total annual operating cost at full operation.
2. An additional 25 percent of total fuel at full capacity for one month of operation.
3. Two percent of the total plant costs (PCT) to cover expected changes and modifications of equipment to reach full capacity.

These costs cannot be determined until the expected operating costs are evaluated. The operating cost calculations are in the following section on operating cost estimation.

The spare parts costs represent the cost of the spare parts needed to minimize shutdown for repairs. The AACE Recommended Practice suggests an allowance of 0.5 percent of the total plant cost (PCT).

The sum of the total plant cost (PCT) and the prepaid royalties, start-up costs, and spare part costs (RSS) represent the depreciable capital expenses (DCE) which can be represented as:

$$
\begin{array}{l}
\text{Depreciable} \\
\text{Capital Expenses} \\
\text{(DCE)}
\end{array}
=
\begin{array}{l}
\text{Total Plant Cost} \\
\text{(PCT)}
\end{array}
+
\begin{array}{l}
\text{Prepaid Royalties, Start-up Costs,} \\
\text{and Spare Part Costs (RSS)} \\
\hfill \text{(14–9)}
\end{array}
$$

Land and Working Capital

The final two cost items for the total capital requirements are the land cost and the working capital. The land cost (L) is based on the specific site and facility land requirements. These costs vary considerably by location, and the prevailing local land costs should be utilized. The sum of the depreciable capital expenses (DCE) and the land cost (L) is the fixed capital investment (FCI), and this can be expressed as:

$$
\begin{array}{l}
\text{Fixed Capital} \\
\text{Investment} \\
\text{(FCI)}
\end{array}
=
\begin{array}{l}
\text{Depreciable Capital} \\
\text{Expenses} \\
\text{(DCE)}
\end{array}
+
\begin{array}{l}
\text{Land Cost} \\
\text{(L)} \\
\hfill \text{(14–10)}
\end{array}
$$

The working capital (WC) represents the funds that a company must contribute, in addition to the fixed capital investment (FCI), to get the project started and meet subsequent obligations as they come due (2). These funds include inventories, cash, and accounts receivable less accounts payable. These funds can readily be converted to cash and are assumed to be recovered at the end of the project. The AACE Recommended Practice suggests that two months of the annual operating cost at full operation (9). The sum of the fixed capital investment and the working capital is the total capital investment (TCI). This can be represented in equation from by:

$$
\begin{array}{l}
\text{Total Capital} \\
\text{Investment} \\
\text{(TCI)}
\end{array}
=
\begin{array}{l}
\text{Fixed Capital} \\
\text{Investment} \\
\text{(FCI)}
\end{array}
+
\begin{array}{l}
\text{Working Capital} \\
\text{(WC)} \\
\hfill \text{(14–11)}
\end{array}
$$

Example 14–4

Use the AACE Recommended Practice to estimate the total process capital and total plant cost for the die-casting problem in Example 14–2. Consider all of the equipment to be class three for estimating the labor factor to handle the bare equipment costs. The average field direct labor cost is 15 $/hr. Compare the results with those obtained by the single factor method in Example 14–2.
Solution:

The procedure followed will be that illustrated in the first part of Table 14–3. The total purchased equipment cost, that is a(1), is $ 700,000.

The installed material cost, $a(2)$, is determined from the sum of the material factors in Table 14–5 and $a(1)$; it is:

$$
\begin{aligned}
a(2) &= 0.315 \times a(1) \\
&= 0.315 \times \$\,700,000 \\
&= \$\,220,500
\end{aligned}
$$

The total direct material cost (TDMC) is then;

$$
\begin{aligned}
\text{TDMC} &= a(1) + a(2) \\
&= \$\,700,000 + \$\,220,500 \\
&= \$\,920,500
\end{aligned}
$$

This value, converted to million dollar units (0.9204), is the first item in Table 14–8. The labor cost to handle and place the bare equipment, $b(1)$, is determined from the labor factor in Table 14–4 for the specific equipment class and the purchased equipment cost. Since all equipment is class three, the labor cost to handle and place the bare equipment, $b(1)$, is:

$$
\begin{aligned}
b(1) &= 0.25 \times \$\,220,000 + 0.25 \times \$\,400,000 + 0.25 \times \$\,80,000 \\
&= \$\,175,000
\end{aligned}
$$

The installation labor, $b(2)$, is obtained from the total labor factor of Table 14–5 and total purchased equipment cost, $a(1)$, and is:

$$
\begin{aligned}
b(2) &= 0.255 \times a(1) \\
&= 0.255 \times \$\,700,000 \\
&= \$\,178,500
\end{aligned}
$$

The total direct labor cost, TDLC, is:

$$
\begin{aligned}
\text{TDLC} &= b(1) + b(2) \\
&= \$\,175,000 + \$\,178,500 \\
&= \$\,353,500
\end{aligned}
$$

The total direct cost, TDC, is the sum of the total direct material cost and the total direct labor cost and is:

$$
\begin{aligned}
\text{TDC} &= \text{TDMC} + \text{TDLC} \\
&= \$\,920,500 + \$\,353,500 \\
&= \$\,1,274,000
\end{aligned}
$$

Table 14–8 Total Capital Requirements Estimate for the Die-Casting Example Problem

Item and Description	Value (million dollar units)		
I. Total Plant Cost			
Total Direct Material Cost	0.9205		
Total Direct Labor Cost	0.3535		
Total Direct Cost		1.274	
Total Indirect Field Cost		0.3871	
Total Process Capital			1.661
General Facilities			0.249
Home Office Overhead and Fee			0.249
Contingencies			0.581
Total Plant Cost			2.740
II. Prepaid Royalties			
(0.5% of Total Process Capital)			0.083
(0.005 × 1.661)			
III. Start-Up Costs			
a. 1 Month Annual Operating Cost			
($3.16 million / 12 months)		0.263	
b. 25% of Total Fuel Costs			
(0.25 × $10,000 / 12 months)		0.0002	
c. 2% of Total Plant Cost			
(0.02 × $2.74 million)		0.0548	
Total Start-up Costs			0.318
IV. Spare Parts			
(0.5% of Total Plant Cost)			
(0.005 × 2.74)			0.014
VI. Land			
($ 10,000)			0.010
V. Working Capital			
(2 months annual operating cost)			
(2 / 12 × $ 3.16 million)			0.527
Total Capital Investment (TCI)			3.692

Notes: Fixed Capital Investment = I + II + III + IV + V = $ 3.165 million; Depreciable Capital Expense = I + II + III + IV = $ 3.105 million

The direct field labor cost of $ 353,500 is 0.3535, or when rounded to three digits is 0.354 million dollar units, and appears in Table 14–10. This value is in the range of 0.25 to 1.2, so Equation 14–4 should be used to determine the percentage of indirect field labor costs. Using the field labor cost of $ 15.00/hr, this gives

$$IFC(\%) = 51 \times (0.354 \times 20 / 15)^{-0.25}$$
$$= 61.5 \%$$

The indirect field cost is:

$$IFC = (61.5 / 100) \times \$ 353,500$$
$$= \$ 217,400$$

The percentage of the indirect field labor cost is obtained from Equation 14–6, and is:

$$IFLC(\%) = 21 \times (0.354 \times 20 / 15)^{(-0.34)}$$
$$= 27.1 \%$$

The indirect field labor cost becomes:

$$IFLC = (27.1 / 100) \times \$ 353,500$$
$$= \$ 95,800$$

The labor benefits, using the recommended value of 35 percent, is:

$$LB(\text{labor benefits}) = 0.35 \times (\$ 95,800 + \$ 353,500)$$
$$= \$ 157,300$$

Using the data of Table 14–6, the small tool cost is 3.5 percent of the total direct field labor cost; that is:

$$STC(\text{small tool cost}) = 0.035 \times \$ 353,500$$
$$= \$ 12,400$$

The total indirect field costs, TIFC, is:

$$TIFC = IFC + LB + STC$$
$$= \$ 217,400 + \$ 157,300 + \$ 12,400$$
$$\doteq \$ 387,100$$

The total process capital, TPC, is the sum of the total direct cost (TDC) and the total indirect field costs (TIFC), and is:

$$TPC = \$ 1,274,000 + \$ 387,100$$

$$= \$ 1,661,100$$
$$= \$ 1.66 \text{ million}$$

This value is considerably lower than that obtained by the single factor method. One of the main reasons is that the single factor method, which gives a value of $ 2.35 million, includes the general facilities and some of the home office overhead. Therefore, the AACE Recommended Practice should be lower than the single factor method for the total process capital calculation.

The general facilities cost (GF) is estimated as 15 percent of the total process capital (TPC) and thus:

$$GF = 0.15 \times \$ 1,661,000$$
$$= \$ 249,000$$

The home office overhead and fees (HOOF) are also estimated as 15 percent of the total process capital (TPC) and thus:

$$HOOF = 0.15 \times \$ 1,661,000$$
$$= \$ 249,000$$

The process contingency fee for a commercial process varies from 0 to 10 percent, and a value of 5 percent of the total process capital will be used. Therefore, the process contingency is:

$$Process\ Contingency = 0.05 \times \$ 1,661,000$$
$$= \$ 83,100$$

The project contingency factor is 25 percent of the total process capital, plus the home office overhead and fee, plus the process contingency fee; thus the project contingency is:

$$Project\ Contingency = 0.25 \times (\$ 1,661,100 + \$ 249,000 + \$ 83,100)$$
$$= \$ 498,300$$

The total contingency cost, CCPP, is the sum of the process contingency cost and the project contingency cost, and is:

$$CCPP = \$ 83,100 + \$ 498,300$$
$$= \$ 581,400$$

The total plant cost, PCT, can now be calculated as the sum of the total process capital, the general facilities cost, the home office overhead and fee cost, and the total contingency cost. It is calculated from Equation 14-8 as:

$$
\begin{aligned}
PCT &= TPC + GF + HOOF + CCPP \\
&= \$ 1,661,100 + \$ 249,000 + \$ 249,000 + \$ 581,400 \\
&= \$ 2,740,500 \\
&= \$ 2.74 \text{ million}
\end{aligned}
$$

These values are presented in Table 14-8. The value of the total plant cost is approximately equal to the fixed capital investment value of $ 2.71 million of the single factor method.

OPERATING COST ESTIMATING

The detailed calculation of the operating cost estimation was presented in Chapter 2, Cost Estimation. AACE Recommended Practice 16R-90 also suggests a less complex method of operation cost estimation. The AACE method is primarily for use in the chemical process industry, and some modifications have been made for its application in the manufacturing industry. Table 14-9 is a summary of the manufacturing version of the recommended practice. The operating cost estimation is necessary for the calculation of the start-up cost and working capital items for the determination of the fixed capital investment and the total capital investment.

The four main categories of the annual operating cost are: the raw material costs, the utility and fuel costs, the labor costs, and the "other" costs. The raw material costs are often the largest component of the operating costs and, as indicated in the costing for materials chapter, may account for over half of the manufacturing cost. The material costs are determined to a large extent by the product requirements and the plant quality performance. The waste material disposal costs can be high, and often approach the indirect material costs.

The utility and fuel costs are primarily used to determine the energy costs to produce the product. However, in low intensity energy industries, the space heating and lighting costs and the transportation energy costs may be a substantial portion of the total energy costs. The space heating, lighting, and transportation energy costs should be separated from the product energy costs when a detailed cost analysis of the product is made for evaluating product profitability.

The labor costs were the cause of high manufacturing costs in the early 1900s, but today the labor costs, and in particular the direct labor cost, have decreased substantially. In many plants the maintenance and indirect labor

Table 14–9 Annual Operating Cost Summary Estimate Form for Manufacturing

Item	Quantity units/yr	Unit cost $/unit	Annual costs subtotal total
A Materials			
Direct Materials			
Raw Material No. 1			
Raw Material No. 2			
. . .			
Indirect Materials			
Indirect Material No. 11			
Indirect Material No. 12			
. . .			
(Indirect Materials can be estimated as 25 % of the Total Direct Labor)			
Scrap Materials			
Scrap Material No. 21			
Scrap Material No. 22			
. . .			
Waste Material			
Waste Material No. 31			
Waste Material No. 32			
. . . .			_____
Total Raw Materials			
B Utilities and Fuels			
Solid Fuels			
Solid Fuel No. 1			
Liquid Fuels			
Liquid Fuel No. 11			
Liquid Fuel No. 12			
Gaseous Fuels			
Natural Gas No. 21			
Steam No. 31			
Electrical Energy			
Electrical–Shop/Machine 1			
Electrical–Shop/Machine 2			
. . .			_____
Total Utilities and Fuels			
C Direct and Indirect Labor			
Direct Operating Labor			
Direct Labor–Product 1			
Direct Labor–Product 2			
. . .			_____
Direct Labor			
Direct Supervision Labor			
(estimated as 15% of			
Direct Labor			_____

Table 14-9   (Continued)

Maintenance Labor (estimated as 3% of Total Plant Cost)	_____
Total Direct Labor (sum of Direct Labor, Direct Supervision, and Maintenance Labor)	_____
Indirect Labor (estimated as 75% of Total Direct Labor)	
Total Labor (Sum of Total Direct Labor and Indirect Labor)	

D   Other Costs
   Payroll (Benefits) Overhead
      (35% of Total Labor)
   Maintenance Material Costs
      (3% of Total Plant Cost)
   Property Taxes and Insurance
      (2% of Total Plant Cost)
   Administration and Corporate Expense
      (60% of Total Labor)
   Selling Expense
      (10% of Total Sales)
      Total Other Costs
         Total Annual Operating Costs

Adapted from Ref. 9. Reprinted with special permission of AACE.

constitute the major labor costs, as increased automation tends to decrease direct labor costs and increase maintenance and indirect labor costs. The AACE Recommended Practice suggests that direct supervision labor can be estimated as 15 percent of the direct labor; the maintenance labor can be estimated as 3 percent of the total plant cost (PCT); and the indirect labor can be estimated as 75 percent of the total of the direct labor, the direct labor supervision, and the maintenance labor.

The "other" costs represent the labor benefit costs, maintenance material costs, property taxes and insurance, administration and corporate expense, and the selling expenses. The AACE recommends the benefits as 35 percent of the total labor cost; the maintenance material costs as 3 percent of the total plant cost (PCT); the property taxes and insurance as 2 percent of the total plant cost; the administration and corporate expense as 60 percent of the total labor cost; and the selling expense as 10 percent of the total sales.

Example 14-5

Estimate the annual operating costs for the die casting problem of Example 14-4. The information in Table 14-10 is to be used for the operating cost estimation. The total plant cost (PCT) was $ 2.74 million and the estimated die casting sales is $ 4.0 million. The scrap (returns) is estimated to be 10 percent of the direct materials and the waste material is estimated at 2 percent of the direct materials.

Find the fixed capital investment and the total capital investment if the land cost is $ 10,000. The royalties are estimated at 0.5 percent of the total process capital.

Solution:

The total annual operating costs are calculated in Table 14-10. The $ 3.16 million does not include the depreciation expense associated with the capital investment. The total capital investment can now be determined, as the annual operating cost value has been determined. Table 14-8 has the total capital requirements for the die casting example problem.

The total capital investment of $ 3.69 million is much greater than the single factor estimate of $ 3.19 million. This difference is due to the relatively high annual operating costs when compared to the total plant cost. The annual operating cost is usually lower than the total plant cost, but in this example the annual operating cost was greater than the total plant cost. This led to high values for the working capital and start-up costs.

SUMMARY AND CONCLUSIONS

The estimation techniques for the capital cost of a manufacturing facility have not been developed and the use of the techniques for estimating in the chemical industry have been presented. The techniques have been modified slightly for some of the differences between the manufacturing industry and the chemical industry.

The five general techniques for making a capital cost estimate were presented, and four methods were illustrated using example problems. The three methods that indicate the greatest potential for success were the single factor (or Lang) method, the knowledge and experience method, and AACE Recommended Practice No. 16R-90. All three methods are based upon the delivered equipment costs.

The single factor method was faster and easier to apply than the other methods. The knowledge and experience method (K and E) is the newest approach for equipment estimating and needs more validation. The AACE method required the estimation of the annual operating costs before the fixed or total capital investment values could be calculated. The greater detail of the AACE method would lead to greater accuracy on the average estimate. The

Table 14-10 Die-Casting Data for Example Problem 14-5 and Annual Operating Cost Calculation

Item	Quantity units/yr	Unit Cost $/unit	Annual Subtotal $	Costs Total $
A Materials				
Direct Material(DM)	1,000,000 lb	$ 2/lb	2,000,000	
Indirect (25% DL)			46, 425	
(see total Direct Labor)				
Scrap (10% DM)	100,000 lb	− $1.5/lb	− 150,000	
(credit)				
Waste Material (2% DM)	20,000 lb	$2.5/lb	50,000	
Total Materials				$ 1, 946, 425
B Utilities and Fuels				
Electricity	200,000 KWH	$.05/KWH	10,000	
Total Utilities and Fuels				$ 10,000
C Labor				
Direct Operating Labor				
(3 persons)	6,000 hr	$15/hr	90,000	
Direct Supervision				
(15% Direct Labor)			13,500	
Maintenance Labor				
(3% Total Plant Cost)			82,200	
Total Direct Labor			185,700	
Indirect Labor				
(75% Total Direct Labor)			139,275	
Total Annual Labor				$ 324,975
D Other Costs				
Payroll (Benefits) Overhead				
(35% of Total Annual Labor)			113,741	
Maintenance Materials				
(3% of Total Plant Cost)			82,200	
Property Taxes and Insurance				
(2% of Total Plant Cost)			54,800	
Administration and Corporate Expense				
(60% of Total Annual Labor)			194,985	
Selling Expense				
(10% of Total Sales)			400,000	
Total Other Costs				$ 845,726
Total Annual Operating Costs				$ 3, 127, 126
				($ 3. 13

Notes: Direct Labor = 0.090 M
Total Plant Cost = 2.740 M
Total Direct Labor = 0.1857M
Total Annual Labor = 0.3250M
(M = million)

factors used for the single factor and AACE methods need to be revised for the various types of manufacturing facilities, but such information is not available.

The AACE Recommended Practice 16R-90 also gives a procedure for estimating the annual operating costs. It presents recommended values for factors that are difficult to evaluate. This recommended practice is presented in a modified manner to make it more applicable to the manufacturing industry.

There is opportunity for considerable improvement in the estimation of the capital costs of a manufacturing facility and in the estimation of its annual operating costs. Since the methods presented are based upon the delivered equipment costs, there is a need for cost capacity equations for the different types of manufacturing equipment to improve these estimating procedures.

EVALUATIVE QUESTIONS

1. What are the two different types of cost estimates presented?
2. What are the five methods used to estimate the capital cost requirements?
3. What is the base factor for the single factor method and the AACE method?
4. Rework Example 14-2 if the die-casting machine cost $ 800,000 instead of $ 400,000.
5. Rework Example 14-3 if the knowledge and experience level is 4 instead of 2.
6. Rework Example 14-4 if the die-casting machine cost $ 800,000 instead of $ 400,000. Compare the results with Question 4.
7. Rework Example 14-5 if the die-casting machine cost $ 800,000 instead of $ 400,000. Compare the results with Question 4.

BIBLIOGRAPHY

1. *Industrial Engineering Terminology—ANSI Standard Z94.0-1989*, Industrial Engineering and Management Press, Norcross, GA, 1990, pp. 2-9.
2. *Standard Cost Engineering Terminology*, AACE Standard No. 10S-90, American Association of Cost Engineers, Morgantown, WV, 1990, pp. 14, 38, 80.
3. Dieter, G. E., *Engineering Design*, 2nd Edition, McGraw Hill, 1991, pp. 412-413.
4. Park, W. R. and Jackson, D. E., *Cost Engineering Analysis,* 2nd Ed., Wiley Interscience, 1984, pp. 137-38.
5. Humphreys, K. K., Editor. *Jelen's Cost and Optimization Engineering*, 3rd Edition, McGraw Hill, 1991, pp. 399-400.

6. Peters, M. S. and Timmerhaus, K. D., *Plant Design and Economics for Chemical Engineers*, 3rd Edition, McGraw Hill, 1980, pp. 179–180.
7. Stamp, G. L., "Estimating the Cost of Developmental Equipment", *1991 AACE Transactions*, American Association of Cost Engineers, Morgantown, WV, 1991, pp. F.1.1–F.1.4.
8. Private communication from Greg Stamp.
9. *Conducting Technical and Economic Evaluations in the Process and Utility Industries*, AACE Recommended Practice No. 16R-90, American Association of Cost Engineers, Morgantown, WV, 1990, pp. 1–84.
10. Frazier, A. M., *Process Design and Economic Evaluation of Preparing a MSW/Coal Fuel for Existing Combustion Facilities*, M.S. Thesis, Civil Engineering Department, West Virginia University, 1991, pp. 47–73.
11. Electric Power Research Institute, *Technical Assessment Guides*, Vol. 1-4, EPRI P-4493-SR, Palo Alto, CA.

Appendix
A Generalized Metal Cutting Economics Model for Single-Pass Cutting in Turning, Drilling, Shaping, and Milling Operations

INTRODUCTION

The optimization for the metal cutting economics models has generally only been successfully applied to the turning operation (1). Only recently has it been extended to other cutting operations (2,3,4) such as milling, shaping, and drilling. The development of a generalized model makes the optimization of a specific metal cutting process easier to perform. The model can be utilized for both the minimum cost or maximum production model conditions, or for any specified cutting speed or any specified tool life.

The previous extensions have some errors that can lead to incorrect conclusions. The author's previous attempt (3) at adjusting the cutting path length was successful with the shaping operation, but failed for the milling operation. The approach by Boothroyd and Knight (2) calculated the interrupted tool life rather than the actual tool life; however, they adjusted the tool life when calculating the cutting velocity and thus obtained the correct cost values. The correct tool life expression is published by Dewhurst and Boothroyd in a separate report (4). The adjustments for the fraction of the cutting time that the tool is actually cutting, or Q, in the following work does include minor adjustments for the lead, which is not included in the expressions developed by Boothroyd (2,4). The expressions for cutting speed and tool life are more clearly developed here than in previously mentioned works.

The model is similar to that used for the basic metal cutting optimization models; the major difference is a term which adjusts for the difference between the machining time and the time during which the edge is actually cutting. This difference is small for the turning process, but it is considerable for the milling process. This somewhat explains the success of the previous models for turning and their failure when applied to milling. The nomenclature used for the model is presented in Table A-1. The models are based upon Taylor's tool life equation, which is:

$$V T^n = C \tag{1}$$

where

V = Cutting speed (ft/min or m/min)
T = Tool life (min)
n = Taylor's tool life exponent
C = Taylor's tool life constant (ft/min or m/min)

Table A–1 Nomenclature for Metal Cutting Economic Models

Symbol	Description and Units
t_l	Handling (nonproductive) time (minutes) per unit
t_{ch}	Tool changing time (minutes) per unit
t_c	Cutting (machining) time (minutes) per unit
t_p	Total unit time (minutes)
M	Total Machine and operator rate (including overheads) in \$/minute
C_t	Average tool Cost (average of original tool cost plus resharpening costs) in \$/tool
C_p	Unit Cost per piece in \$/unit
V	Cutting speed (velocity) in ft/min or m/min
T	Tool life in minutes
n	Taylor's tool life exponent
C	Taylor's tool life constant in ft/min or m/min
B	Total cutting path length in ft or m
n_t	Tools per unit
C_u	Total unit cost in \$/unit
Q	Fraction of cutting time when cutting edge is cutting
L	Total Length of cut including lead and overtravel
L_c	Length of cut when tool is actually cutting material (metal)
d	Depth of cut in inches or mm
W	Piece Width for shaping in inches or mm

MINIMUM COST MODEL

The cost components traditionally considered in the metal cutting economics model are the handling (nonproductive) costs, the cutting costs, the tool costs, and the tool changing costs. These components can be expressed in the following equations:

$$\text{Handling Cost} = M \times t_l \tag{2}$$

$$\text{Cutting Cost} = M \times t_c \tag{3}$$

$$\text{Tool Cost} = C_t \times n_t \tag{4}$$

$$\text{Tool Changing Cost} = M \times t_{ch} \times n_t \tag{5}$$

The total unit cost can be expressed as the sum of Equations 2 through 5, that is

$$C_u = M \times t_l + M \times t_c + n_t(C_t + M \times t_{ch}) \tag{6}$$

where

M = Total machine and operator rate (\$/min)
t_l = Handling (nonproductive) time (min)
t_c = Cutting time (min)
t_{ch} = Tool changing time (min)
C_t = Tool cost/cutting edge (\$/edge)
n_t = Tool changes/unit
C_u = Total unit cost

However,

$$t_c = B / V \tag{7}$$

where

B = Cutting path length (ft or m)
V = Cutting speed (ft/min or m/min)

and, for uninterrupted cutting

$$n_t = t_c/T \tag{8}$$

where

t_c = Cutting time per unit (min/unit)
T = Tool life (minutes/edge)

However, for interrupted cutting, which is the usual cutting condition,

$$n_t = Q \times t_c/T \tag{9}$$

where

Q = Fraction of cutting time that the tool is actually cutting

Substituting the results of Equations 7, 8, 9, and 1 into Equation 6 and expressing T in terms of V results in:

$$C_u = M \times t_l + M \times B \times V^{(-1)} + M \times B \times Q(C_t/M + t_{ch})\, C^{(-1/n)} V^{(1/n-1)} \tag{10}$$

Note that the Q term directly affects the tool costs and tool changing costs, but not the cutting time costs or the handling costs. If one takes the derivative of Equation 10 with respect to V, sets the derivative to zero and solves for V one obtains:

$$V = [(1/[Q \times (C_t/M + t_{ch})]) \times (n/[1-n])]^n \times C \tag{11}$$

If one evaluates T from Equation 1, the following is obtained:

$$T = Q[C_t/M + t_{ch}] \times [(1-n)/n] \tag{12}$$

The expressions of Equations 11 and 12 are similar to the traditional metal cutting economics model except for the Q term. Since the tool life expression is easier to evaluate, the total unit cost of Equation 10 can be represented as:

$$C_u = M \times t_l + (B/C) \times T^{(n-1)}[Q(M \times t_{ch} + C_t) + M \times T] \tag{13}$$

$$= M \times t_l + (B/C) \times M \times T^{(n)}[1 + (Q/T) \times (t_{ch} + C_t/M)] \tag{14}$$

$$= M \times t_l + (B/C) \times M \times T^{(n)} + (B/C) \times M \times T^{(n)}(Q/T)$$
$$\times (t_{ch} + C_t/M)] \tag{15}$$

The different forms of the unit cost equation can be used for different purposes. Equation 13 is the simplest form and gives the result faster; Equation 14 has the tool costs (tool plus tool changing time) as a ratio of the cutting costs; and Equation 15 has the costs broken into the three main components. The equations can be used to determine the unit cost at any desired tool life and not only at the optimal value. Equation 15 can be descriptively written as:

$$C_u = \text{Nonproductive Costs} + \text{Machining Costs} + \text{Tooling Costs} \tag{16}$$

It is important to note that although the Q factor appears directly only in the tooling cost term, it is also a factor in the tool life expression, Equation 12, so it does affect the machining costs. Equations 13 to 15 can be used to evaluate the unit costs at any tool life value, not only at the minimum cost tool life. Equation 15 can also be written in terms of the cutting speed rather than the tool life, and that is:

$$C_u = M \times t_1 + M \times (B/V) + M \times (B/V) \times Q \times (t_{ch} + C_t/M) \times (V/C)^{1/n} \quad (17)$$

The three terms of Equation 17 are the same components as expressed in Equation 16. Equation 17 can be used to evaluate the unit costs at any cutting speed, not only at the minimum cost cutting speed of Equation 11.

MAXIMUM PRODUCTION MODEL

The maximum production model minimizes the total unit time to produce a unit. The total unit time can be expressed as:

$$t_p = t_1 + t_c + t_{ch} \times n_t \quad (18)$$

where

t_p = Total unit time
t_1 = Handling (nonproductive) time
t_c = Cutting time
t_{ch} = Tool changing time
n_t = Tool changes/unit

If one substitutes the values of t_c, n_t, and T via Equations 7, 9, and 1 into Equation 18, the result is:

$$t_p = t_1 + (B/V) + Q \times B \times C^{(-1/n)} \times V^{(1/n-1)} \times t_{ch} \quad (19)$$

If one takes the derivative of Equation 19 with respect to V, sets the derivative to zero, and solves for V one obtains:

$$V = [1/(Q \times t_{ch}) \times (n/(1-n))]^n C \quad (20)$$

If one uses the Taylor relationship of Equation 1 and solves for T, the expression obtained is:

$$T = Q \times t_{ch} \times (1-n)/n \quad (21)$$

The expressions in Equations 20 and 21 represent the value for the optimal cutting speed and tool life for the maximum production model. These values can be substituted into Equations 15 or 17 to determine the unit cost for this set of conditions. The cutting speeds determined by Equations 11 and 20 are often used to define the lower and upper limits of the high efficiency cutting speed range for cutting.

CUTTING PATH LENGTH AND CUTTING FRACTION

Two parameters that are needed for the calculations for the unit cost are the cutting path length (B) and the cutting fraction (Q). The cutting fraction represents the portion of the machining cycle that the tool is actually cutting, and this is used for determining the tool life and tool costs. The total machining cycle time is required for determining the machining costs of the unit cost. The expressions for the cutting path length and cutting fraction are presented in Table A-2 for the turning, drilling, shaping, and milling processes. Table A-3 contains the nomenclature for the parameters used in Table A-2. Table A-2 also lists the typical ranges for the cutting fraction for the four processes. These parameters, cutting path length and cutting fraction, permit the extension of the traditional metal cutting economics model for turning to these other metal cutting processes.

SLAB MILLING EXAMPLE

To illustrate the application of the formulas, an example for slab milling has been developed. The piece is illustrated in Figure A-1 and the data used is presented in Table A-4. The dimensions are shown in inches and centimeters. The cutting parameters B and Q require the evaluation of L and the angle theta.

Table A–2   Cutting Path Length(B) and Cutting Fraction(Q) Values for Four Cutting Processes

Cutting Process	Expression for Cutting Path Length (B)		Cutting Fraction(Q)		
	US-ENGLISH	ISO-METRIC	Typical Value	Typical Range	Expressions for Calculation
Turning	$\pi DL/(12\ f_r)$	$\pi DL/(10\ f_r)$	1	.95-1.0	L_c/L
Drilling	$\pi DL/(12\ f_r)$	$\pi DL/(10\ f_r)$	1	75-.95	L_c/L
Shaping	$WL/(12\ f_s Z)$	$WL/(10\ f_s Z)$	.67	55-.70	$Z(L_c/L)$
Milling	$\pi DL/(12\ n_t f_t)$	$\pi DL/(10\ n_t f_t)$	.15	.03-.50	$(\theta/360)(L_c/L)$

Note: $Z=R/[R+1]$. $\theta=$ Angle of Contact of Cutter.

Table A–3 Nomenclature for B and Q Parameters in Table 2

Symbol	Description	Units (English or ISO)
D	Diameter (tool or workpiece)	in or cm
L	Length of cut plus lead and overtravel	in or cm
L_c	Cutting length	in or cm
f	Feed per revolution	in/rev or m m/rev
W	Width of sample	in or cm
R	Return velocity: cutting velocity (for Shaper)	
f_s	Feed per stroke	in/stroke or mm/stroke
f_t	Feed per tooth	in/tooth or m m/stroke
n_{tr}	Number of teeth/rev	
θ	Angle of engagement (milling)	degrees

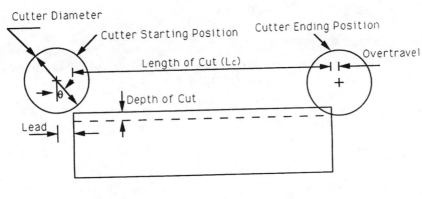

d=0.20 inches L_c=10 inches
Overtravel=0.25 inches   L=11.12 inches
Lead=0.87 inches   D=4.0 inches
θ=25.8 Degrees

Figure A–1 Slab milling example problem to illustrate cutting parameters and new calculation procedure.

Table A–4 Cutting Parameters for Slab Milling Example Problem

Symbol	Description	Value
M	Machine and operator rate ($/min)	$ 0.80/min
c_t	Average tool cost ($/tool)	$ 25.00/tool
L_c	Length of cut (in,cm)	10 in, 25.4 c m
f_t	Feed per tooth (in, mm/tooth)	0.004 in, 0.102 mm
n_{tr}	Number of teeth/revolution	6
n	Taylor's tool life exponent	0.10
C	Taylor's tool life constant (ft/min, m/min)	200 ft/min, 61 m/min
d	Depth of cut (in,mm)	0.200 in, 5.1 mm
X	Overtravel (in, cm)	0.25 in, 0.6 cm
D	Cutter Diameter (in, cm)	4 in, 10.2 cm
t_l	Handling time (min)	1.5 min
t_{ch}	Tool changing time (min)	2.0 min

$$L = L_c + X + Y \tag{22}$$

where

X = amount of overtravel (inches or cm)
Y = Lead (inches or cm)
L_c = Length of Cut (inches or cm)

The lead for slab milling is found from the geometry of the depth of cut and tool diameter as indicated in Figure A-1. It is:

$$
\begin{aligned}
Y &= [d \times (D - d)]^{(1/2)} \\
&= [0.200 \times (4.00 - 0.200)]^{(1/2)} \\
&= 0.87 \text{ inches}
\end{aligned}
\tag{23}
$$

From the geometry of Figure A-1, the angle θ can be evaluated as

$$
\begin{aligned}
\theta &= \text{Arc Sin } [Y / (D / 2)] \\
&= \text{Arc Sin } [0.87 / (4.00 / 2)] \\
&= 25.8 \text{ degrees}
\end{aligned}
\tag{24}
$$

Thus the value of L can be determined using Equation 22:

L = 10.00 + 0.25 + 0.87

= 11.12 inches

The value of the cutting path length B can be determined from the expression in Table A-2 for milling, that is:

B = π × (4.0 in) × (11.12 in) / (12 × 6 × 0.004 in)

= 485 ft

or

B = π × (10.2 cm) × (28.2 cm) / (10 × 6 × 0.102 mm)

= 148 m

The cutting fraction Q is obtained from the expressions in Table A-2 for milling and is:

Q = (25.8 / 360) × (10.0 / 11.12)

= 0.064

The tool life for the minimum cost model can be evaluated using Equation 12 and is:

T = 0.064 ($ 25.00 / $ 0.80/min + 2.00 min) × (1.0 − 0.1) / 0.1

= 19.15 min

The corresponding cutting speed is obtained by rearranging Equation (1) and solving for V and is:

V = C / T^n

= (200 ft/min) / $(19.15)^{(0.1)}$

= 149 ft/min

If the ISO values are used, then

V = (61 m/min) / $(19.15)^{(0.1)}$

= 45.4 m/min

The unit cost for machining can be evaluated using Equation 15 and the result is:

$$C_u = \$\,0.8/min \times 1.5\,min$$

$$+ \$\,0.8/min \times (485\,ft\,/\,200\,ft/min) \times (19.15)^{(0.1)}$$
$$+ \$\,0.8/min \times (485\,ft\,/\,200\,ft/min) \times (19.15)^{(0.1)} \times$$
$$(0.064\,/\,19.15) \times (2.0\,min\,+\,\$\,25\,/\,\$\,0.8/min)$$

$$= \$\,1.20\,+\,\$\,2.61\,+\,\$\,0.29$$

$$= \$\,4.10$$

The unit production time can be obtained from Equations 1, 7, 9, and 18 which result in:

$$t_p = t_l + t_c + t_{ch} \times n_t$$
$$= t_l + t_c + t_{ch} \times Q \times t_c\,/\,T$$
$$= t_l + t_c \times [1 + (Q\,/\,T) \times t_{ch}]$$
$$= t_l + (B\,/\,V) \times [1 + (Q\,/\,T) \times t_{ch}]$$
$$= t_l + (B\,/\,C) \times T^{(n)} \times [1 + (Q\,/\,T) \times t_{ch}] \qquad (25)$$

Equation 25 can be used to determine the unit production time for any tool life and is not restricted to optimal tool life values. For the minimum cost model for the slab milling example, the value of t_p is:

$$t_p = 1.5\,min\,+\,(485\,ft\,/\,200\,ft/min) \times (19.15)^{(0.1)}$$
$$\times [1 + (0.064\,/\,19.15\,min) \times 2\,min]$$
$$= 1.5\,min\,+\,3.28\,min$$
$$= 4.78\,min$$

The production rate, in pieces/hour, is:

$$P = 60\,/\,t_p$$
$$= 60\,min/hr\,/\,4.78\,min/piece$$
$$= 12.6\,pieces/hr \qquad (26)$$

If the maximum production model is considered, T is evaluated by using Equation 21 and the result is:

$$T = 0.064 \times (2min) \times [(1 - 0.1)\,/\,0.1]$$
$$= 1.15\,min$$

The corresponding cutting speed would be, from Equation:

$$V = 200 \text{ ft/min} / (1.152)^{(0.1)}$$
$$= 197 \text{ ft/min}$$

The corresponding unit cost would be:

$$
\begin{aligned}
C_u = \ & \$\,0.8/\text{min} \times 1.5 \text{ min} + \\
& \$\,0.8/\text{min} \times (485 \text{ ft} / 200 \text{ ft/min}) \times (1.152)^{(0.1)} + \\
& \$\,0.8/\text{min} \times (485 \text{ ft} / 200 \text{ ft/min}) \times (1.152)^{(0.1)} \times \\
& (0.064 / 1.152) \times (2.0 \text{ min} + \$\,25/\$\,0.8/\text{min}) \\
= \ & \$\,1.20 + \$\,1.97 + \$\,3.63 \\
= \ & \$\,6.80
\end{aligned}
$$

The unit production time and production rate for the maximum production case can be determined from Equations 25 and 26, and the results are:

$$
\begin{aligned}
t_p = \ & 1.5 \text{ min} + \\
& (485 \text{ ft} / 200 \text{ ft/min}) \times (1.152)^{(0.1)} \, [1 + (0.064 / 1.152 \text{ min}) \times 2 \text{ min}] \\
= \ & 1.5 \text{ min} + 2.73 \text{ min} \\
= \ & 4.23 \text{ min}
\end{aligned}
$$

$$
\begin{aligned}
P = \ & 60 \text{ min/hr} / 4.23 \text{ min/piece} \\
= \ & 14.2 \text{ pieces/hr}
\end{aligned}
$$

This indicates that although the cutting cost decreases from \$ 2.61 to \$ 1.97 for the maximum production case versus the minimum cost case, the tooling costs increase per unit from \$ 0.29 to \$ 3.63 and thus the total unit cost increases from \$ 4.10 to \$ 6.80. The production rate increases from 12.6 in the minimum cost case to 14.2 for the maximum production case.

COMPARISON WITH TRADITIONAL ECONOMICS MODEL

If the traditional metal cutting economics model expressions are used for tool life and cutting speed (which is the same as using a value of 1.0 for Q), the tool life and corresponding cutting speed values would be:

$$T = (\$\,25 / \$\,0.8/\text{min} + 2 \text{ min}) \times [(1 - 0.1) / 0.1]$$
$$= 299 \text{ min}$$

and

$$V = 200 \text{ ft/min} / (299)^{(0.1)}$$
$$= 113 \text{ ft/min}$$

The total unit cost can be determined from Equation 15 and is:

$$C_u = \$\,0.8/\text{min} \times 1.5 \text{ min} +$$
$$\$\,0.8/\text{min} \times (485 \text{ ft} / 200 \text{ ft/min}) \times (299)^{(0.1)} +$$
$$\$\,0.8/\text{min} \times (485 \text{ ft} / 200 \text{ ft/min}) \times 299^{(0.1)} (1/299) \times$$
$$(2.0 \text{ min} + \$\,25 / \$\,0.8/\text{min})$$
$$= \$\,1.20 + \$\,3.43 + \$\,0.38$$
$$= \$\,5.01$$

The corresponding unit time and production rate for the traditional minimum cost economics model are:

$$t_p = 1.5 \text{ min} + (485 \text{ ft} / 200 \text{ ft/min}) \times 9299)^{(0.1)} \times [1 + 2 \text{ min} / 299 \text{ min}]$$
$$= 1.5 \text{ min} + 4.32 \text{ min}$$
$$= 5.82 \text{ min}$$

$$P = 60 \text{ min/hr} / 5.82 \text{ min/piece}$$
$$= 10.3 \text{ pieces/hr}$$

The traditional optimization approach gives an increased unit cost (\$ 5.01 versus \$ 4.10) and a decreased production rate (10.3 versus 12.6 pieces/hr). This discrepancy between the traditional unadjusted model and the proposed model is large because of the small value of Q, which is associated with milling operations.

COMPUTERIZED MODEL

A computer spread sheet model has been developed by John Mansuy while taking a special topics course in his Graduate Program in the Industrial Engineering Department at West Virginia University. The model uses the Lotus spread sheet and calculates the unit costs for both the minimum cost and maximum production cutting speeds. It also determines the tool life, production rates, and pieces per tool for both cases.

SUMMARY AND CONCLUSIONS

A new generalized metal cutting economics model has been developed and applied to the turning, drilling, shaping, and milling processes. The model has been developed for single-pass cutting. The adjustment for the time when the tool is not cutting results in an increase of the cutting speed. The cutting fraction Q varies not only for the process but also for the particular cutting conditions.

The milling operations have the lowest values of Q whereas turning operations tend to have the highest values for Q. This analysis, and the sample problem, illustrates that previous attempts to optimize the metal cutting operations for milling would have given incorrect cutting speeds (too low), higher unit costs, and lower production rates. As the cutting fraction approaches unity, the errors are reduced and thus the errors in turning and drilling operations would have been smaller.

The optimal values for tool life and cutting speed for the Taylor tool life model are developed for the minimum cost model and the maximum production model. The cost and unit time expressions developed can be used for any cutting speed or tool life, and not only for the two optimal cases.

BIBLIOGRAPHY

1. Kalpakjian, S., *Manufacturing Processes for Engineering Materials*, 2nd Edition, 1989, Addison Wesley, pp. 571–575.
2. Boothroyd, G. and Knight, W. A., *Fundamentals of Machining and Machine Tools*, 2nd Edition, 1989, Marcel Dekker, Inc. pp. 175–201.
3. Creese, R.C., "Standards for the Minimum Cost and Maximum Production Metal Cutting Models: Turning, Shaping, Drilling, and Milling" *AFS Transaction*, 1985, Vol. 93, pp. 183–186.
4. Dewhurst, P. and Boothroyd, G., *Early Cost Estimating in Product Design*, Report # 11, Department of Industrial and Manufacturing Engineering, University of Rhode Island, March 1987, p. 7.

Index

ISBN 0-8247-8712-9

90000

9 780824 787127